MW00812934

To our parents, Hop Mui and Kan Sau Chung and Daphne Hsu and Dean Chang, who we disobeyed, first by doing fine art degrees instead of business studies and then by opening a restaurant instead of getting office jobs, but who still supported us and brought us a gazebo and an icebox to kick-start BAO, and who ran around Taiwan buying us custom steamers and queueing for goose fat.

BAO

BAO: THE COOKBOOK

ERCHEN CHANG   SHING TAT CHUNG   WAI TING CHUNG

KEY

ERCHEN CHANG – EC

SHING TAT CHUNG – STC

WAI TING CHUNG – WTC

(N) NUTS   (S) SPICY   (C) COLD

(V) VEGETARIAN   (VE) VEGAN

A Quick Word

BAO. A humble three-letter word steeped in history, its literal meaning is simply 'steamed bun'.

Yet those three letters mean so much more to us. After our first trip to Taiwan together, the three of us sitting in the back of a Volkswagen Polo on our way back from the airport, we chose BAO as the name for the next chapter of our lives. At the time, the word felt so trivial to us, but fast forward to the present day and you can't walk down the street without seeing it, from restaurant menus to advertisements.

Since then, BAO has become not just our personal project, but a collection of restaurants, each with their own identity. And now here we are, writing BAO's story. This book serves as a cookbook-cum-manifesto: a declaration of our intentions, what's important to us and an explanation of why and how we do the things we do and cook the dishes you might have had the chance to eat. In the following pages, we write about our journey in becoming specialists and our aspirations to push the boundaries of a traditional product, and we travel together back to where the Lonely Man – the character pictured gracefully eating a BAO on our logo – originated from. First and foremost, our aim is to be storytellers, and when you sit in our restaurants you become part of our world – the world created for the Lonely Man. Each of our voices is dotted around the book, Shing in the first parts, talking about our history and manifesto, Wai Ting on our beginnings and Erchen discussing food culture and upbringing in the recipes. We tell stories of culture through mastery and artistry, crafted in, and embodied by, that three-letter word – BAO.

A History Lesson

**Before the beginning of the beginning:
first to third generation**

While Erchen is from Taiwan, Wai Ting and I were born in the UK. Erchen grew up in Muzha, Taipei, where food played a large part in her upbringing. With both her parents focusing on their careers during a golden time for the Taiwanese economy, she spent her time with her grandma, who was tasked with cooking epic family banquets each day. Erchen would tag along on the back of her grandmother's bike, whizzing through the streets of Muzha picking up supplies and ending up in the local wet markets. She was the kid with an appetite big enough to finish all the remaining dishes when everyone else had already left the dinner table. Her upbringing and stories of Taiwan are interwoven into the recipe sections of the book (see pages 41–233). Wai Ting and I, however, have a less exotic history. We pretty much lived the classic Cantonese immigration story.

Our grandfather first moved to London in 1960, where he took a job as a pot washer at a Chinese restaurant in London's Chelsea. He worked his way up to head chef at Golden Palace on Hyde Park Corner before moving to Nottingham, where he started what would become a family of ever-changing restaurants and takeaways over the next sixty years.

We were born into restaurant life, hopping from our parents' latest restaurants to new takeaways. We lived above the restaurants, pot washed from the age of nine and spent weekends working. Staff meals were our family dinners. Ingrained in our early memories is the dread of manoeuvring a sizzler plate off the wooden tray and onto a hot plate. Or the moment when I was washing and drying plates at the age of five and accidently took a sip from the permanently smiley pot washer's Coca-Cola. He had Yakuza-style tattoos from head to toe (although they were never visible under his clothes) and was allocated one iced Coke per shift. He never smiled or spoke to me again after that.

Naturally, all the sweat and tears involved in working in restaurants meant our family, who endured the hardship of immigrating to England and living that life so that we could afford a better education, tried to steer us away from a career in restaurants. We lived through our family's journey in this industry, with restaurant opening upon restaurant opening and a bankruptcy somewhere in the middle. As kids, we would sneak onto our parents' much-needed massage equipment, watching them evolve from manual wooden beads to old-school automatic foot massage machines and finally to fully-automatic massage chairs over the span of thirty years. It's ironic that when we began our own journey into restaurants, those massage chairs became our go-to therapy when we did find the time to escape back up north, cradling our stressed, work-worn bodies like a mother holding a child, rocking us back and forth on shiatsu mode before we ventured back to our restaurant life in London (see page 15, image 06).

So, yes, we didn't quite obey our family's wishes. After a long period of education in the arts, we found ourselves drawn back to the allure of food. It's where we belonged. But we embarked on our own journey, this time with the ambition to use food to inspire using our background in art and design.

First Generation

1960
At the age of 27, Shing and Wai Ting's grandfather, Pai Wan Tang, who was a rice paddy farmer in Hong Kong at the time, took a month-long boat journey to London by himself. He started as a pot washer at Choice (Chung Ying) restaurant on King's Road in London's Chelsea.

1964
Pai Wan worked in six restaurants before he became head chef at Golden Palace, Hyde Park Corner.

01: PAI WAN, LEFT, HYDE PARK, LONDON.

1965
Pai Wan moved to Nottingham and opened Dragoness (Long Jee) restaurant, as a partner. The restaurant later relaunched as Pagoda.

02, 03: HOP MUI, DAUGHTER OF PAI WAN, PAGODA RESTAURANT, NOTTINGHAM.

1973
Pai Wan opened Hong Kong House Takeaway in Hucknall, Nottinghamshire. Shing and Wai Ting's grandmother, Lin Tai, also moved to Nottinghamshire to reunite with Pai Wan after twelve years apart. Lin Tai became the wok chef, while Pai Wan took the orders and worked the fryer.

04: PAI WAN AND LIN TAI, HONG KONG HOUSE TAKEAWAY, NOTTINGHAM.

1982
Pai Wan opened Wing Wah restaurant in Beeston, Nottinghamshire, before selling it. Having saved up money and invested in property he retired at the age of 55 in the UK.

01

02, 03

04

01

02

03

Second Generation

1970
On the other side of the family, Shing and Wai Ting's father, Kan Sau, worked at a fish and chip restaurant in Kowloon, Hong Kong, before moving to Grantham in Lincolnshire.
01: THE ORIGINAL NAKED CHEF, GRANTHAM.

1972
Shing and Wai Ting's mother, Hop Mui, moved to Grantham in 1972, aged 16, where she met Kan Sau.

1981
Kan Sau and Hop Mui opened The Willows in Nottingham, which became the best Chinese takeaway in town.

1988
With profits from selling The Willows, Hop Mui opened Oriental Pearl in Nottingham with her eldest brother Ken. She sold her half of the business after five years.
02: SHING AND WAI TING EATING A FAMILY MEAL WITH HOP MUI AT ORIENTAL PEARL, NOTTINGHAM.

1992
Hop Mui had the opportunity to acquire the original Wing Wah, turning it into the Golden Crown (Fu Sing) in Beeston, named after Aaron Kwok – one of the four gods of pop culture in Hong Kong.
03: GOLDEN CROWN RESTAURANT, BEESTON.

1999
Hop Mui took over Oriental Pearl and relaunched it as the Pearl with brother King. At one point, they were so tired that Shing and Wai Ting had to take a black cab to school every morning.

2002
Hop Mui opened Opium in the Lace Market, with brother King and sister Jackie. It later won the Nottingham Restaurant Award for Best Non-European Restaurant.

2004
Hop Mui relaunched Golden Crown as The Republic (including karaoke) with King and brother-in-law Martin. Wai Ting became the manager.

2009
Hop Mui and Kan Sau opened Orient Takeaway in Nottingham.

2014
Hop Mui, King and Jade, a previous employee, opened Yumacha restaurant in Nottingham.

2019
Hop Mui, King and Jade acquired the original Willows takeaway site from 1981 and opened the Japanese restaurant Uchi in Nottingham.

Third Generation

2013
Shing, Wai Ting and Shing's partner Erchen created BAO as a street food and pop-up project in London.
04: OUR MARKET STALL AT KERB, KING'S CROSS.

2014
The trio opened BAO BAR shack in a car park in Hackney. Erchen was the heart of the kitchen, while Shing was the fryer chef and Wai Ting was the maître d'.
05: SHING AND WAI TING INSTALLING THE BAO BAR LIGHTBOX THAT SHING MADE AT NETIL MARKET.

2015
Opened BAO Soho, the first restaurant on Lexington Street, attracting an infamous queue.
06: THE INFAMOUS QUEUE AT BAO SOHO.

2016
Opened BAO Fitz in Fitzrovia.
07: ERCHEN AND WAI TING DURING THE BAO FITZ BUILD.

2017
Opened XU Teahouse & Restaurant on the edges of London's Chinatown (XU closed after the Covid-19 pandemic).

2019
Opened BAO Borough in Borough Market.
08: BAO BOROUGH IN ACTION.

2020
Tried to open BAO King's Cross, but the Covid-19 pandemic halted plans. Instead, launched delivery brand Rice Error and E-commerce brand Convni.

2021
Opened BAO King's Cross and BAO Noodle Shop in Shoreditch.
09: THE GRAND RIBBON CUTTING AT BAO NOODLE SHOP.

2023
Opened BAO Marylebone on St Christopher's Place.

04,05

07

06

08, 09

Erchen and I met at the Slade School of Fine Art in 2008, after Wai Ting and I had both moved to London. I had always felt an affinity with the arts, having memories that have stayed with me from an early age. I have my Mum to thank for it. She sent off my drawings to the local art competition when I was a toddler and unknowingly I won; she negotiated a bursary for me in primary school while we were going through bankruptcy; and she haggled an art scholarship so I could go to our chosen secondary school (although only because she had forgotten to apply for it). So, while pushed to do the opposite in higher education, it was really the arts, which had sustained my early education, that propelled me to continue down that path. When I finished my art foundation in Loughborough, I moved down to London at just about the same time as Wai Ting moved from Manchester to pursue a career in the fashion industry as a pattern cutter. At the same time, Erchen had moved from Taiwan to study in London and was actually facing the opposite rhetoric – her mum supported her ambition to pursue the arts and knew that studying abroad would be beneficial.

Artistically, Erchen and my styles were wildly different: Erchen is an artist, whereas I thrive on creative solutions. I like straight lines; she likes sketchy lines. Future–nostalgia; concept driven – craft driven. There is real beauty where our styles collide and, in my view, the differences between us create necessary nuance. Whether it is sleekness with soul beneath it, or a loose, undesigned nature with sharp thinking behind it, this is what gives BAO its integrity.

Humour is important to both of us, too. It's important to be able to have a bit of fun, as that feeling of fun ultimately makes its way into the product. In 2012, prior to starting BAO, Erchen's performative installation, *Rules to be a Lonely Man*, was exhibited at a group exhibition in New York. The work featured five lonely men dressed in oversized suits, gathered on a riverbed and gazing into the sky, with melancholic filmic music in the background. Though we didn't know it at the time, this was the piece that would later influence the birth of BAO. At the same time, I had graduated with a masters from the Royal College of Art with The Superstitious Fund – a one-year project that involved a live trading robot that operated an investment fund from investors around the world, trading the equity automatically on superstitious behaviours. The fund lost 25 per cent that year... So, you can probably see that hint of satire in our works.

The summer after we graduated, Erchen, Wai Ting and I travelled around Taiwan. Wai Ting and I travel to Hong Kong nearly every year, so it felt fitting that having met Erchen we would travel around Taiwan together. We spent time visiting the night markets and favourite street food stalls that Erchen had grown up frequenting. Upon returning to London, we created BAO. Originally it was conceived as a supplement to our own practices: mine being design and Erchen's, art. It was never our intention to open a restaurant. Rather, it was a route to bring together our creative backgrounds through the commonality of food. It started out as a project through which we could utilize our skills, from pattern-cutting the uniforms and building the flat-pack stall, to branding and coding the website. We weren't sure what to expect or what we

were venturing into, but we had time to dream and build up the skeleton of a brand. This golden time wouldn't last, however. As soon as we pushed the button, it evolved much faster and quicker than we expected. I remember vividly the first time we traded at a night market in Dalston and from there, there was no going back. The adrenaline was mixed with confusion as to why the queue snaked around the corner. I remember a woman crying and hugging Wai Ting after she took a bite of a BAO, and people re-joining the never-ending queue to order a second one. Maybe people were a little drunk, but from that moment BAO took over, and while we left behind our individual practices, we remained adamant about keeping our passions and interests alive in BAO.

Naturally, in the early stages of BAO, we were asked countless times why we had ventured from our creative backgrounds into restaurants. Not long after we started BAO, travelling to Hong Kong with my father, we visited his home village north of Tai Po and he had to explain to the head of the village that his kids couldn't get jobs anymore so they had resorted to selling steamed buns from a market stall. It's quite hard for some to understand our motives – after all, I spent nearly seven years at university to then go and sell baos in a car park. In my father's eyes it was probably akin to what is seen in Chinese dramas – the vendors selling mantou in ancient times – and just like when I did my art degree and he could only visualize me selling paintings on Hyde Park Corner. I guess there was always a small part of me that wanted to succeed in the language that was common to our family. So much of our lives revolved around restaurant culture. We would talk numbers with my mum when she came home to cash up while watching Chinese TV, and I watched the second generation (my mother and her siblings) develop their method of modernizing Cantonese restaurants. It felt natural that we would take that mantle and carry it forwards to another stage. And, in reality it was not too dissimilar to art school, which had drilled into us that mentality of quick-fire idea materialization and solutions in a highly pressurized and competitive system. When we graduated, the process of creating BAO from idea to reality wasn't all that different to what we'd already been doing, from the micro level of design to the macro level of ideation. It's just that now we were combining two passions: food and design.

Following that formative trip to Taiwan, Erchen and Shing had a bit of time on their hands. They had recently graduated, so they put their time to good use, beginning the process of perfecting the BAO recipe. None of us were chefs; we had no idea how to work or run a kitchen cook-line, all we had were two things: drive and three honed palates. We wanted to perfect each component of the classic pork belly gua bao and make it our own. Shing and Erchen even made a huge block of peanut brittle to shave with a wooden plane, so we could create the peanut powder for the BAO. This is how they do it back in Taiwan. What we wouldn't advise is to do this at home. Not just because of the high boiling point needed to make the caramel, from which bubbles of air continuously try to escape and spit out at you, but also because it is very sticky and very painful if it gets on your skin. This is what happened to Erchen; she still has the scars.

While Erchen and Shing focused on the recipes, I was in charge of getting us into a market. At the time, Street Feast, Kerb and Broadway Market were the most popular and exciting food markets in London. I tried to reach out but never heard anything back. Competition was so fierce, as it seemed that everyone had had the bright idea of starting out in street food at the same time. Those were the peak street food years, mainly because of the low overheads. I even contacted council-run markets, and I remember finally getting a response from one of them six months later, just to be put on a six-month waiting list... It was a bit of a catch 22, as we hadn't traded a single day; so no one knew what our food was like, or was able to try it.

Pop-ups or residencies in London were also becoming popular at the time, so we decided to take another approach and see if anyone would take us on for one night. We lucked out and managed to take over the Pacific Social Club in Hackney for one evening. We sent our menu and posters for the event to the founders of Kerb and Street Feast and the manager of Netil Market (near Broadway Market), and amazingly they all came down. It was booked out for both sittings (see page 15, image 05).

We were steaming the BAOs off a gas camping stove, as the coffee shop had no kitchen equipment. We had no clue how to work the gas canister, so of course it set alight a metre in front of a table of four Japanese ladies, who laughed hysterically as though it was all part of the pop-up mania.

That night, we were accepted into all three of the markets we had invited to try our food – it was a pivotal moment that kick-started our journey into street food.

When we started trading as a street food stall, there were three items on the menu: the Classic Pork BAO (see page 51), Taiwanese Fried Chicken (see page 92) and a pomelo salad. We had huge queues at our stall that would snake around the corner, and we would take pictures and send them home to our parents. My dad could never get over how we sold only three things and people would still queue for it. He is so used to having 100 items on a menu. He would constantly refresh the Instagram app for new photos – his way of saying, I think, how proud he was.

I was doing the street food events on my 'holiday' days off from my day job. When Kerb asked us to join them as permanent traders, I remember having to make the calculations of how many BAOs we needed to sell a week in order for the three of us to survive living in London. After some back-of-an-envelope calculations, and much deliberation, I made the leap from day job to full-time street food trader. That was probably one of the best decisions I have ever made.

And so we began our full-time street food life. The first half of the week would be spent steaming all the BAOs and prepping for the weekend trading at Street Feast and Kerb, and a Saturday at Netil Market. Every week, after a long day of steaming 800 BAOs, we would religiously venture to our local, Silk Road in Camberwell, with Employee Number 1, Alice. We would call ahead to pre-order, creating our own Set A and Set B to alternate the flavours.

The BAO BAR in Netil Market was our first baby, and was different to the roaming street food events we did at Kerb and Street Feast, as it was a permanent stall. It was also a place of refuge, a home – one that didn't need to be set up and packed away like our other street food stalls. It was a thing of beauty: a small shack that we designed and built, which was inspired by the Golden Gai bars in the alleys of Shinjuku, Japan. We have a great respect for and interest in Japanese culture and design, and this is something that would go on to echo through the BAO world, though at that time we had no idea what was in store for us. The BAO BAR was something that, at the time, you would not have come across anywhere else in London: a six-seater shack, where you could sit in a cosy wooden environment and eat your BAO, and where we also performed ritualistic Taiwanese tea ceremonies for the regulars. You felt like you had been transported somewhere far away, not sitting in a car park in East London. It is this transportive feeling that we have since tried to replicate in all our restaurants.

Street food life was crazy – the heavy lifting; the intricate jigsaw puzzle of how the van had to be packed in order to fit the big steamer throne and the green wooden stall; the times when we'd venture past tiredness, packing up at midnight after a food festival, not to go home to sleep before the next 6.00 a.m. start, but instead to steam another 400 BAOs because we oversold on the first night. And there are many other stories we chuckle about now (although we didn't at the time): the 3.00 a.m. pomelo hunt driving around East London, scraping the van on the Netil Market gate, reversing into a tree stump that took out the back window of the van, the swellings in uncomfortable places – but you don't need to know about all of those.

Although it was tiring, we loved what we were doing. It was incredibly satisfying to be doing something that we had built ourselves, and to be introducing something new to London. We collected a few awards along the way, the YBFs (Young British Foodie) award and Street Food awards, which made up for all those scars.

When we opened our first permanent restaurant in 2015, we knew the stress and exhaustion would kick into another gear. But even with this in mind, there was a sense of relief. We were dreaming of the days when we wouldn't have to physically set up and break down a stall just for a couple of hours of trading, never knowing if it was going to rain or not. I mean, it was probably our fault – we had designed a flat-pack stall that was a bit over the top, with nuts and bolts that had to be drilled in each time (see opposite page, image 01). At the same time, our prep kitchens were our own open-plan kitchens at home and I can tell you that the constant smell of braised pork and deep-frying really does permeate into the fabric of your life. The straw that broke us was a mini Christmas market for an office block. It was the kind of Christmas party that featured a sad little donkey dressed up as a reindeer. There was a biblical-level storm: picture equipment flying around and us holding onto the gazebo to stop it from blowing away into the storm. Everyone else was laughing from the comfort of their vans. We had only sold 15 BAOs. That was the last event we did. It marked the moment when we were ready to open a restaurant and swap market-stall trading for a dry roof over our heads.

This is when the second part of our journey began. We received an email from Karam Sethi, who was one of the three sibling founders behind JKS Restaurants – Jyo, Karam and Sue – with just one line, 'Do you guys want to open a restaurant?'. We didn't really think anything would come of it, but after a few meetings, they started looking for a site while we spent about six months planning, designing and testing our recipes at home. Looking back, they really took a punt on us, considering we had only been trading for about 6 months. I still remember our first tasting we did with Jyo and Karam inside our shack. Netil Market back then wasn't as lively and full as it is now and our shack sat next to a burger van and another market stall in an empty car park. We had to arrange the chains to be taken off the main gates to allow Karam's car in. I can picture the scene to this day: a dark green Classic BMW 8 E31 parked in front of our lonesome shack, in a deserted car park, on a cold mid-autumn's night in East London.

It took over a year to find the right site that would become our first restaurant – a dark French café with a tiny basement on Lexington Street in Soho. I vividly remember counting how many people passed the café as a way to figure out how many covers we might be able to get through the doors. At the time, Lexington Street, wasn't a particularly busy street in Soho.

Nothing can really prepare you for the challenge of running a non-stop restaurant machine. It's so very different to running the market stalls we were used to, where selling out of food, to preserve wastage, was the norm. When we finally opened our doors on Lexington Street, the very same emotion we had when we first traded in the night market came rushing back, with the queue snaking down the road and around the corner. Understandably, neighbouring restaurants were upset. We had to control the queue and create gaps at intervals for each shop front to make walkways into their entrances. Then we moved the queue across the road, but there was no winning there – a well-known sandwich chain got upset. It was surreal, but there

was a real sense of pride, especially for the team. When they set up the restaurant in the morning, they would see a queue already forming half an hour before we opened. I remember Erchen getting upset as her grandma, who had flown halfway around the world to visit BAO, got up to leave after 10 minutes because she felt so uncomfortable knowing that she was occupying a seat while people were impatiently queuing outside (see opposite page, image 04).

You've probably heard all the stories of opening a restaurant. The hours, the exhaustion, the hurdles and dramas – there is no way round it. Yes, once you've done it, you'll never want to do it again (until six months later). When we opened, we were doing 100 hours a week in a short-staffed restaurant and driving up to Nottingham and back every Sunday (the day we were closed) due to a family illness. The weekend before the opening, our sous chef emailed to say he was in a car on his way to Cornwall and he wasn't coming back. That was the icing on the cake of what it takes to open a restaurant.

I still remember the countless 'laughing-but-really-crying' moments. Especially because after all that exhaustion we remained so committed to keeping our recipes secret that we would come in early or stay late to quietly make them. We'd spent so long perfecting them that we held their secrets close to our chests, covertly topping up buckets of hot sauce with secret ingredients and mixing the spice for the fried chicken once everyone had gone home (see opposite page, image 03). What we didn't know was that years later, all those secret recipes would be here, laid in front of you to read and cook from.

OPPOSITE PAGE
01: THE FLAT-PACKABLE STALL.
02: THE SNAKING QUEUE THAT WE MOVED ACROSS THE STREET.
03: WAI TING MIXING THE SECRET SPICE MIX FOR THE CHICKEN.
04: ERCHEN'S GRANDMOTHER, CHEN HSIU HSU, AT BAO SOHO.
05: FIRST POP-UP IN PACIFIC SOCIAL CLUB WHERE A GAS CANNISTER WAS SET ALIGHT.
06: SHING ON A MASSAGE CHAIR IN NOTTINGHAM.

01

04

02

05

03

06

BAO Manifesto: Inspiring Your Inner Lonely Man

You'll have likely seen our logo, the illustration of a Lonely Man eating a BAO that was born from Erchen's artwork, *Rules to be a Lonely Man*. You have probably wondered why he's sad. The answer is that he isn't – he's filled with joy because he's found a perfect moment in his BAO. As we travel back to the beginnings of what this artwork symbolized, we will explore how the five lonely men searching for a perfect moment of solitude in the original artwork would become the foundation of what BAO came to be.

Our purpose in opening restaurants was not just to fill empty stomachs, but to inspire lonely mouths with perfect moments. We built a world to be explored, through which we could equip our community to thrive by connecting with their inner Lonely Man. We are all here to find our place in the world and mastering our own role in life is part of being the Lonely Man. In this manifesto we first explore the inspiration behind BAO, the world we have tried to create and why we set out to do the things we do, and then we take a closer at look at how we achieve that vision.

Build a World
    Rules to be a Lonely Man by Erchen Chang
    Riverbed to BAOverse
    Experiences for the single diner
    Expanding BAOverse
    A community of searchers
    School of BAO

Inspiring Lonely Mouths
    Become a specialist
    Mastery
    Think food, serve design
    The BAO centimetre
    Rare Taiwanese produce
    Sourcing beef
    The vessel: Ozu plate
    Artistic experimentations
    BAO artist dinners
    BAO: bakery of artistic objects

Build a World

When we first opened BAO, we always sought to connect it to our backgrounds in the arts. Early on, people often asked if BAO was one big art piece, having seen the connection between Erchen's original 2012 artwork and the restaurant. Erchen's work was always about creating an immersive, dreamlike fantasy. Such 'worlds' resemble an alternate space, and so world-building was the creative approach that we adopted to allow us to distil our inspirations into these dream spaces. There is a quote from the artist and designer Isamu Noguchi that really hits the mark for us: to 'take the essence of nature and distil it – just as a poet does. And that's what I'm interested in – the poetic translation'. We take the essence of the Taiwanese way of life and apply our poetic translation to create a world for the Lonely Man. It's this process of translation that is integral to how we create.

If you've eaten our food, you've most likely been to our restaurants. The restaurants are part of this world, and this world is full of stories driven by a narrative. Ultimately, you are sitting in a story that came from that defining moment back in 2012.

Picture a riverbed with five lonely men, all in specific poised positions, gazing into the shimmering river on a dark night, with a melancholic soundtrack playing in the background. As a spectator, you can't help but let out a small smirk as you recognize that these singular lonely men, in search of themselves, have gathered in the same spot. Looking past that comical moment, a carefully curated collection of objects in the surrounding scene has created a platform that allows the lonely men to search for a perfect moment in solitude. Each finds themselves in a community of some sort with a shared mission.

01, 02

This mini world that was created by Erchen would become the most important factor in why BAO exists, and the transition from artwork to real life would lead to us serving nearly half a million lonely men a year. Whether you are on a riverbed gazing into the night or in our restaurant looking for a perfect moment in solitude, like it or not, both exist in the same world. The Lonely Man sitting under the single cheese plant on a step crafted for him became the man eating the BAO. It's worth noting here that when we refer to the lonely man, we're referring to anyone who resonates or who searches for their innermost Lonely Man.

We sometimes take a step back and chuckle knowing that what was once an artwork in a gallery in New York has evolved into something that is so intrinsic to the BAO world. As years go by, this world evolves and mutates. Is mutating a good or bad thing? Who knows? We draw a lot of inspiration from a manga film trilogy called *20th Century Boys* about a group of kids that illustrate a comic book prophecy, which thirty years later becomes reality. In the present day, the characters try to unlock who the mysterious villain really is as they battle against the sci-fi apocalypse. We draw a connection between the comic book prophecy and Erchen's manual that taught performers in her artwork how to embody the Lonely Man characteristics. We joke that the artwork is the prophecy that created BAO and the manual is how we built this dreamlike world.

01, 02: THE ORIGINAL RULES TO BE A LONELY MAN ARTWORK AND PERFORMANCE.

Riverbed to BAOverse   STC

We have long been inspired by Walt Disney's unrealized Experimental Prototype Community of Tomorrow (EPCOT), a prototype city for the future. However, as we expand our world, instead of looking forwards to the perfect city of the future, we look inwards and envisage a world suited to finding oneself. From the Lonely Man riverbed, we expand to a world containing eateries, shops and delivery. When we first opened BAO Soho, we sketched out a BAO World Map for ourselves that represented what we now call the BAOverse. While it did get lost along the way (you know, running restaurants is a pretty full-time gig) it remained integral to how we envisaged our world. Sometimes we would put ourselves in the shoes of the Lonely Man to try to understand what he would want or where he would find his perfect moment. This meant giving a purpose to each of our touchpoints – from the design of our spaces to how our retail shop supplies the Lonely Man.

Back in the 1990s, I was hooked on world-building and strategy games. Think Command & Conquer and Theme Hospital as some classic examples. This world-view element is something that seeped into our visual language. It was about providing a world for you to discover, that you could view in its entirety. We later started working with illustrators Doug John Miller and Marcelo Colmenero, who create these inviting worlds so successfully. Through these detailed depictions of our worlds, we become voyeurs, whether it's through an isometric God's-eye view of the restaurant buildings or an ambient atmospheric illustration of the interiors. Those scenes achieve the exact same ambience as the original artwork of the Lonely Man on the riverbed. So, when we build our restaurants, we build them for the Lonely Man, making them places where diners can be transported into a narrative moment in time, inspired by the different ways of life in Taiwan.

When we approach the design of these spaces, it's essential that we take inspiration from Taiwanese eating cultures and distil these into the world we have created for the Lonely Man. We get very excited and nostalgic about the food culture back in Taiwan – having now travelled there together many times since that first trip – from *xiao chi* houses, which serve a collection of 'small eats', to Taiwanese cafés, beef noodle shops and fast-food ventures. But it's equally important that we don't try to directly import authentic experiences, as what's crucial is the process of how we translate this way of life while still maintaining an element of feeling transported. We don't want to transport people back to Taiwan, but to another world – an uncanny version of Taiwan. For us, it has been about building a philosophy that is anchored in Taiwanese culture but completely comfortable in London.

BAO Soho
Escape the hustle of Soho with the bustle
of a Soho *xiao chi* house
Inspired by Taiwanese *xiao chi* houses
and street food culture

BAO Fitz
Perch at a Fitzrovian bar feeling like you are in an
Edward Hopper scene
Inspired by heritage and quick-fry Taiwanese flavours
that pair well with drinks

BAO Borough
Grab a skewer and a highball on the way home via the
train that rumbles past the Borough Grill House
Inspired by Taiwanese and Asian grill house culture

BAO King's Cross
Loose yourself in a place where you can simply be,
in the all-rounder King's Cross Café
Inspired by nostalgic Taiwan and non-spaces

BAO BAR
Inspired by Tokyo's Golden Gai bars that have
only 6 seats

BAO Noodle Shop
A moment to restore yourself with soul warming
bowls of noodles
Inspired by Taiwan's famous beef noodle culture

Convni
The supply company for the lonely man
Inspired by 7-Eleven convenience stores

Rice Error
Time for a TV dinner for one
Inspired by the *Chishang bian dang* – rice houses
across Taiwan

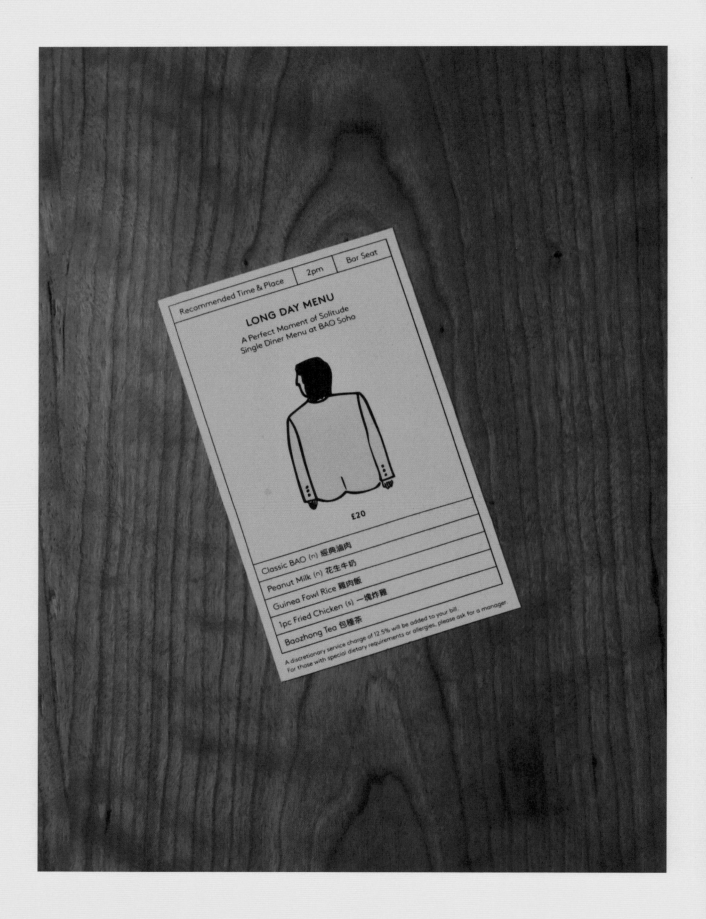

建造一個世界

Throughout the world of BAO, we create experiences specifically for the single diner. We all have our perfect, private moments. One of mine is lunch at Paul Rothe & Son, an old-school sandwich shop in Marylebone where staff dressed in old-fashioned workwear jackets and shirts blend into the furniture of Formica tables and floor-to-ceiling shelves. I'll order a bacon mayo sandwich with salt and vinegar Walker's crisps (chips) emptied onto the plate and a cup of builder's tea, served in a porcelain cup with a lid to preserve the temperature. I dress semi-smart to blend into the surroundings and, most importantly, I'll be by myself. In that moment, everything is in its perfect place, and I am transported to a place of solitude and reflection, escaping from the fast-moving world for a short while, right before a long meeting. As humans, we take pleasure from things feeling like they are just as they should be – when your socks finally don't have holes in them, or when you drink your British brew from the right porcelain china at the optimum temperature, experiencing the ideal 'aah' moment. This is the same 'aah' moment we reference when talking about Taiwanese beef noodles, and it's what we aspire to in our restaurants – putting everything in its right place, in the hope that guests can experience that perfect moment we always refer to.

It's a little-known secret that if you are a single diner in the queue, you most likely will be fast-tracked. We make sure that when we design our restaurants, we accommodate single diners – this might be by including a certain number of well-placed counter seats that have a view into the theatre of the kitchen or a quirky single seat positioned in the window for gazing out into the world. We then layer these spaces with experiences for the single diner. An example is the single diner menu we have at all our restaurants, which we call the 'Long Day' menu (see opposite page). It is a ritualistic menu that is tailored to each restaurant. Not too big or too small, it's an experience that we will want to return to again and again. Along with the menu we provide instructions on how to be a Lonely Man, so that the diner can experience the meal as intended, aided by the stories that explain why and how those dishes were created.

BAO has its roots in Erchen's iconic Lonely Man, searching for his perfect moment of solitude. It's important to note that this is what we're aiming for – finding moments for yourself and appreciating those moments. We want to validate an appreciation of solitude, provide the tools to find this appreciation and encourage the happiness that comes from it. Think about the 2008 Disney film *Wall-E*, in which everyone is hooked into their own world of augmented reality. While they remain 'connected' to a digital sphere, at the same time they become detached. There is a phrase in Taiwan, 'little happiness', which references all those perfect little humble moments that keep us connected to real-world experiences. The Lonely Man is not lonely in the way we might usually think of it, he is rather a reflection of the power of a solitary experience to keep us in tune with the simple pleasures of life. We want to channel that inner Lonely Man and help others to do so.

There are some amazing stories from our BAO history that will always remain with me. One that stands out is of the two single diners who met in the queue, ended up getting married and revisited BAO Soho on their anniversary. Another is the pregnant woman dining alone whose water broke and who still insisted on staying for her guinea fowl rice to come before she went to hospital. There are our single diner regulars, too – Khalid who loves whisky and brings different types for staff to try, or the peanut milk man who loves going to Soho to tell them their peanut milk isn't as good as at Fitz.

OPPOSITE PAGE: THE LONG DAY MENU

Expanding BAOverse   STC

When expanding our world outside of the restaurant zone, it was important to us that purposeful experiences for the single diner weren't bound to these physical locations. We want to make sure that this purpose continued into other manifestations that would emerge in our world in the future.

When the pandemic hit in 2020, we had to react quickly and we launched a takeaway and delivery brand, Rice Error, and an E-commerce at-home brand, Convni. With nearly everyone around the world focused on one thing – that awful word, 'pivoting' – these offshoots could have gone either way, and we might easily have left behind our values by churning something out at high speed. But, despite the fast turnaround, everything still had to be right – the straight-edged bamboo boxes from Taiwan, the cobalt blue paper bags, and, most importantly, the common thread of what each brand means. We wanted these offshoots to still have a shared purpose of equipping our community with single diner experiences that tapped into their inner Lonely Man – whether that was via Convni, our Lonely Man supply company, which equips one with the necessary items at home for one, or Rice Error, which gives purpose to having the TV dinner for one.

Many dismiss or frown upon eating in front of the TV, but we wanted to give purpose to that experience. Why is it any different to mindlessly sitting at a table and ploughing through a meal to satisfy your hunger? We should celebrate those moments; that unbeatable feeling of ordering a dish that's perfectly suited to eating in front of the TV and enjoying it while watching just the right film. When we launched our limited-edition Guest Box Series, working with chefs such as Ixta Belfrage, Fuchsia Dunlop, Margot Henderson, Victor Liong and Junya Yamasaki, the idea was to not only create a knock out, exciting dish, but to pair it with an episode or film to watch with the meal that provides further insight into the food. There is a Japanese word, *kuchisabishii*, which describes the concept of eating not because you are hungry but because your mouth is lonely. This idea of inspiring lonely mouths is one that feeds into much of our practice.

As our world grows and spaces multiply, the spaces must come to life. There is a famous breakfast restaurant in Hong Kong that we often visit when we're there called Australia Dairy Company. When we sit in their dining room, at first it feels like chaos, but there is a harmonious, chaotic rhythm to it all that is like theatre – a performance of around fifteen waiters standing in the middle of the room casually shouting this way and that or looking at their phones. This performative quality really activates the space. We can spend all the time in the world fantasizing and building beautiful settings, but they are lifeless without people.

When we first started trading with our market stall, we must have been doing something right, because we attracted a fan base – maybe it was just a case of right time, right place. People would take pictures of their BAO tote bags and T-shirts around the world and friends would send us messages when they spotted a BAO bag on their travels. There was always a sense of pride when we spotted one ourselves, too, especially overseas. This feeling of a connected community even later evolved into a tradition in which our core community would tattoo themselves with our artworks. We created a certified tattoo list that functions as a 'get what you tattoo' pass, with a complimentary item from us when they dine in. The weeping sake man = a glass of sake, the original Lonely Man = a BAO and so on.

Starting out on the riverbed in 2012, it was then about developing a larger world that recognized our community. When you join our world, you join a collective pursuit to thrive by connecting with your inner Lonely Man. We provide the tools to do so, and along the way we try to gamify the journey, turning diners and staff from people into characters. We find a lot of joy in games, and there is this real addictiveness in seeing a population grow, like watching your visitor count multiply in Rollercoaster Tycoon, but from a guest perspective, it's about how people discover our world and how they might feel a sense of belonging in this community. All games have communities, whether that's in a multiplayer game or having to join a random team to progress further. You all have one collective mission, sometimes with strangers – the only difference is that with BAO, the aim is to identify with your inner Lonely Man. We're here to provide the platform and the nudge needed to make that happen.

As abstract and serious as finding your inner Lonely Man sounds, it's important that this concept is fundamentally about having fun and figuring out how we can channel that light-heartedness into the systems and cultures we have in place, from our loyalty app, which rewards single dining with double points, to the journey our team members experience, with rewards based around perfect moments in solitude. In the end, we want everyone – our guests and employees, and everyone who dips into the BAOverse – to enjoy a moment in solitude, fun and creativity in the everyday.

OPPOSITE PAGE: THE BAOVERSE. ILLUSTRATION BY MARCELO COLMENERO

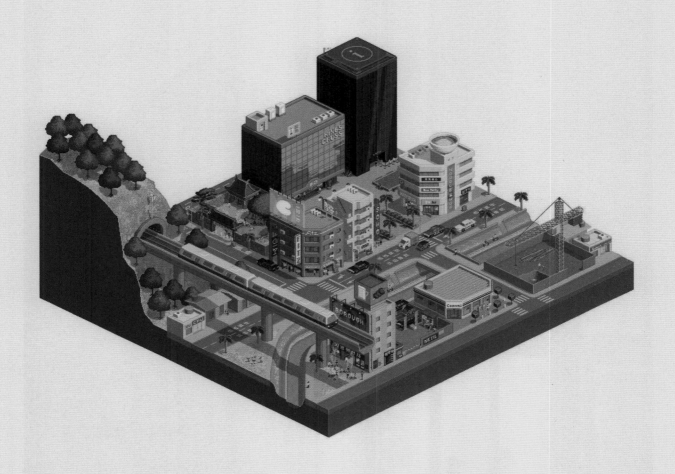

建造一個世界

After opening Soho and Fitz, we wanted to shift our focus on to creating something meaningful for our team. We thought about why people seem to want to work at BAO, clearly food plays an integral part in this, but also design. This was how School of BAO came about, our way of combining our philosophies of hospitality, art and design through a curated series of workshops, talks and field trips. The idea was to offer something that was more than just an average hospitality learning and development path.

Funnily, the acronym for School of BAO is SOB, which we found fitting, bringing to mind a lonely tear falling down the curve of the Lonely Man's cheek.

We started with trips to our suppliers and talks from industry peers, such as Zan Kaufman, Founder of Bleecker Burger and Jeremy Lee, Chef Proprietor of Quo Vadis. We combined these with workshops and talks related to art and design, such as a Riso Press workshop with Hato Press and a talk by Doug John Miller, an artist we commissioned to do the BAO night series.

02

I remember when we sat down after a year or two of School of BAO and we tried to develop it past just being a calendar of events. We came up with some abstract stuff like linking it to the Bauhaus philosophy – this must have blown some minds. But really philosophies, cultures... they all build steadily over time and in hindsight trying to capture it at the start probably was a little too keen to do. Through the years, we slowly evolved and crafted what School of BAO means, how it can be beneficial for our team for their everyday learning, but also quite simply for them to gain insight into Taiwanese culture, the BAO pursuit in becoming a specialist and let's not forget the most important thing, parties and get togethers.

One of the most rewarding parts of owning a business, is watching how it has grown and developed over the years, in terms of creating and building a culture. School of BAO is a big part of shaping the culture at BAO. Every year we take our managers to a place of architectural interest for our 'No Managers at Home' getaway – Walmer Yard, Shingle House (see opposite page), Norfolk House – each designed by a famous architect. The first one we ever did, we invited a learning and development specialist in to workshop together what we believe, who we are, and the characteristics we celebrate. While understandably these things can end up quite generic, what's been great to see is how that seed of a workshop was planted and grew from a bunch of words to how we create belonging and culture in our own unique way.

03

Rewinding to the beginning, we always had illustrations of the three of us, Shing, Erchen and me, illustrated as the Lonely Man eating the BAO – living our best Lonely Man lives. We put these on our business cards, and no one took me seriously because Shing gave me an eye patch and my job title was Oops Director instead of Ops Director. Something like this is so small but can be so big in terms of feeling a sense of belonging, and so this portraiture and characterization spread to managers who had been with us for 2 years. None of the staff know that for Erchen to illustrate them and achieve their Lonely Man portrait, she has to get intimate, studying their faces by trawling through photos or stalking them through social media. That love and care that transports itself into their Lonely Man portraits creates a warmth that connects the team.

OPPOSITE PAGE: THE FIRST 'NO MANAGERS AT HOME' AT SHINGLE HOUSE, DUNGENESS, DESIGNED BY NORD.
02: THE BAO JACKET.
03: STAFF IN OUR HIGHBALL MANIA T-SHIRTS, BAO BOROUGH.

Inspiring Lonely Mouths

When we started BAO, our aim was to inspire people by bringing together food, art and design. The stories behind how we do this are just as important in inspiring others as the final product itself. The processes of how we translate and distil the Taiwanese way of life and food culture into a world to be explored using our own unique perspectives are an important part of what BAO means. We're here to spark people's imaginations through stories and bring them together in the shared mission of finding our own inner Lonely Man.

When we moved into our first restaurant, BAO Soho, we painted the letters 刈包專門店 on our shop front (some of you might have seen this on our logo). It means 'gua bao specialist shop'. We respect and look up to the vendors in Taiwan who hone their products over decades, producing something seemingly simple with such elegance. From the way their utensils are exactly the right measurements to the flick of condiments, there is such precision in both technique and flavour.

We strive to bring a specialist approach into everything we do at BAO by mastering both the micro and the macro elements of design, sourcing and skill. This can be seen in the tongs we get from Taiwan that pick up just the right amount of meat to place into the BAO, the kitchen trays we import from Hong Kong that are much smaller than standard gastronorms, and the traditional handmade steamers that Erchen's mother still personally orders from a one-man specialist shop in Taipei. Being a specialist is about obsessing over the details and about innovating and pushing the boundaries, in this case, of a humble and traditional product. When we started, we weren't chefs, we were more like craftspeople, which meant we compensated for any lack of experience with our commitment to deliver quality through dedication. It took us a long time to get our BAOs to even a respectable level in the very early stages. It's important that as we recount our stories and processes, we also tell the stories of our failures, as they are all part of mastering our craft, which in turn becomes part of a holistic approach to becoming specialists.

The concept of mastery can be quite alien in our culture, especially during the time of Instagram and social media, in which young people are much more interested in pursuing their final goals as quickly as possible. Who can blame us, when day in, day out these aspirations are plastered all over Instagram? We admire and are inspired by the vendors in Taiwan – the way they perfect one product their whole lives and serve casual food with such elegance. That elegance is only achieved through decades of mastery and is often overlooked. In Japan, the term for this mastery of your profession is *shokunin*. It takes ten years before you can call yourself a sushi chef in Tokyo. I'm sure in London it only takes you to put on a uniform. When we create, execute and repeat, we are always pushing to pursue the finer details and make things better. Not just the taste and the execution of a dish, everything surrounding it – it is a holistic approach. It's often the journey and the processes that make who you are rather than the product itself.

The 'think food, serve design' approach is one we describe internally to ground us and remind us of our aims when we create. When we use the word 'design', it doesn't just refer to making things look aesthetically pleasing, rather, it's the creative solution for how we distil our inspirations into the narrative for our world.

Firstly, it's important to note that our creative foundation – 'think food' – is rooted in the Taiwanese way of life. This is where we draw our inspiration from. Taiwan has a diverse history from the indigenous Taiwanese heritage to the influence of mainland China and the Japanese. This is what makes Taiwan a true melting pot. It's the daily way of life that inspires us, not just Taiwanese cuisine, but the places people frequent, their habits and lifestyle.

When we create, there is a logical approach that we follow, all the way from our overall world view, making sure the guiding narrative underpins the 'why', to the rules that we follow in dish designs. For the first several years, we couldn't articulate how we were creating, probably because we had no idea what we were doing in the first place. Without being able to put the process on paper, the term 'The BAO Way' organically appeared. Our team would learn The BAO Way through trial and error, and later laugh when they realized it had taken them two years to understand. This initial, nebulous concept of The BAO Way was the prequel to think food, serve design. Naturally, as the brand grew, it became ever more important to paint a clearer definition of our philosophies on how we create.

Our processes aren't based on the entrenched rules of cookery that chefs learn at culinary school – what ingredients should go with what, etc. Just as we don't rigidly follow the functionalities of interior design as the 'right' way to design. That used to weigh us down, but over the years, we learned to appreciate and take advantage of the fact that we had different processes and perspectives, not trying to deliver like for like, we could take pride in creating something that had our own imprinted artistry, however flawed it sometimes was.

First of all, we look at the narrative – the purpose of the dish, and what context it should be eaten in. We design the dish to work with each restaurant's story, then we apply our logic onto the actual dish, trying to tick off at least two or three of the key details that make us who we are: a small touch of innovation, a specially sourced product or a foundation that is based on heritage or a personal experience.

This is how we translate, and how we question the notion of authenticity – by taking Taiwanese culture, by way of our travels and upbringings, and distilling it into our world for the Lonely Man. When people ask why we don't serve 'authentic' traditional food, the answer is that this is not what we are here to do. It's not that our aim is to 'Westernize' Taiwanese food, but as Noguchi put it, it's the nuance of the 'poetic translations' that resonates with us.

Yes, sometimes things are lost in translation, sometimes Wai Ting's and my Hong Kong heritage seeps in. And there are a lot of setbacks and uncertainties along the way, too. But ultimately, it's these impurities that truly make us who we are.

Sometimes you don't realize that the push to improve and perfect happens organically without you paying attention. When we look back at photos of when we first opened, our BAOs looked crazy. But as time went on, chef by chef, the rhythm and language of the kitchen naturally shifted the trajectory of the product into a better and better form. We've seen this repeatedly through the different iterations of the product and by literally serving thousands over time. Put a master behind the making and watch as time goes by.

The BAO centimetre is a term we use to describe the making of our BAOs. There always needs to be a 1 cm (½ inch) gap between the filling and the edge of the BAO. In the case of our Classic BAO (see page 51), this term is only the tip of the iceberg – there are other detailed processes that follow suit: the way we sprinkle the peanut powder so that the coriander (cilantro) is just peeking out slightly to indicate every layer of filling; the way you have to hold the BAO so that when dismounting the BAO, it doesn't knock off all your hard work; and how the BAO must be rotated to face the diner when set down on the dining table. These might read as being easy, but the challenge is that one person needs to deliver this 400 times a day, which roughly equates to a BAO every thirty seconds.

Taiwan is an amazing country that yields quality produce. Due to the altitude and climate, Taiwanese tea is prized, so much so that they have tea competitions. A lot of the tea is drunk by the islanders themselves, so much of the best tea doesn't make it off the island. The rice farmers from Chishang each have to pass stringent tests and prove the provenance of their product before getting their stamp of authenticity and quality, just like Champagne. We're always on the hunt for highly selective produce to use in our dishes, and one that's especially close to our hearts is our 400-day aged white soy sauce. It's a soy sauce that Erchen's grandma has been buying from a local small-batch producer since the 1970s in the south of Taiwan. She would have stacks of boxes in her kitchen and she swore by this soy sauce. It is such a beautiful and elegant sauce, made from the first pressing of white soybeans that is then aged for 400 days. Lightly salty yet heavy in umami, it's also a touch sweeter than other soy sauces. It is rare, and you have to get on a waiting list to purchase it. When we first opened, Erchen's mother had to stockpile the boxes and send them over – picture the scene of crates of soy sauce packed high in the living room. Six restaurants in, obviously this wasn't a sustainable method of importing, so we had to find a more realistic solution. Luckily, due to Erchen's grandma's history and relationship with the company, they were happy to bulk supply us. We are put on a waiting list once a year and we feel so privileged to be able to import it. Once, one of our ex-staff who went back to Taiwan mentioned they couldn't get any as we had cornered all the supply. This aged soy sauce embodies our focus on importing perfect produce to the UK via our family stories and strands of history.

When we first began to think about opening our own restaurant, we knew we wanted to work with the best suppliers. We had heard of The Cornwall Project, set up by Matt Chatfield. His mission was to supply London's restaurants with the best Cornish produce and in return create long-term jobs in that part of the country. I remember hounding him to get him to work with us – I called him up and he pretended he had to take a call from his office. In reality he had no office, and he was just trying to evade me. My persistence paid off when someone he was supposed to show around Cornwall cancelled on him, so he gave in and let us come to see him. That began our relationship with Matt, with the help of a bottle of whisky. We went to see Philip Warren & Son and saw the incredible amount of care and detail that is put into the ageing process of their beef.

Matt was instrumental in supporting us. Before we opened BAO Soho, we were doing a lot of tasting and menu development, and he would drop off my ridiculously small order of twelve duck hearts, one tongue, three trotters (pig's feet), different cuts and different aged specifications of meat on his delivery run to my flat, before heading off to deliver to The Clove Club in Shoreditch. We were only a street food business at the time, so he must have seen some potential in us.

Matt then took over his family farm in Devon a few years ago. His family farmed it on behalf of a big estate for 360 years before his grandad was able to buy it 40 years ago. Inspired by the Iberico pigs of Spain, he realized he could apply the same logic to sheep, he started farming *cull yaw* (older female sheep). He takes on old ewes that would otherwise be destined for the abattoir and gives them a good feeding on his land for six months, getting a nice fat coverage. The meat is then aged by Philip Warren & Son. We use *cull yaw* in our dumplings at BAO Noodle Shop (see page 204), which has really elevated the humble dumpling through the incredible flavour and quality of the meat.

All our pottery is made by local ceramicists, the majority by Owen Wall and Anna Hodgson. We use different pieces for different dishes at different sites, but not all of our dishes have unique tableware suited to them. One of the dishes that does is 40-day Aged Beef Rump Cap with Aged White Soy (see page 102), which is a delicate and simple dish needing an elegant solution. The dish is served on a plate that Erchen designed with Owen, inspired by a dining scene in the Yasujirō Ozu film *An Autumn Afternoon* in which dishes seem to be raised off a table. His films welcome the audience through a low perspective, positioning the viewpoint at eye level, as if you are with the characters in the scene and they are speaking to you. As such, the mise-en-scène of the dining scene is crafted over different tiers, from the beer bottles on the floor to the different levels of ceramics on the table. The Ozu plate we created is raised off the table, echoing the floating ceramics in the film. The height gives focus to the food while casting a shadow below. With a slightly matte, speckled finish, the plate is made uniquely for BAO Soho.

The three of us came from artistic backgrounds, and having founded BAO quite quickly after graduation, there was a part of us that tried not to lose the thread that connected us to our backgrounds, in part as a kind of justification of our studies. As time went on, we came to realize that it wasn't so black and white as art being our past and restaurants our future, and it became much less important to force through a connection. In fact, the journey in the next stage of our lives was a continuation of what we had already been doing – applying our unique perspectives to our creations and craft. BAO is a journey, one in which we can see our own tastes morph and develop over the years, leaving behind a trail of restaurants inspired by those very same changes. And at the same time, from an artistic perspective, we can see the journey of BAO as shaped by my creative direction, observing the progression of what BAO means – both as a brand and as a physical form that can be playfully manipulated.

OPPOSITE: BAOBRA HEPWORTH (ERCHEN) WITH BAO SCULPTURES.
02: BAO SKETCHES AND DIAGRAMS.
03: SCULPTURAL BAOS.
04: BEHIND THE SCENES.

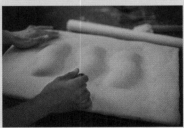

02, 03, 04

鼓舞孤獨胃口

We were drawn to the idea of putting on an event in which the importance of the dinner wasn't actually the attendance or the consumption of the food but the process of creating it and the parts of it that could live on afterwards as artefacts – like a time stamp or a form of documentation. Our first Artist Dinner was held in 2016, in the basement of BAO Fitz in collaboration with the artist Yuyu Wang, who had been working in our bakery. We love her eye and she was acclimatized to BAO as a material, so was the perfect choice to host the first dinner.

Developing the menu was eye-opening. We're not trained chefs, which means we approach dish creation in a different manner – but this process pushed the boat out even more, creating a new set of rules in which to create a dish. The whole process was very experimental, working with and reflecting Yuyu's approach to materials, her love for textures and her sensuality.

The menu featured a bouncy prawn-ball-filled Boobie BAO (see image opposite), a pink marbled bubble-gum BAO with slow-cooked ox tongue (image 02), a silken egg with salmon roe and a table setting that included Yuyu's objects and installations. It was interesting to see the collision of her artistic language with her kitchen language, and to see that cross-pollination produce new objects – for example, by using the vacuum-pack machine for her prints, which preserved moments from the dinner as a nod to the short-lived experience. The dinner and collaboration served as a way to further explore the connections between artistic perspectives and food. For us, these events and out-of-the-ordinary menus are an exciting way to incorporate different processes, stories and creative restrictions in food. The rawness of the collaboration allows us to explore and drives us to new places.

Several months later, we curated a show with six international artists. While it was a great project, it was less successful because the two languages did not hit that sweet spot wherein the artist process collides with food. It becomes much more interesting when pursuing a space where the two speak to each other and therefore push the boundaries of each other's craft and discipline. A couple of years and a couple of restaurants later, our friends, Ken and Em, at design studio HATO, invited me to do a collaborative dinner to launch their cookbook *Cooking with Scorsese vol. 3*. They were very open to the suggestions I had, and we decided to host a small immersive dining experience. When I was at the Slade School of Fine Art, I held a few immersive performances – notably one where I impersonated my favourite singer, Momoe Yamaguchi, for a seminar in a small dark room, transitioning the atmosphere from serious art discussions to a full-blasted mini concert. What I love doing is making people feel intimidated in a small space. There may be a feeling of discomfort but there is always a hint of warmth at the end. And so, for this dinner, unlike Yuyu's, there was a performative edge. I chose the 90s Korean thriller *301 302* by Park Chul Soo – an eccentric cult classic and a feast for the eyes – and from there created a dining experience inspired by the film. I was in front of the screen performing a butchery session of a steamed Halibut BAO, which mirrored the film clip behind me; the food was

served on warped blue BAO plates that the knife would cut straight through (see page 39, image 02); and at the end of the meal, we went around smashing food into a bin. What seemingly felt like an uncomfortable gesture to the diners, as though we were tired chefs wanting to go home, was actually a motion to make them realize that these plates were made from steamed bread. (Afterwards we would go through the bin in the kitchen to pick out the metal cutlery.) It was both an intimate and surreal dinner and something I treasure having done. A lot of my processes are inspired by filmic references, so I found it extremely satisfying to create a dinner that directly referenced one.

OPPOSITE PAGE: BOOBIE BAO FILLED WITH PRAWN MINCE.
02: OX TONGUE REUBEN BUBBLEGUM BAO.

02

At the start of BAO, I would often make my own BAOs using leftover dough, either just to try things out or to give to friends when they came in. As time went on, they started evolving into larger, more experimental forms. For me, it was when we made a giant longevity peach BAO filled with lots of mini longevity peach BAOs for the fashion designer Simone Rocha that my investigation and exploration of BAO as a physical form began. I started to manipulate the BAO into more and more experimental structures. When using BAO as a material, one challenge is that it is a living ingredient that must prove and therefore grow. When it proves, it grows and when it steams it rises into a new form. That living element introduces complexity, but in a fun way, as it gives more room to experiment, from using live dough to already steamed dough to produce what I want. What this also meant was changing the recipe of the dough in order to yield different forms and to allow the structure to hold its shape better.

Just like most forms of craft, working with dough is a meditative process, in which I can get lost in time. There are two ways I experiment with dough: one is a pure, freeform type of experimentation in which I push the boundaries of BAO as a sculptural, living, cookable form, and the other is a more design-led approach, for which there is a very specific visual end point in my mind. This latter type involves drawing out the BAO, planning and making structural equipment that allows it to form and holds it in certain ways. It's such a naughty material – it does unexpected things and definitely doesn't want to come out the way you want it to. Over the years when we have collaborated with chefs, friends and artists, I have always tried to sneak in an element of BAO experimentation – sometimes it's planned and sometimes I surprise our collaborator. There's the experimental jewellery display for Simone Rocha that had growing pink BAO dough for the hair slides; the nose-to-tail BAO that was a set of deconstructed BAO pig parts for our dinner collaboration with Fergus and Margot Henderson, and the mini faces of Wong Ping's illustrations in BAO form for his solo show at Camden Arts Centre.

The purpose of these experimentations is to push the boundaries of what BAO can do. I'll work the material just to investigate its limits and also to have fun and produce something for an occasion. One of my favourites is when our ex-head baker, Keegan, who is also a pro 'body builder', was moving on to new pastures, we made him a giant six-pack torso and mini torsos filled with chocolate.

While experimenting can prove useful and result in a new item we can serve in the restaurant, I also hope the process itself can inspire. Like all true research and development projects, we experiment to fail – and the 1 per cent that does make it out will be truly innovative. For example, without the Artist Dinner, the Boobie BAO would not have been created. It now lives on as our Boobie and Penis Valentine's Special BAO. Similarly, the six-pack torso that I created for Keegan's leaving ceremony is now being planned as a hen party pre-order special in our karaoke rooms. What I love about all these investigations is that BAO is ultimately a humble form, which many people think of as a cheap snack. This drives me to push the boundaries of what it can do and to represent it in a new light.

01: VISAGE DE SHING BAO.
02: BLUE BAO PLATES.
03: BUTCHERED HALIBUT BAO.
04: SUCKLING PIG BAO.
05: GIANT LONGEVITY PEACH BAO FOR SIMONE ROCHA.
06: SIX-PACK TORSO BAO MADE AS A LEAVING PRESENT FOR KEEGAN.

01

02

04, 05

03

06

A Note from Erchen

BAO started as a small market stall with just a handful of recipes. Now we have multiple restaurants, and the recipes that we share in the following pages tell the stories of each of them in much the same way as the restaurants themselves represent our translations of the Taiwanese way of life.

Each recipe chapter is introduced by a handful of pages that explain the inspiration behind the restaurants, their stories and identities. There are strong connections to my upbringing in Taiwan and to my travels with Wai Ting and Shing after having moved to London. It's fascinating for me to connect to both the nostalgia of my childhood and daily life in Taiwan as well as to the new interactions I have with Taiwanese culture when I return with a different perspective. Things change and develop, and those dual connections are something that we use as building blocks to create and build what we have in London.

At the beginning, we would develop the dishes ourselves. As we started to grow, we had some brilliant minds work with us as development chefs. Many recipes could not have been created without them, thank you Eryk, Anaïs and Hsuan.

BAO

SHING SEARCHING FOR THE PERFECT BAO RECIPE IN THE TAIWANESE MOUNTAINS.

We once wrote in a social media post that we had travelled the mountains of Taiwan to become steamed bun masters. A few people latched on to the idea that we had spent the last decade mastering the art of making baos in the mountains, obviously not getting our deadpan English humour. What was true, however, was that we developed our BAO in reference to two styles in Taiwan: the *baozi* (a bao that is stuffed with a filling before steaming) and the typical *gua bao* (a folded bao that is stuffed after steaming) that you find in the night markets. While you find baos for sale in a lot of the night markets, they tend to focus on the filling and their gua baos are normally bought in and factory-made. We witnessed this in the basement of old Nanmen Market where we saw them being made on a mass scale, then be loaded into bags ready for the street vendors. On our travels around Taiwan, Shing, Wai Ting and I visited a famous *baozi* vendor, Jiaoxi Baozi, in Yilan, near the mountains and roughly an hour's drive from Taipei. They make fresh *baozi*, which are much fluffier than the regular gua bao, perhaps due to the method of steaming from raw dough. In these baos, the bread takes centre stage, with a much smaller filling. Now, the phrase 'like biting into a cloud' is used frequently, but this experience really fit that description to a T. It was one of those perfect first-bite moments – the kind that expands the range of what you thought was possible, in this case both in terms of how beautiful the *baozi* looked but also how incredibly subtle and elegant it tasted. The shop itself is nothing remarkable, but it is so popular that they limit how many baos an individual customer can order at any one time.

SHING AND ERCHEN'S FAMILIES QUEUEING FOR THE FAMOUS JIAOXI BAOZI IN YILAN.

包

When developing our BAO, we wanted to combine the best of both worlds: the softness of the Yilan *baozi* with the classic filling from the night-market gua bao. This is something we have worked hard to achieve. I remember when my friend Wei Ting visited us from Taiwan and she tasted one of our BAOs, her response was, 'Wow, you can't even get baos this soft back in Taiwan!'

SHING EATING GUA BAO FOR THE FIRST TIME AT LAN JIA GUA BAO, TAIPEI.

LAN JIA GUA BAO, GONGGUAN NIGHT MARKET, TAIPEI.

Many people ask why we chose BAO. That's a hard question to answer, but what we can say is that this dish connected all three of us – Shing, Wai Ting and me – on our travels. As Wai Ting explained earlier (see page 13), we had found ourselves with a bit of time after graduating in 2012. Naturally, I went back to Taiwan to spend time with family and it was a great opportunity for Shing and Wai Ting to join me and explore the country. There was no great plan to open a business at that point, rather, it evolved organically after I was able to introduce them to the unknown foods and places of Taiwan. Bao was one of the dishes that we all ate together on that trip. For me, it was a dish embedded in my childhood memories, having regularly eaten it as an after-school snack, and when Shing and Wai Ting tried it for the first time, it sparked a perfect moment of inspiration. The first time you take that bite – with the savouriness of the pork, the sweetness of the peanut powder and the sourness of the fermented mustard greens – it is perfect.

BAO

The holy grail recipe – a humble product with a humble history. I'm inspired by the craftspeople who push to perfection a single product over the course of their careers, becoming specialists of one form. BAO is the dish that represents that specialism to us, in which our role is to keep developing and improving what BAO means to us. This recipe is only one form that is ever morphing and adapting to new circumstances and new developments.

Our BAOs are made using the tangzhong technique. Tangzhong is an Asian culinary technique that helps dough absorb more liquid and retain moisture, resulting in a softer fluffier bread. All you need to do is cook a portion of flour and water into a thick consistency, similar to a roux.

The BAOs can be frozen in batches for later use, or, for those who want to skip making their own BAOs altogether, we sell our Gua BAO on our online shop (see page 233).

Makes about 20 BAOs

For the tangzhong:
100 g plain (all-purpose) flour
500 ml cold filtered water

For the BAO dough:
100 g tangzhong (see above)
420 g plain (all-purpose) flour, plus extra for dusting
90 g caster (superfine) sugar
40 g milk powder
2.5 g fast-action dried (active dry) yeast
5 g baking powder
pinch of salt
80 ml milk, at room temperature
80 ml water, at room temperature
10 ml vegetable oil, plus extra for brushing

Tangzhong

Put the flour into a small saucepan, pour in the cold water a little at a time, and mix in the flour until smooth. Slowly warm over a low heat until it becomes gluey and you can draw a line on the surface. Remove from the heat, cover tightly with cling film (plastic wrap) so that the film touches the surface of the tangzhong and leave to cool.

The tangzhong can be stored in the refrigerator, covered, for up to 3 days. Any leftover mixture can be used to make more BAOs or our Sesame BAO (see page 49).

BAO dough

Put 100 g of the tangzhong and all the dry ingredients into the bowl of a stand mixer fitted with a dough hook. Start mixing on a low setting and then slowly add the milk and water. Finally, add the oil and continue mixing until the dough is smooth. Cover with a damp cloth or cling film and leave to prove somewhere warm for 2–3 hours depending on the temperature, until doubled in size.

Turn the dough out onto a lightly floured surface and knead for 5 minutes – it will gradually become more elastic and the surface of the dough will become smooth. You can now use this dough to make Gua BAOs, Hot Dog BAOs and Round BAOs.

Shaping the BAO

Divide the dough into pieces of the specified weight for your chosen BAO (see below). Give each a strong knead, then roll into smooth balls. Cover with baking (parchment) paper to prevent them drying out while you roll the rest.

Gua BAO (40 g)
Flatten one of the dough balls with the palm of your hand, then using a rolling pin, roll it into an oval shape 8 cm (3¼ inches) long. Brush the top with oil, then, with a short edge facing you, place a chopstick horizontally across the middle and fold the oval in half over the chopstick. Remove the chopstick and repeat with the remaining dough balls.

Hot Dog BAO (45 g)
Using your palm and the work counter, roll the dough balls back and forth to create hot-dog-bun-shaped BAOs.

Round BAO (40 g)
No need to shape as they are already in smooth balls.

包

Place each BAO on a square of baking paper a little bigger than the size of the BAO, then transfer to a large tray. Cover with a sheet of baking paper and leave to prove somewhere warm for 15–20 minutes until the BAOs have doubled in height. They they should look relaxed, puffed up and the surface should no longer be damp. Imagine touching a smooth baby's skin. (Alternatively, you can do this final prove directly inside the bamboo steamers.)

<u>Steaming the BAOs</u>

When the BAOs are ready, carefully transfer them, on their squares of paper, to a prepared bamboo steamer (see below). Cover and steam over a medium-high heat for 15 minutes until they look soft and podgy, not firm, and their surface glistens with a satin sheen. If you feel any resistant patches in the centre that don't bounce back, keep steaming. Remove from the steamer and either eat straight away or leave to rest at room temperature until the steam has fully evaporated and the BAOs are completely cool. If your steamer doesn't fit all the BAOs, shape them for the second prove only after you have put the first batch in to steam. Over proved dough results in over expansion and will look flat and bubbly. The BAOs can be stored in the refrigerator in an airtight container for up to 5 days or they can be frozen for up to 1 month.

If you are reheating cooked BAOs, add them to the prepared steamer (see below), cover and steam over a high heat for about 10 minutes until they bounce back nicely when pressed with a finger. If you feel any resistant patches in the centre that don't bounce back, keep steaming. If steaming from frozen, it's the same process but add another 2–3 minutes in the steamer.

<u>How to prepare a steamer</u>

Use a deep saucepan that fits your bamboo steamer snugly.

If you are steaming fresh dough, there is no need to line the steamer basket/s – you need only use the squares of baking paper that the BAOs are on. If you are reheating BAOs, use muslin (cheesecloth) or a sheet of baking paper to line the basket/s.

Fill the pan with about 5 cm (2 inches) of water, place the empty steamer on top and bring to the boil. This will warm the steamer so that when you place your BAOs (or other food) inside, it will start steaming straight away.

KEEGAN, OUR EX-HEAD BAKER, ROLLING THE DOUGH.

SHAPING GUA BAOS BY HAND.

BAO

FRESHLY STEAMED SESAME BAOS ON BESPOKE BAMBOO TRAYS.

MIXING THE SESAME BAO DOUGH.

Sesame BAO

The black sesame BAO came about because we wanted to create a BAO that would look similar to a burger bun. The white BAO in the form of a burger bun just didn't look great to us, so we decided to experiment with mixing a sesame paste into the dough and it turned out not only looking beautiful, but also full of nutty flavour with amazing fragrance. We've used the black sesame BAO for 'sandwiching' fillings at BAO ever since.

Makes about 20 BAOs

For the sesame paste:
100 g black sesame seeds
50 ml vegetable or rapeseed (canola) oil

For the sesame BAO dough:
100 g Tangzhong (see page 46)
420 g plain (all-purpose) flour, plus extra for dusting
90 g caster (superfine) sugar
40 g milk powder
2.5 g fast-action dried (active dry) yeast
5 g baking powder
pinch of salt
80 ml milk, at room temperature
80 ml filtered water, at room temperature
10 ml vegetable oil
10 ml sesame paste (see above)

Sesame paste

Toast the sesame seeds in a dry frying pan (skillet) over a low heat for 2–3 minutes or until fragrant and nutty. Tip into a blender, add the oil and pulse until you have a smooth paste. Leave to infuse overnight, or for 8 hours. There will be more paste than is needed for this recipe, but it can be stored in a sterilized jar (see page 89) or airtight container in the refrigerator for up to 1 month or in the freezer for up to 3 months.

Sesame BAO dough

Put the tangzhong and all the dry ingredients into the bowl of a stand mixer fitted with a dough hook. Start mixing on a low setting and then slowly add the milk and water. Finally, add the oil and 10 ml of the sesame paste and continue mixing until the dough is smooth. Cover the bowl with a damp cloth or cling film (plastic wrap) and leave to prove somewhere warm for 2–3 hours depending on the temperature, until doubled in size.

Turn the dough out onto a lightly floured surface and knead for 5 minutes – it will gradually become more elastic and the surface of the dough will become smooth. Divide the dough into 40 g pieces. Give each a strong knead, then roll into tight balls. Cover with baking (parchment) paper to prevent them drying out while you roll the rest.

Place each BAO on a square of baking paper a little bigger than the size of the ball, then transfer to a large tray. Cover loosely with a sheet of baking paper and leave to prove somewhere warm for 15–20 minutes until the BAOs have doubled in height. (Alternatively, you can do this final prove directly inside the bamboo steamers, covered.)

Steaming the BAOs

When the BAOs are ready, carefully transfer them, on their squares of paper, to a prepared bamboo steamer (see page 47), cover and steam over a medium-high heat for 15 minutes until the edges look soft and podgy, not firm, and the surface of the BAOs glisten with a satin sheen. If you feel any resistant patches in the centre that don't bounce back, keep steaming. Remove from the steamer and either eat straight away or leave to rest at room temperature until the steam has fully evaporated and the BAOs are completely cool. If your steamer doesn't fit all the BAOs, shape them for the second prove only after you have put the first batch in to steam. Over proved dough results in over expansion and will look flat and bubbly. The BAOs can be stored in an airtight container in the refrigerator for up to 5 days or frozen for up to 1 month.

If you are reheating cooked BAOs, halve them, add to the prepared steamer (see page 47), cover and steam over a high heat for about 10 minutes until they bounce back nicely when pressed with a finger. If you feel any resistant patches in the centre that don't bounce back, keep steaming. If steaming from frozen, it's the same process but add another 2–3 minutes in the steamer.

Classic Pork BAO

This is the BAO that defines who we are. It is the BAO that is in our logo and the BAO that embodies all our values. It is our pursuit of perfection. The processes and techniques that go into it and the ways in which we have translated the traditional Taiwanese gua bao into our BAO makes it who we are. At home in Taiwan, the gua bao is normally two to three times larger. At that size, it is all about filling your stomach – the opposite of *kuchisabishii* (see page 24). A lot of people ask why we serve it smaller. Well, firstly it's because we want diners to sample a range of dishes, not just one. But most importantly, we serve it this way to facilitate that perfect moment of solitude. Our BAOs are the ideal 3–4 bites for the Lonely Man.

The Classic Pork BAO is perfectly formed, with a clean 1 cm (½ inch) gap between the edge of the bun and the edge of the meat. It is filled with twelve-hour braised pork that yields no resistance, melting in your mouth with the cloud-like BAO, the flavour notes of the ferments and sweet peanut powder lingering on in your mouth. In this recipe the pork is braised for 3 hours at a higher temperature but it still produces a great braise.

The Fermented Mustard Greens are a crucial component of this BAO and you will need to prepare them at least 2 weeks in advance (see page 231). If you don't have the time or desire to ferment your own, however, you can buy them from any Asian supermarket. They tend to be vacuum-packed in a bag with their own juices and are a pleasing yellowish-green colour.

Makes 10–12 BAOs

For the soy-braised pork belly:
1 kg pork belly (side), cut into 5 cm (2 inch) cubes
50 ml light soy sauce
40 ml dark soy sauce
60 ml Shaoxing rice wine
20 g spring onion (scallion)
1 clove garlic, crushed
20 g fresh ginger, peeled, sliced and crushed
1 star anise
20 g rock sugar
pinch of garlic powder
4 dried red chillies
6 g cinnamon bark

For the fried mustard greens:
2 tablespoons vegetable oil
½ teaspoon *doubanjiang* (fermented chilli bean paste)
100 g drained Fermented Mustard Greens (see page 231), chopped
a few drops of rice vinegar

To serve:
10–12 Gua BAOs (see page 46, or use our ready-made BAOs, see page 233)
1 small bunch coriander (cilantro), chopped
90 g Peanut Powder (see page 228)

The first time we served this BAO at a night market in Dalston, a customer cried and hugged Wai Ting.

Soy-braised pork belly

Bring a large saucepan of water to the boil. Add the pork cubes and blanch for 2–3 minutes to get rid of any impurities. Drain, then place in a flameproof clay pot or large saucepan.

Add the remaining ingredients to the pot or pan and pour over enough water to just cover the ingredients. Bring to the boil, then reduce the heat to low and simmer gently for 3 hours. There should just be small bubbles on the surface of the liquid. Halfway through cooking, flip the pork cubes to ensure they are evenly cooked.

Transfer the pork to a plate and leave to cool. Strain the braising liquid, then bring to the boil and cook until it is a light, sticky consistency, reducing it by about half. When the pork has cooled slightly, chop it into cubes of about 1 cm (½ inch). Put the cubes into the reduced sauce, give it a good stir and remove from the heat.

Warm the pork with the sauce over a medium heat for about 10 minutes before serving.

Fried mustard greens

Heat the oil in a frying pan over a medium-high heat. Add the *doubanjiang* (fermented chilli bean paste) and, when the oil starts to turn red, add the fermented mustard greens. Stir-fry for 5 minutes until super fragrant and wilted. Season the greens with a few drops of the vinegar.

To assemble

While the pork is reheating and the greens are cooking, steam the gua BAOs following the directions on page 47.

Open a BAO and line the bottom with 45 g of the piping-hot, glistening pork, then top with 1 teaspoon of the fried mustard greens. Finish with 1 teaspoon of the chopped coriander (cilantro) and 1 tablespoon of the golden, sweet peanut powder. Repeat with the remaining BAOs and fillings.

Hold a BAO lovingly in your hand. Open your mouth fully, like the BAO, and eat from the side.

Confit Pork BAO

We've been serving this pork BAO since 2014. It's important to use good-quality meat that has evenly distributed fat. We work closely with Swaledale Butchers in Yorkshire, who age our pork for 28 days. The edges of the meat are trimmed to make a neat square (we braise the trimmings to use in other dishes). While we don't usually like fancy kitchen equipment like tweezers and brushes, in this instance, using a brush means we can add exactly the right amount of sauce in one go.

Makes 5 BAOs

For the confit pork belly:
1 x 250-g piece of pork belly (side), cut into 5-cm (2-inch) thick slices
rapeseed (canola) oil, to cover

To serve:
5 Gua BAOs (see page 46, or use our ready-made BAO, see page 233)
5 teaspoons diced onion
5 teaspoons Black Garlic Glaze (see page 229)
7½ teaspoons Hot Sauce, or to taste (see page 231)
5 teaspoons Crispy Shallots (see page 228)

No detail is too small
Ensure there is a clear 1 cm (½ inch) gap between the BAO filling and the edge of the BAO. Squeeze the hot sauce in a W shape, trying not to break the flow of the lines.

Confit pork belly

Preheat the oven to 150°C/300°F/Gas Mark 2.

Put the pork into a lidded casserole dish (Dutch oven) and pour over rapeseed (canola) oil until the meat is completely covered. Make a baking (parchment) paper lid, lay it on top of the oil, then put the lid on the dish and cook in the oven for 3 hours. Remove the pork from the oil straight away and transfer to a plate to cool. When it is cool enough to handle, cut into 25 g slices, about 1 cm (½ inch) thick (you should get 10 slices out of the pork belly strip).

If the confit pork is still warm when you are ready to assemble, then you can put it straight into the steaming BAO. Otherwise, reheat it gently for about 5 minutes before serving, either by steaming over a low heat or in a low-temperature oven (about 100°C/210°F).

To assemble

Steam the gua BAOs following the directions on page 47. Open a BAO and spoon 1 teaspoon of the diced onion over the bottom, making sure to cover the entire bottom of the BAO and not to let the onion fall to the back (you want every mouthful to have that sharp, peppery onion flavour to balance the tender and fatty confit pork).

Layer 2 slices of pork in the BAO, arranging them like a step. Dab the pork with 1 teaspoon of the black garlic glaze with a brush, making sure to cover the entire slice but without smudging it onto the BAO. Cover with generous squiggly lines of hot sauce (especially if you love spicy food – tighten the lines to add more) and finish with 1 teaspoon of the crispy shallots. Repeat with the remaining BAOs and fillings.

包

Daikon BAO

This was a dish born from a mistake. At our first pop-up, we had wanted to serve pan-fried turnip cake with a sunny-side-up egg. When we made a batch, we accidentally used plain (all-purpose) flour instead of rice flour. The latter gives the cake the solid, waxy consistency that is traditional, but this version came out softer with a looser structure that broke up when pan-frying. How could we fix it? The answer was to deep-fry it. We don't put any *lap yuk* (cured pork belly/side) in our daikon cake, which is also traditional, as we prefer to keep it vegetarian, but feel free to experiment by adding diced cured meats.

What most people don't know is that at BAO Soho we have three different versions of the Daikon BAO, even though on the menu we only list this original preparation. If a table orders a lot of Daikon BAOs, then we offer them the two other preparations: Green Monster and Golden Kimchi. To make a Green Monster Daikon BAO we add a squeeze of Burnt Chilli Sauce (see page 230) and two pieces of Soy-pickled Chillies (see page 231), just overlapping. The Golden Kimchi Daikon BAO uses hot sauce like the original, but we substitute the pickled daikon with the Taiwanese Golden Kimchi that we use in our Fried Chicken BAO (see page 63).

Makes 4 BAOs

For the daikon cake:
275 g daikon, peeled and coarsely grated
130 g plain (all-purpose) flour
½ teaspoon salt
2 eggs, beaten
100 g panko breadcrumbs
vegetable oil, for deep-frying

To serve:
4 Gua BAOs (see page 46, or use our ready-made BAO, see page 233)
4 tablespoons coriander (cilantro), finely chopped
2½ tablespoons Hot Sauce (see page 231)
4 slices Pickled Daikon (see page 192)

Daikon cake

Prepare the daikon cake a day in advance. Put the grated daikon into a dry frying pan (skillet) and cook over a medium heat until most of the liquid has evaporated and you have a ratio of about 1:3 liquid to daikon. Transfer the daikon and liquid to a large bowl, then add 33 g of the flour and the salt and mix thoroughly.

Prepare a steamer (see page 47) and line a 10 x 10 cm (4 × 4 inch) baking pan with cling film (plastic wrap). Press the daikon mixture into the pan, to a depth of about 1.5 cm (⅝ inch), then transfer to the prepared steamer, cover and steam over a medium heat for 30 minutes, making sure that the water does not boil dry. Leave to cool, then wrap the baking pan in cling film and freeze overnight.

The next day, remove the daikon cake from the freezer and leave to rest at room temperature for 30 minutes (you want it to be partially defrosted before you cut it, but not fully defrosted or it will be too difficult to work with). Cut the daikon cake into quarters.

Put the remaining flour, the eggs and the panko breadcrumbs into 3 separate shallow dishes and position them in front of you so you can move easily between them, from left to right. Toss one of the daikon cakes in the flour, then use your left hand to coat it in the egg mixture before placing it into the breadcrumbs (be careful that your left hand does not touch the panko itself). Using your right hand, coat the eggy daikon cake in the breadcrumbs. (This method allows you to work as efficiently as possible, and means the breadcrumbs won't become clumpy.) Repeat with the remaining daikon cakes.

Heat the oil in a deep, heavy-based saucepan to 160°C/325°F, or until a cube of ginger sizzles and browns in 20 seconds. Carefully place the daikon cakes in the hot oil and deep-fry for 2 minutes. Remove with the tongs or a slotted spoon, drain on paper towels and leave to cool completely. When cool, reheat the oil to 190°C/375°F and deep-fry again for 1 minute, then remove with a slotted spoon and drain on paper towels.

To assemble

While you coat and deep-fry the daikon cake portions, steam the gua BAOs following the directions on page 47. Open a BAO and place 1 tablespoon of the chopped coriander (cilantro) on the bottom, then top with a daikon cake. Drizzle or squeeze over 2 teaspoons of the hot sauce. Finish with a slice of pickled daikon, pushing it down a little at the back so that it sits perfectly on top. Repeat with the remaining BAOs and fillings.

Curry Cheese BAO

The idea for this BAO came about when we knew we wanted to do a cheese croquette and decided to add some texture by adding tapioca pearls. Tapioca pearls are often used in desserts or drinks. We use the unwanted trimmings of Neal's Yard Dairy cheese to make the croquettes – we call it the 'sad cheese' – which is a mix of cheeses that are never the same.

The fermented red chillies for this BAO need to be made at least 2 weeks in advance.

Makes 9 BAOs

For the cheese croquettes:
225 ml milk
110 g small tapioca pearls
150 g Cheddar, grated
1 teaspoon salt
pinch of ground white pepper
pinch of ground red Sichuan peppercorns
vegetable oil, for greasing and deep-frying
15 g cornflour (cornstarch)

For the curry sauce:
40 ml rapeseed (canola) oil
115 g onions, diced
4 g fresh ginger, peeled and very finely chopped
4 g garlic, very finely chopped
3 pinches of Kashmiri chilli powder
5 pinches of mild curry powder
2 pinches of Madras curry powder
4 pinches of garam masala
10 g Granny Smith apple, peeled, cored and chopped
2 teaspoons light soy sauce
15 ml coconut milk
10 ml Sichuan Chilli Oil (see page 229)

To serve:
9 Gua BAOs (see page 46, or use our ready-made BAO, see page 233)
3 tablespoons Fermented Red Chillies (see page 228)

Cheese croquettes

Put the milk and tapioca pearls into a saucepan and bring to a low simmer over a low heat, whisking constantly so that the milk and tapioca do not catch. Cook for about 10 minutes until just cooked but not mushy.

Put the remaining ingredients except the oil and cornflour (cornstarch) into a mixing bowl. When the tapioca is tender, pour the milk and pearls into the bowl. Mix well, then set aside to cool a little.

Grease a 12 × 15 cm (4½ × 6 inch) baking pan with oil. Pour in the cooled cheese mixture, making sure to spread it out evenly. Cover with cling film (plastic wrap) to prevent a skin forming on top. Leave to stand at room temperature for 1 hour, then transfer to the refrigerator for a couple of hours to firm up.

Curry sauce

Heat the oil in a deep frying pan (skillet) or saucepan over a medium heat, add the onions and fry for 5–10 minutes until golden. Add the ginger and garlic and cook for another couple of minutes, then add the spices and apple and cook for another 10 minutes. Pour in 325 ml water and the soy sauce and continue to cook for 20 minutes. Finally, add the coconut milk and cook for 5 minutes. Pour the mixture into a blender and blend until smooth. Add the Sichuan chilli oil to the sauce and blend again.

There will be more curry sauce than is needed for this recipe, but it can be stored in an airtight container in the refrigerator for up to 3 days and works well with rice and a boiled egg.

To assemble

Cut the chilled cheese mixture into nine 4 × 5 cm (1½ × 2 inch) pieces, then toss them in the cornflour. Heat the oil in a deep, heavy-based saucepan to 180°C/350°F, or until a cube of ginger sizzles and browns in 10 seconds. Carefully place the cheese croquettes in the hot oil and deep-fry for 1½ minutes on each side, or until golden, then remove with a slotted spoon and drain on paper towels.

Meanwhile, steam the gua BAOs following the directions on page 47. Open a BAO and place a cheese croquette on the bottom, then spoon over 1 tablespoon of the curry sauce and 1 teaspoon of the fermented red chillies. Repeat with the remaining BAOs and fillings.

包

Prawn Shia Song BAO

Prawn (shrimp) shia song is a classic Taiwanese dish that is often served at weddings and banquets as an appetizer. Chopped prawns are combined with crunchy vegetables, such as water chestnut and carrot, then tossed through with a mixture of cornflour (cornstarch) and egg white to create a fluffy texture. Traditionally, this is spooned into lettuce cups that have a refreshing crunch, but who needs lettuce when you can use it to fill a deep-fried, doughnut-like BAO?

The fermented green chillies for this BAO need to be made at least 2 weeks in advance.

Makes 6 BAOs

For the sweet mayonnaise:
1 egg yolk
1½ teaspoons Dijon mustard
1 tablespoon rice vinegar
1 tablespoon caster (superfine) sugar
¼ teaspoon salt
200 ml rapeseed (canola) oil

For the prawn shia song:
230 g uncooked prawns (shrimp), shelled and deveined
20 g carrot, finely chopped
20 g celery, finely chopped
20 g water chestnut, finely chopped
1 teaspoon caster (superfine) sugar
1½ teaspoons salt
35 g egg white (from about 1 egg)
½ teaspoon ground white pepper
7 g cornflour (cornstarch)
2 cloves garlic, minced
vegetable oil, for cooking
1 teaspoon Fermented Green Chillies (see page 228, or use shop-bought)

To serve:
vegetable oil, for deep-frying
6 unsteamed Hot Dog BAOs (see page 46)
30 g coriander (cilantro) stalks, finely chopped

Sweet mayonnaise

Put all the ingredients except the oil into a food processor or blender and pulse until combined. With the motor running, slowly pour in the oil through the funnel, making sure it is incorporated before adding more. Blend until the mixture is a stiff, creamy texture and all the oil is fully incorporated. The mayo can be stored in a jar in the refrigerator for up to 3 days. It is great with prawns (shrimp), chicken dishes or in sandwiches.

Prawn shia song

Combine all the ingredients except the oil and fermented green chillies in a bowl.

Heat the oil in a deep, heavy-based saucepan to 130°C/265°F (this is hot enough for the prawns to gently cook, releasing a few bubbles, but not so hot that they deep-fry). Carefully add the prawn mix to the pot and stir. When the prawns turn opaque, about 2–3 minutes, they are ready.

Place a sieve over a heatproof metal bowl or another saucepan and strain the prawns, then transfer to a bowl. Add the fermented chillies and mix through, then set aside and keep warm.

To assemble

Heat the oil in a deep, heavy-based saucepan to 180°C/350°F, or until a cube of ginger sizzles and browns in 10 seconds. Carefully place the hot dog BAOs, in batches, in the hot oil and deep-fry for 1 minute on each side until golden brown, then remove with a slotted spoon and drain on paper towels.

Cut a slit in the BAOs lengthways, like hot-dog buns. Gently prise open a BAO to make sure you have enough room for the filling, being careful not to overextend the bun and break it. Line the bottom with 2 teaspoons of the sweet mayo, then spoon 3 heaped tablespoons of the prawn mix on top and sprinkle with 1 teaspoon coriander stalks. Repeat with the remaining BAOs and fillings.

包

Cod Black BAO

One of the most popular BAOs at BAO Fitz was only dreamed up just before we opened our doors. This was a dream-team collaboration from our chefs Sagar Desai and James Ng. Sagar came up with the idea of the black batter for the cod and James magically whipped up (quite literally) a sauce that we named after him – Ng sauce. The real beauty of this BAO relies on the three sauces: Ng sauce, hot sauce and mayo.

Makes 4 BAOs

For the Ng sauce:
1 cloves garlic, finely grated
½ shallot, coarsely chopped
10 ml vegetable oil
15 ml sesame oil
25 ml Sichuan Chilli Oil (see page 229)
15 g caster (superfine) sugar
10 ml rice vinegar
20 g cornichons, finely diced

For the cuttlefish-ink battered cod:
250 g plain (all-purpose) flour, plus extra for dredging
2 g salt
1 teaspoon baking powder
330 ml Taiwan Beer (or light lager)
35 ml cuttlefish ink
vegetable oil, for deep-frying
1 x 180-g skinless and boneless cod fillet, cut into 4 pieces

To serve:
4 steamed Sesame BAOs (see page 49)
vegetable oil, for toasting
4 tablespoons Homemade Mayonnaise (see page 230)
4 tablespoons Hot Sauce (see page 231)
40 g finely sliced flat cabbage

Tip
When transferring the fish pieces from the batter to the oil, keep hold of the fish in the oil with the tongs for a few seconds to ensure the batter seals around the fish – this will stop it sticking to the bottom of the pan.

Ng sauce

Put all the ingredients, except the cornichons, into a food processor or blender and blend at medium speed for 3 minutes until combined. Then turn up the speed and blend for another few minutes until the consistency is very smooth. Add the finely diced cornichons and mix well. Store in the refrigerator until ready to use.

Cuttlefish-ink battered cod

Make the cuttlefish ink batter. In a large bowl, whisk together all the dry ingredients. Make a well in the middle of the ingredients and gradually add the beer, whisking to avoid lumps. When all the beer has been added, gradually whisk in the cuttlefish ink.

Heat the oil in a deep, heavy-based saucepan to 180°C/350°F, or until a cube of ginger sizzles and browns in 10 seconds. Pour some flour into a shallow dish. Dip the cod pieces in the flour and then into the cuttlefish-ink batter. Using tongs, carefully lower the cod into the hot oil and deep-fry for 1–2 minutes until the fish is cooked through and the batter is crunchy. Remove the fish with the tongs and drain on paper towels.

To assemble

While you prepare and deep-fry the cod, reheat the sesame BAOs following the directions on page 49.

Heat a little oil in a frying pan (skillet) over a medium heat. Remove the BAOs from the steamer, then toast, cut sides down, in the pan.

Spread first 1 tablespoon of the mayonnaise on the bottom half of a toasted BAO, followed by 1 tablespoon of the Ng sauce. Place a piece of cod on top, then add 1 tablespoon of the hot sauce. Top with a three-finger pinch of sliced flat cabbage and close off with a BAO lid. Repeat with the remaining BAOs and fillings.

包

Fried Chicken BAO

While fried chicken is incredibly popular in Taiwan, it isn't commonly found in a bao. This is our own take on the dish, for which we use our house-made kimchi. Taiwan has a big culture of pickles and ferments, but *huang jin pao tsai* (golden kimchi), is not one of the most famous. Ours is made with turmeric, apple and green snub-nose chillies. The addition of carrot gives it a light golden colour. It's not particularly spicy, but it really lifts the flavour of the juicy chicken. Having a pot of this kimchi in your refrigerator is perfect for when you want an easy accompaniment for a meat dish, or simply to eat with rice.

There are a lot of components in this BAO, and it can seem as if there is no way that this amount of stuff will hold itself together in the BAO. But that's the genius of the mayo and the hot sauce, which not only provide flavour and colour but also help to hold the ingredients in place. This is how we manage to send out trays of these structurally complex BAOs throughout service without them collapsing all over the place.

Makes 5 BAOs

1 quantity Taiwanese Fried Chicken (see page 92)
5 steamed Sesame BAOs (see page 49)
5 tablespoons Sichuan Mayonnaise (see page 230)
5 teaspoons finely chopped coriander (cilantro)
5 tablespoons Taiwanese Golden Kimchi (see page 232)
5 tablespoons Hot Sauce (see page 231), or to taste

(S)

While you deep-fry the Taiwanese Fried Chicken (see page 92), reheat the sesame BAOs following the directions on page 49.

Heat a dry frying pan (skillet) over a medium heat. Remove the BAOs from the steamer, then toast, cut sides down, in the pan.

Spread the bottom half of a BAO with 1 tablespoon of the Sichuan mayo and sprinkle with 1 teaspoon of the coriander (cilantro). Take 2 pieces of fried chicken and lay them on top, side by side, using the mayo to hold them in place. If they teeter, push them down into the bun.

Sterilize a fork with boiling water (you don't want to accidentally contaminate the kimchi jar with a dirty fork), then carefully remove a few pieces of golden kimchi from the jar. Lay 1 tablespoon of the kimchi on top of the chicken, then add 1 tablespoon of the hot sauce. Top with a BAO lid, using your palm to gently press down so everything is held in place. Repeat with the remaining BAOs and fillings.

Chicken Nugget BAO

Nothing beats a juicy spiced chicken nugget with a crisp lettuce leaf and a punchy slice of raw onion. It's a small, perfectly formed BAO with just the right amount of seasoning, spice and juiciness from the chicken. The nuggets are so good by themselves, too; just mop them up with our hot sauce.

Makes 5 BAOs

For the chicken nugget seasoning:
2 teaspoons chicken spiced flour mix (see page 92)
2 g onion powder
2 g garlic powder
3 g caster (superfine) sugar
2 g salt
pinch of lemon zest
9 g sesame oil
3 g premium soy sauce
3 g cornflour (cornstarch)

For the chicken nuggets:
90 g minced (ground) chicken breast
90 g minced (ground) chicken thighs
¼ teaspoon onion powder
¼ teaspoon garlic powder
1 teaspoon chicken nugget seasoning (see above)
¼ teaspoon caster (superfine) sugar
pinch of salt
a light grating of lemon zest
¾ teaspoon sesame oil
¼ teaspoon premium soy sauce
¼ teaspoon cornflour (cornstarch)
vegetable oil, for deep-frying

For the panko coating:
3 eggs, beaten
100 g plain (all-purpose) flour
100 g panko breadcrumbs
50 g tapioca flour (starch)
15 g chicken spiced flour mix (see page 92)

To serve:
5 steamed Sesame BAOs (see page 49)
5 iceberg lettuce leaves
5 tablespoons Sichuan Mayonnaise (see page 230)
Hot Sauce (see page 231), to taste
5 slices onion

Chicken nugget seasoning

First make the chicken nugget seasoning by mixing all the ingredients in a bowl. It will make a little more than you need for this recipe.

Chicken nuggets

Mix together all the ingredients, except the oil, in a large bowl. Shape the mixture into five 35 g balls.

Panko coating

Put the eggs and the plain (all-purpose) flour into separate shallow dishes, then combine the panko breadcrumbs, tapioca flour (starch) and chicken spice in a third dish. Position the dishes in front of you so you can move easily between them, from left to right. Toss one of the chicken nuggets in the flour, then use your left hand to coat it in the egg mixture before placing it into the breadcrumbs (be careful that your left hand does not touch the breadcrumbs itself). Using your right hand, coat the eggy nugget in the breadcrumbs, then transfer to a plate. (This method allows you to work as efficiently as possible, and means the breadcrumbs won't become clumpy.) Repeat with the remaining chicken nuggets.

To assemble

Reheat the sesame BAOs following the directions on page 49.

Meanwhile, heat the oil in a deep, heavy-based saucepan to 180°C/350°F, or until a cube of ginger sizzles and browns in 10 seconds. Carefully place the nuggets, in two batches, in the hot oil and deep-fry for 2½ minutes until cooked through, golden brown and crisp, then remove with a slotted spoon and drain on paper towels.

Heat a dry frying pan (skillet) over a medium heat. Remove the BAOs from the steamer, then toast, cut sides down, in the pan.

Place a leaf of iceberg lettuce on the bottom half of a BAO, followed by a chicken nugget, then top with 1 tablespoon of the Sichuan mayo, a drizzle of hot sauce and finish with a sliced onion ring. Top with a BAO lid. Repeat with the remaining BAOs and fillings.

Breakfast Sausage BAO

Since day one, we have always wanted to make an all-day breakfast sausage BAO. Who knows why, maybe the nostalgic attachment to the 'dirty' sausage breakfast muffins? I worked with Anais, our development chef at the time, to re-create the feeling of biting into a sausage muffin – that sweet, soft bread with the meatiness of a juicy sausage patty.

Makes 6 BAOs

For the potato rosti and sausage patties:
145 g waxy potatoes
1 teaspoon flaky sea salt
1 egg yolk
1½ teaspoons plain (all-purpose) flour
40 g Cheddar, grated
210 g sausage meat (bulk fresh pork sausage)
3 eggs, beaten
splash of vegetable oil

To serve:
6 Gua BAOs (see page 46, or use our ready-made BAO, see page 233)
60 ml Black Garlic Glaze (see page 229)

Potato rosti and sausage patties

Prepare a steamer (see page 47) and steam the potatoes for 12 minutes, then using a box grater, coarsely grate them into a bowl while still hot. Combine with the salt, egg yolk, flour and cheese, then divide the mixture into three 60 g balls.

Divide the sausage meat (bulk fresh pork sausage) into three 70 g balls, then press them into thin patties less than 1 cm (½ inch) thick. Place a rosti ball on top of a sausage patty, then shape into a patty so the rosti and sausage meat are layered one on top of the other. Cut each patty in half horizontally, to make 2 semicircles. Repeat with the remaining rosti balls and sausage patties.

Pour the beaten eggs into a squeezy bottle ready for when you need them.

Heat a splash of oil in a large frying pan (skillet) over a low heat. Fry the patty semicircles, potato side down, until crisp, about 1½ minutes, then flip and cook on the sausage side for another 1½–2 minutes, or until cooked through. Gently lift the patties and squeeze some of the beaten egg mixture underneath, then place the patties back on top of the thin layer of egg.

To assemble

Meanwhile, steam the gua BAOs following the directions on page 47. Open each BAO and place a fried patty on the bottom, then drizzle with the black garlic glaze.

包

Lamb Shoulder BAO

At our first pop-up, we served Xinjiang lamb ribs, inspired by the food stands in Taiwan that serve lamb skewers barbecued with a spice mix used in the northeastern region of China, Xinjiang. The ribs we made were braised slowly with this spice mix and then fried to order. Later on, when we opened BAO Soho, we wanted to keep that same spirit but put it into a BAO. We achieve this by slow-cooking lamb shoulder with Shaoxing rice wine, which gives the dish a sherry-like sweetness. We then shred and refry the lamb in the same Xinjiang spice mix with some of the leftover lamb juices.

Makes 10 BAOs

For the Xinjiang spice mix:
5 g red Sichuan peppercorns
10 g black peppercorns
50 g cumin seeds
5 g dried red chillies
1½ teaspoons flaky sea salt
¾ tablespoons garlic powder
1 teaspoon ground ginger

For the Xinjiang lamb shoulder:
½ bone-in lamb shoulder (about 1.5 kg), cut into 3 pieces
vegetable oil, for rubbing
500 ml Shaoxing rice wine
salt

To serve:
10 Gua BAOs (see page 46, or use our ready-made BAO, see page 233)
3½ tablespoons Garlic Mayonnaise (see Homemade Mayonnaise tip, page 230)
3½ tablespoons Green Sauce (see page 230)
20 pieces of Soy-pickled Chillies (see page 231)

Tip
Any leftovers of the Xinjiang lamb shoulder can be served over rice or noodles.

Xinjiang spice mix

Toast the Sichuan peppercorns in a dry frying pan (skillet) or wok over a medium heat for 1 minute until the aromas are released, being careful they don't burn. Remove and set aside. Toast the black peppercorns and cumin seeds in the same pan for 2 minutes, then remove and set aside, and finally toast the dried chillies for 3 minutes. Leave to cool.

Put the toasted spices and salt into a spice grinder or pestle and mortar and grind to a powder. Tip into a bowl and stir in the garlic powder and ginger. The spice mix can be stored in a jar in a cool, dry cupboard for up to 3 months.

Xinjiang lamb shoulder

Preheat the oven to 200°C/400°F/Gas Mark 6 and rub the pieces of lamb with oil and salt.

Put the lamb pieces into a roasting pan and roast for 15 minutes until browned, then turn them over and cook on the other side for 10 minutes. The lamb needs to have developed a strong colour before slow cooking. Transfer to a casserole dish (Dutch oven) and pour over the Shaoxing wine and 500 ml water. Put the lid on the dish, turn the oven down to 160°C/325°F/Gas Mark 3 and cook for 2 hours 40 minutes.

Remove from the oven and transfer the lamb to a plate. Pass the braising liquid through a sieve into a measuring jug (large measuring cup) and reserve. When cool enough to handle, remove the meat from the bones, cut into 2.5 cm (1 inch) cubes and put into a bowl. Heat a saucepan and fry the cubed lamb with the Xinjiang spice mix followed by the braising liquid. (For every 100 g of cooked chopped lamb, add 40 ml of the braising liquid and 8 g of the Xinjiang spice mix.) Fry for a couple of minutes until everything combines nicely. The cooked lamb can be stored in an airtight container in the refrigerator for up to 3 days.

To assemble

Steam the gua BAOs following the directions on page 47. Open a BAO and spread 1 teaspoon of the garlic mayonnaise on the bottom, then top with 45 g of the lamb shoulder. Add 1 teaspoon of the green sauce, then place 2 pieces of soy-pickled chilli on top. Repeat with the remaining BAOs and fillings.

Shortrib BAO

This is infamously known as the 'Big Mac' BAO. Secretly, all we do is try to cook up McDonald's flavours and then when we achieve them, we nod knowingly at each other, pleased with our accomplishment. The short rib we use here is the prime fore rib from Philip Warren & Son butchers in Cornwall, which is aged for 40 days, giving it a really punchy beef flavour.

Makes 5 BAOs

For the braised short ribs:
500 g bone-in beef short ribs
1 teaspoon salt
3 cloves garlic
60 g honey
50 g *doubanjiang* (fermented chilli bean paste)
1 bunch spring onions (scallions), roots trimmed
25 g chilli powder

For the egg emulsion:
85 g egg yolks (about 15 yolks)
1¼ teaspoons Dijon mustard
½ a pinch chilli powder
pinch of fine salt
2 teaspoons Chinese red vinegar

To serve:
5 Gua BAOs (see page 46, or use our ready-made BAO, see page 233)
1 large gherkin (dill pickle), sliced
5 tablespoons Crispy Shallots (see page 228)

Braised short rib

Preheat the oven to 180°C/350°F/Gas Mark 4. Season the short ribs with the salt and put into a flameproof casserole dish (Dutch oven) with the garlic. Place in the oven for 15–20 minutes until browned, then remove and cover the ribs with water. Add the honey, *doubanjiang* (fermented chilli bean paste), spring onions (scallions) and chilli powder. Put the lid on the dish, turn down the oven to 90°C/195°F/Gas Mark ¼ and cook overnight, or for 8 hours.

Remove the short ribs from the braising liquid, reserving the liquid, and shred the meat from the bones. To make the short rib sauce, reduce the braising liquid down to about 145 ml, then pass through a fine-mesh sieve into a clean saucepan.

When ready to serve, add the meat to the short rib sauce and reheat over a medium heat. You don't want to cook the meat further, so as soon as it is warmed through, take it off the heat.

Egg emulsion

Bring a saucepan of water to a low simmer. In a heatproof bowl set on top of the pan, whisk together all the ingredients until combined and the mixture resembles the consistency of mayonnaise, nice and smooth. You may need to add a splash of water if it gets too thick.

To assemble

While you make the egg emulsion and reheat the beef, steam the gua BAOs following the directions on page 47. Open a BAO and put a slice of gherkin (dill pickle) on the bottom, then top with 1 tablespoon of the crispy shallots. Add 50 g of the short rib and finish with 1 tablespoon of the egg emulsion. Repeat with the remaining BAOs and fillings.

包

包

Fried Horlicks Ice Cream BAO

Food has a magical ability to transport you back to certain points in your life. I love those nostalgic flavours that seem to hold within them a special memory of a time and a place. The malted milk drink Horlicks seems to be connected to deep-rooted sensory memories for lots of people both in the UK and Asia. The time and place of those memories might be worlds apart but they are united by this creamy, malty flavour. For me, it takes me back to a glorified, worry-free childhood moment in which my euphoria is encompassed in a warm cup of malty goodness. This recipe is inspired by the deep-fried *yin si juan* (a style of bread roll) that you find at most fried chicken stalls across Taiwan. In our dish, the pure, sweet indulgence of Horlicks ice cream is sandwiched between hot, freshly fried BAO.

Makes 4 BAOs

For the Horlicks ice cream:
250 ml double (heavy) cream
10 g Horlicks malted milk powder
150 ml milk
60 g caster (superfine) sugar
3 egg yolks

For the deep-fried BAOs:
vegetable oil, for deep-frying
4 unsteamed Round BAOs (see page 46)

Horlicks ice cream

Make the ice cream at least a day in advance. Combine the cream and malted milk powder in a saucepan and heat gently over a low heat. When the cream starts to simmer and the powder is fully dissolved, remove from the heat and leave to cool.

Pour the flavoured cream and the milk into a heatproof bowl and set it over a saucepan of gently simmering water. Add 45 g of the sugar and stir until dissolved. Remove the bowl from the pan.

Prepare an ice bath and set another bowl on top of it. Put the egg yolks and remaining sugar into the top bowl and whisk until the sugar has dissolved. Using a ladle, spoon some of the hot cream mixture onto the cold yolks (the ice bath will prevent the eggs scrambling). Keep mixing in the cream mixture until you have incorporated about half of it. The egg and cream mixture should be thick, smooth and lump-free.

Slowly pour the egg mixture into the heatproof bowl with the remaining half of the hot cream mixture, whisking until fully combined. Cook the custard gently over a medium heat, whisking regularly, for about 25 minutes until it is about 78°C/172°F, coats the back of a spoon and you can run your finger across the spoon without creating drips. Remove the custard from the heat, transfer into an airtight container and allow to cool to room temperature with the lid ajar. Close the lid before chilling in the refrigerator overnight.

The next day, pour the custard into an ice-cream maker and churn according to the manufacturer's directions until the ice cream is smooth and aerated. There will be more ice cream than is needed for this recipe, but it can be stored in an airtight container in the freezer for up to 3 months. To serve, transfer to the refrigerator for 15 minutes to let it soften very slightly, which will make it easier to scoop.

Deep-fried BAO

Heat the oil in a deep, heavy-based saucepan to 180°C/350°F, or until a cube of ginger sizzles and browns in 10 seconds. Carefully add the round BAOs to the hot oil and deep-fry for about 2 minutes until golden, flipping them over like a doughnut halfway through cooking. Remove with a slotted spoon and drain on paper towels.

To assemble

Cut each of the deep-fried BAOs in half and make a depression in the bottom half with a teaspoon. Place a scoop of Horlicks ice cream in the depressions and top with the other half of the BAOs.

Sad Face BAO

The BAO that represented all of us in 2020 during the pandemic, this is a classic salted-egg-yolk custard bun that actually makes you happy when you look at it. One of my all-time favourites, it is great for breakfast, snacking or as dessert.

Makes 8 BAOs

For the salted egg custard:
4 Salted Duck Egg yolks (see page 228) or frozen salted duck egg yolks (found in most Asian supermarkets)
40 g caster (superfine) sugar
30 ml milk
75 g salted butter, softened
30 g milk powder
15 g custard powder

For the BAO Bakery Goods dough:
90 g Tangzhong (see page 46)
420 g plain (all-purpose) flour, plus extra for dusting
1 teaspoon baking powder
pinch of salt
35 g milk powder
80 g caster (superfine) sugar
¾ teaspoon fast-action dried (active dry) yeast
70 ml milk
70 ml warm water
10 ml vegetable oil

For the sad faces:
2 g food-grade charcoal powder

Tip
To use up the salted egg white, you could stir fry it with some rice for a quick lunch.

Salted egg custard

Prepare the filling the day before. Prepare a steamer (see page 47). Put the salted egg yolks into a heatproof bowl. Transfer the bowl to the steamer, cover and steam the yolks for 15 minutes, then allow to cool. Using a hand blender, blend the cooked yolks with the sugar and milk.

In a bowl, cream the butter until light and fluffy, then add the yolk mixture, a little at a time, and mix well – you don't want to see any lumps of butter or the mix inside the BAOs will split). Mix in the milk powder and custard powder and blitz until fully incorporated. Chill in the refrigerator overnight, or for at least 8 hours. When ready to use, divide the mixture into eight 25 g balls.

Bao Bakery Goods dough

Put the tangzhong and all the dry ingredients into the bowl of a stand mixer fitted with a dough hook. Start mixing on a low setting and then slowly add the milk and warm water. Finally, add the oil and continue mixing until the dough is smooth. Cover with a damp cloth or cling film (plastic wrap) and leave to prove somewhere warm for at least 2 hours, or until doubled in size.

Turn the dough out onto a lightly floured surface and knead for 5 minutes – it will gradually become more elastic and the surface of the dough will become smooth. Divide into eight 65 g balls, reserving 25 g for the sad faces. Cover loosely with a sheet of baking (parchment) paper to prevent them drying out.

Sad face

Mix the charcoal powder with the reserved dough, kneading until fully incorporated. It should be a dark black – if not, add a touch more charcoal powder. Using a pasta roller or rolling pin, roll out the dough to 2 mm (¹⁄₁₆-inch) thick, then cut out two long 3-mm (¹⁄₁₆-inch) wide strands. Cut the strands into 16 'eyes' with a very sharp knife. Cut out 8 lengths 3–5 cm (1¼–2 inches) for the 'mouths'. Cover loosely with a tea towel to prevent them drying out.

To assemble

Using a rolling pin, roll out the dough balls into 10–12 cm (4–5 inch) circles, allowing the middles to be slightly thicker. Place a salted egg custard ball in the middle of a dough circle and carefully bring the edges of the dough together, enclosing the ball, and pinch the dough so it is firmly closed with no holes. Gently transfer to a cupcake case (paper baking cup) with the seam facing down. Repeat with the remaining dough circles and custard balls. Leave to prove somewhere warm, covered loosely with a sheet of baking paper, for 30–50 minutes until they have risen to fill out the cupcake cases to about 90 per cent. Brush the surface of the proved BAOs with water and gently attach the eyes and mouths to resemble sad faces. Place the proved BAOs in 8 cm (3 inch) metal rings to help them rise upwards when steamed.

Prepare a steamer (see page 47). Transfer half the BAOs in the metal rings to the steamer, cover and steam the BAOs for 15 minutes over a medium-high heat until they bounce back nicely when pressed with a finger. If you feel any resistant patches in the centre that don't bounce back, keep steaming. Remove from the steamer and either eat straight away or leave to rest at room temperature until the steam has fully evaporated and the BAOs are completely cool. Repeat with the remaining BAOs. The BAOs can be stored in an airtight container in the refrigerator for up to 3 days or frozen for up to 1 month. To rehaeat follow the directions on page 47.

Peach BAO

Known as the longevity bun, steamed peach baos are a symbol of long life and are usually eaten during birthday celebrations for the elderly across China, Taiwan and Hong Kong. I was always fascinated by peach baos growing up, which are eaten at outdoor Taiwanese banquets or in hotel dining halls, usually in celebration of some random elder family friends who I hardly knew. Peach baos are usually the last dish that comes out when everybody is full and drunk. We occasionally make a giant longevity peach bun (see page 39, image 05) that's filled with mini longevity peach buns, which makes for a wondrous moment as you cut it open and all the mini buns flow out.

包

Makes 12 BAOs

For the almond cream:
15 flaked (sliced) almonds
15 ml double (heavy) cream

For the white chocolate red bean filling:
65 g canned chickpeas (garbanzo beans) with their liquid
50 g white chocolate pistoles
10 g butter
15 g almond cream (see above)
95 g sweet red bean paste (found in most Asian supermarkets)
pinch of flaky sea salt

For the BAO Bakery Goods dough:
100 g Tangzhong (see page 46)
470 g plain (all-purpose) flour, plus extra for dusting
1 teaspoon baking powder
pinch of salt
40 g milk powder
90 g caster (superfine) sugar
4 g fast-action dried (active dry) yeast
80 ml milk
80 ml warm water
10 ml vegetable oil

For the green leaves:
reserved BAO Bakery Goods dough
¾ teaspoon spirulina powder

To decorate:
20 ml pink food colouring

Almond cream

Preheat the oven to 180°C/350°F/Gas Mark 4. Spread out the almonds on a baking sheet and gently toast in the oven for 5 minutes until golden brown and fragrant, being careful they don't burn. While the almonds are still hot, put them into a bowl with the cream and leave to infuse overnight, or for at least 8 hours. Strain the infused cream through a fine-mesh sieve into a jug (pitcher) and discard the almonds. The cream can be stored in an airtight container in the refrigerator for up to 3 days.

White chocolate red bean filling

Line a sieve with muslin (cheesecloth) and set over a bowl. Put the chickpeas (garbanzo beans) with their liquid into a blender and blend until smooth. Strain through the muslin, removing as much liquid as possible. Discard the liquid.

Melt 25 g of the white chocolate with the butter in a heatproof bowl set over a pan of simmering water. Put the strained chickpea mixture, almond cream, red bean paste and salt into a blender and blend until combined, then add the melted chocolate and butter. When the mixture has cooled, add the remaining chocolate. Transfer to a bowl and chill in the refrigerator for at least 2 hours. When ready to use, divide into twelve 20 g balls. The balls can be frozen for up to 1 month.

BAO Bakery Goods dough

Put the tangzhong and all the dry ingredients into the bowl of a stand mixer fitted with a dough hook. Start mixing on a low setting and then slowly add the milk and water. Finally, add the oil and continue mixing until the dough is smooth. Cover with a damp cloth or cling film (plastic wrap) and leave to prove somewhere warm for at least 2 hours, or until doubled in size.

Turn the dough out onto a lightly floured surface and knead for 10 minutes – it will gradually become more elastic and the surface of the dough will become smooth. Divide into twelve 65 g balls, reserving 150 g for the green leaves. Cover loosely with a tea towel to prevent them drying out.

Green leaves

Mix the reserved dough with the spirulina powder to create a green dough. Using a rolling pin, roll the dough out to 1 mm (¹⁄₁₆ inch) thick. With a leaf cutter or sharp knife, create 24 leaf shapes, about 1 × 2.5 cm (½ × 1 inch).

To assemble

Using a rolling pin, roll out the dough balls into 7–8 cm (2¾–3¼ inch) circles, allowing the middles to be slightly thicker. Place a white chocolate red bean ball in the middle of a dough circle and carefully bring the edges of the dough together, enclosing the ball and pinching the dough so it is firmly closed with no holes. Turn the BAOs over so the seam is facing down and shape to resemble a peach. Repeat with the remaining dough circles and filling balls.

Place the BAOs onto cut squares of baking (parchment) paper then brush the tops with water and place 2 leaves at the top of each. Leave to prove somewhere warm for 30–50 minutes until they have risen, are fluffy and don't bounce back too quickly when poked.

Prepare a steamer (see page 47). Carefully transfer the peach BAOs, including the baking paper, to the steamer and steam over a medium-high heat for 15 minutes until they bounce back nicely when pressed with a finger. If you feel any resistant patches in the centre that don't bounce back, keep steaming. Remove from the steamer. Pour the pink food colouring into a fine-mist spray canister with 60 ml water, then spray the front tip of the still-hot BAOs. Either eat immediately or leave to rest at room temperature until the steam has fully evaporated and the BAO are completely cool if you are eating another time. The BAOs can be stored in an airtight container in the refrigerator for up to 3 days or frozen for up to 1 month.

Coconut BAO Loaf

One of my favourite baked goods is the baked coconut bun, also known as a cocktail bun. It's an iconic Hong Kong style sweet bun with a soft coconut filling. Every time I'm in Chinatown, I make sure to buy some to have the next morning. They are perfect when slightly warmed up for breakfast. We took this classic flavour and put it into our BAO Bakery Goods. A great hack is to cut a slice of the loaf and put it into the toaster.

Makes 1 BAO Loaf

For the coconut filling:
35 g salted butter, softened
15 g caster (superfine) sugar
5 g plain (all-purpose) flour
2.5 g cornflour (cornstarch)
15 g milk powder
20 g desiccated (unsweetened dried shredded) coconut

For the BAO Bakery Goods dough:
45 g Tangzhong (see page 46)
210 g plain (all-purpose) flour, plus extra for dusting
½ teaspoon baking powder
pinch of salt
20 g milk powder
40 g caster (superfine) sugar
2g teaspoon fast-action dried (active dry) yeast
35 ml milk
35 ml warm water
1 teaspoon vegetable oil, plus extra for greasing

To decorate
light brown food colouring
desiccated (unsweetened dried shredded) coconut

Coconut filling

In a bowl, beat the butter, then slowly add the sugar and beat until light and fluffy. Add the remaining ingredients, one by one, making sure they are each fully incorporated before adding the next. Chill in the refrigerator for at least 2 hours until the mixture is easier to handle. When ready to use, divide the filling into six 15 g balls.

BAO Bakery Goods dough

Put the tangzhong and all the dry ingredients into the bowl of a stand mixer fitted with a dough hook. Start mixing on a low setting and then slowly add the milk and water. Finally, add the oil and continue mixing until the dough is smooth. Cover with a damp cloth or cling film (plastic wrap) and leave to prove somewhere warm for at least 2 hours, or until doubled in size.

Turn the dough out onto a lightly floured surface and knead for 10 minutes – it will gradually become more elastic and the surface of the dough will become smooth. Divide the dough into six 55 g balls.

To assemble

Line a 15 × 9 × 7 cm (6 x 3½ x 2¾ inch) non-stick perforated loaf pan with baking (parchment) paper and brush with oil.

Flatten the dough balls a little and put a ball of coconut filling in the middle of each one. Carefully bring the edges of the dough together, enclosing the balls and pinching the dough so they are firmly closed with no holes. Place the BAO balls in the pan in sets of 2, with the seams facing down. Leave to prove somewhere warm for 60–90 minutes until the balls have risen to fill the pan by about 90 per cent.

Prepare a deep pot that will fit the loaf pan so that it sits in shallow water. Place a steamer stand inside. Bring the water to the boil, then reduce to a medium heat. Place the loaf pan on top of the steamer stand and cover. Steam for 15 minutes, then remove the loaf from the pan and steam for another 15 minutes. Remove from the steamer and, while the loaf is still warm, spray the top of it with light brown food colouring and top with sprinkles of desiccated coconut. Either eat immediately or leave to rest at room temperature on a wire rack until the steam has fully evaporated and the BAO loaf is completely cool.

The BAO loaf can be stored in an airtight container in the refrigerator for up to 3 days or the freezer for up to 1 month. If reheating by toasting, first defrost overnight in the refrigerator. If steaming, it is fine to reheat from frozen.

Xiao Chi
BAO Soho

A TYPICAL XIAO CHI HOUSE, ROU BUO TURKEY RICE, TAINAN.

NOT A TYPICAL TAIWANESE FRIED CHICKEN BUT A STALL WE FREQUENTED ON OUR TRAVELS, LONG GE, GONGGUAN NIGHT MARKET.

When we opened our first restaurant in April 2015, we moved from a shack in a car park to a 110 square metre (1,200 square foot) wardrobe-like room on Lexington Street in Soho, London. We like to call it our *xiao chi* house, as it's the home of our *xiao chi* ('small eats'), which are inspired by the *xiao chi* houses and street food in Taiwan. The beauty of *xiao chi* is their size, making them perfect for the mouth of the Lonely Man. You can eat a few, then try some other dishes or move on to somewhere else. Taiwan is famous for its snacking culture, and the city is perfectly designed to hop from place to place, constantly sampling new dishes. One thing my dad always asks me is, why anyone would want to have a meal with just one plate of food. He is referring of course, to the Western way of eating. It's hard to explain to him that there is a beauty and simplicity to a single plate of food, too. But I can understand where he is coming from, because in Taiwan the culture is to have variety in a meal.

It is at BAO Soho where we picture the Lonely Man perched at the end of the bar, eating a bowl of Guinea Fowl Rice (see page 100), sipping Peanut Milk (see page 214), as the aromas of fresh oolong tea float in the air around him – right in the middle of Soho, where he can swap the chaotic hustle of one of the city's busiest neighbourhoods for the organized bustle of our intimate kitchen. He'll be sitting at the Douglas fir bar watching a speedy version of the traditional Taiwanese tea ceremony, which involves the therapeutic washing and pouring of a teapot with steaming hot water, while through a small window at the end of the room a chef hurtles out orders. For me, the sounds of the kitchen bring back treasured memories – of the hostess who rhythmically sang out orders in a soba restaurant in Tokyo or the clatter of our much-loved greasy spoon in Pimlico, the Regency Café. I still remember when we first opened BAO Soho, you could hear Shing's low-pitched voice calling out the orders as soon as you walked into the restaurant.

THE OLD LADY, BOTTOM RIGHT, SINGS ORDERS TO THE KITCHEN AT KANDA YABU SOBA, TOKYO.

When I was growing up in Taipei, I spent my spare time socializing in night markets, walking among the bustling vendors and snacking on *xiao chi*. I much prefer the smaller, local street markets, as often at the more touristic ones you end up walking around in a circuit in a packed-sardine-like formation. My local, or at least my favourite, routine was whizzing through Gongguan night market eating my usual gua bao and then walking around the corner for fried chicken and milk bubble tea.

The culture of street food is so engrained in the Taiwanese way of life. I love walking around markets and observing the grannies who have perfected their singular signature dishes, selling the same thing day in, day out. There is so much elegance in their craft, which I feel is embodied in the perfect one-person portion size. Back in the day, I had my go-to places for each speciality. If I fancied gua bao, I would go to Lan Jia in Taipei. If I wanted turkey rice, I would go to Rou Buo in Tainan (unfortunately the original Tainan shop has closed). Pig heart glass noodles? It's got to be A Ming on Bao'an Road in Tainan, with A Ming himself impressing everyone by remembering queues of orders without writing a single one down. Such a legend.

Many years later, when I returned with Shing and Wai Ting, night markets made up a lot of our first visits. Maybe we could pin down the founding of BAO to the regular market trips I had been accustomed to since I was a child, and which I was able to introduce Shing and Wai Ting to. One memory particularly sticks out, which is of taking Shing to a famous night market in Tainan for the first time. He described the scene as being like a Japanese battlefield, with samurai banners flying on the skyline. There is a constant smoke surrounding you and gleaming lights all around. It's alive and exciting. Another time, in Tainan (back when our metabolisms worked faster), we visited eighteen different *xiao chi* houses and street food vendors in one day. While our restaurants take inspiration from many different Taiwanese eating cultures, Soho, where it all began, was very much inspired by the food in the night markets and these small eats.

A MING PIG HEARTS, BAO'AN ROAD, TAINAN.

HUAYUAN NIGHT MARKET, TAINAN.

When we first opened, you could count how many Taiwanese restaurants there were in London on one hand. We were on a mission to bring *xiao chi* to London, and we found this small, charismatic room in Soho. Small place, a concise menu and a simple, tick-box ordering system – great! Shing's dad, who was used to cooking in restaurants with 100+ à la carte dishes on the menu, was so confused by the idea that we would only sell BAOs and a few other plates, the entire menu amounting to only around twenty items. I remember him querying whether people would actually come if there was only a handful of dishes to choose from. The kitchen was the size of their bathroom, so if they had seen it, they might have understood that our desire to run a short menu was also a reflection of the limited capacity of the kitchen itself.

I love small spaces – they force you to become much more strategic and detail-focused in how you use them. Lots of chefs would come in for a trial and laugh at the size of our kitchen, saying they were too big to work in it. Indeed, many didn't make it, but having such a small, clever space also meant that the team who did stay worked closely together, helping to keep the kitchen extremely streamlined. Everything has to be in the right place. I often talk about the white patch on the floor, worn out by the chef standing on the fryer section, swivelling on the spot so that their arm is in touching distance of the pass. There is something poetic in the transition of this floor, or the glossy stainless steel of a counter that in time becomes buffed and matte. These instances of time-worn beauty grow throughout the years, as the edges of the kitchen become burnished and smooth through use, each chef leaving their indelible mark. It's not surprising that it ended up being our best-functioning kitchen.

When we designed the restaurant with our architect friends, Emma Flynn and Luke Royffe, the challenge we had with the dining room was the same we had with the kitchen. Just 46 square metres (500 square feet) to fit thirty covers? I still remember getting a call from our partners – 'It's not going to work,' they said. 'You walk in and you walk straight into the bar! Why is the hoist on the floor? This isn't workable.' But despite the last-minute scares that always come to the surface when you are mid-build, it's the quirks that make BAO Soho so beautiful. Functional design details in a small space, or those that are added over the course of its history, can be some of the most exciting. I remember sitting in a small dive bar in Tokyo that only fits six people and seeing the shop owner unplug a small hole in the wall and shout to their neighbouring shack for someone to get something – the action was so smooth, so perfectly grounded in that place and moment, that it felt like a piece of cinema. It's exactly that kind of feeling I hope we've created for people in Soho.

Whenever we design interiors, we become very picky about dimensions and materials. We tape up plans and print-outs everywhere around our house – from the height of a ceiling fan to the paint for a door sign. Our house is plastered with them and their purpose becomes integrated into our everyday life before they are signed off. These constant reminders allow the concept to grow into something real – when you become familiar with something it looks and feels different. When travelling, I would sometimes have to pack samples of wood to take with me because I needed the timber to live in the corner of my eye until I could make a decision – and if that meant bringing it on my travels, so be it.

THE SOHO BAR THAT WAS 'TOO CLOSE' TO THE ENTRANCE.

BAO SOHO, LEXINGTON STREET.

THIS SHOP OWNER USES THE SMALL PIPE BEHIND HIS
LEFT SHOULDER TO COMMUNICATE TO HIS NEIGHBOUR.

　　　　　　　　　小吃 ─ 包蘇活店

Soho House Pickles

Pickles are always an important part of the meal at BAO, whether to complement the components of a dish or as a way to kick-start your appetite. They are also great simply eaten with boiled rice.

Makes 1 × 500 ml jar per pickle

For the soy-pickled cucumber:
200 g cucumber, halved, seeded and cut into 5.5 × 1.5 cm (2¼ × ⅝ inch) sticks
pinch of salt
45 g caster (superfine) sugar
200 ml rice vinegar
45 ml light soy sauce
45 ml dark soy sauce

For the pickled daikon:
350 g daikon, peeled
400 ml rice vinegar
100 g caster (superfine) sugar
50 g salt

For the soy-pickled tomatoes:
250 g cherry tomatoes
60 g caster (superfine) sugar
250 ml rice vinegar
60 ml light soy sauce
60 ml dark soy sauce

To serve:
Spring Onion Tofu (see page 229), to taste

How to sterilize jars
Pour about 2.5 cm (1 inch) water into a large saucepan. Place a steam tray on top (the top of the tray should sit just above the waterline). Place your jars and lids upside down on the tray and bring the water to a gentle boil for about 15 minutes. This should generate enough steam inside each jar and lid to sterilize them. Carefully remove, then air dry the jars. The jars are now ready for use – it's best to use them right after sterilizing them.

Soy-pickled cucumber

Put the cucumber sticks into a colander, sprinkle over the salt and leave to drain for 1 hour.

In a small non-reactive bowl, whisk together the sugar, vinegar and both soy sauces until the sugar has dissolved.

Transfer the cucumber sticks to a 500 ml sterilized jar (see below left), then pour over the pickling liquid, leaving a 1 cm (½ inch) head space, and seal. Leave to pickle in the refrigerator for at least 3 days before using and up to 1 week for optimal flavour. The soy-pickled cucumber can be stored in the refrigerator for up to 1 month.

Pickled daikon

Using a mandoline, shave the daikon into circles 3 mm (⅛ inch) thick and 5 cm (2 inch) diameter.

In a large non-reactive bowl, whisk together the vinegar, sugar and salt until the sugar and salt are fully dissolved. Add the daikon slices and mix well. Transfer to a 500 ml sterilized jar (see below left), leaving a 1 cm (½ inch) head space, and seal. Leave to pickle in a cool, dark place for 1 day before using. The pickled daikon can be stored in the refrigerator for up to 1 month.

Soy-pickled tomatoes

Cut a small nick in the skin at the bottom of each tomato.

Prepare a bowl of iced water. Bring a large saucepan of water to the boil, then blanch the tomatoes, in small batches, for 10 seconds. Remove with a slotted spoon and plunge immediately into the iced water. The skins should start to peel back. Drain and peel the tomatoes.

In a small non-reactive bowl, whisk together the sugar, vinegar and both soy sauces until the sugar has dissolved.

Transfer the tomatoes to a 500 ml sterilized jar (see below left), then pour over the pickling liquid, leaving a 1 cm (½ inch) head space, and seal. Leave to pickle in the refrigerator for 2 days before using. The soy-pickled tomatoes can be stored in the refrigerator for up to 10 days.

To assemble

On a small plate, place 2 pieces of pickled cucumber in parallel and on a diagonal. Put 2 pickled tomatoes perpendicular to the cucumbers and add 1 heaped tablespoon of the spring onion tofu between them. Drape 2 slices of pickled daikon over the tomatoes, so that it partially covers the cucumber and spring onion tofu.

House Salad

The BAO House Salad has been on the menu since day one at BAO Soho. Grated salted duck egg is our equivalent to Parmesan, providing that salty and creamy hit. It requires a bit of time to dry out the salted duck eggs so they're easy to grate. If you have more time on your hands, salting your own duck eggs would be even better (see page 228). You can easily buy salted duck eggs from your local Asian supermarket or online.

Serves 2

1 Salted Duck Egg (see page 228)
90 g kale, stems removed and leaves coarsely chopped
100 ml Tiger Dressing (see page 229)

The day before you want to serve the salad, bring a saucepan of water to the boil, then add the duck egg and cook for 10 minutes. Drain, then refresh in cold water to cool.

Line a small chopping (cutting) board with baking (parchment) paper. Cut the cooled egg in half and remove it from the shell. Put the egg onto the prepared board and place in the warmest and driest area of your kitchen. Leave for 24 hours until it has totally dried out and is hard.

To assemble

If you have kitchen gloves you might want to wear them for this part. Combine the kale and dressing in a bowl and massage the dressing into the leaves with your hands, ensuring you get into all of the crinkled parts of the kale. Divide between 2 bowls and grate 1 tablespoon of the duck egg over each salad.

Sweet Potato Chips with Pickled Plum Ketchup

When Shing and Wai Ting first had this, they couldn't get their head around why you would batter a chip (fry) – the same way I couldn't get my head around why the British would put chips in a bread roll to make a chip butty. Either way, they loved it. Traditionally in Taiwan, we sprinkle plum powder on top of these chips, so at BAO we used to pickle plums and dehydrate them before turning them into a powder. However, the humidity in our small restaurant meant that the plums often wouldn't dry thoroughly enough and became like jam in the blender. Because of this, we decided to turn the pickled plums into a ketchup.

Serves 2–3

300 g sweet potatoes (about 2), peeled and cut into 1-cm (½-inch) thick sticks
rapeseed (canola) oil, for deep-frying
2–3 teaspoons Pickled Plum Ketchup (see page 231), to serve

For the batter:
150 g plain (all-purpose) flour
30 g cornflour (cornstarch)
⅛ teaspoon salt
⅛ teaspoon caster (superfine) sugar
⅛ teaspoon baking powder
2 teaspoons rapeseed (canola) oil

Tip
If you don't want to cook the chips (fries) twice, just deep-fry them once at 175°C/345°F for 4 minutes.

Batter

Combine all the dry ingredients in a large bowl, then pour in 210 ml water and whisk until there are no lumps. Add the oil and give it a final stir.

To assemble

Add the sweet potato sticks to the batter and toss to coat.

Heat the oil in a deep, heavy-based saucepan to 165°C/330°F, or until a cube of ginger sizzles and browns in 20 seconds. Working in batches and using a slotted spoon, lift the sticks from the bowl, letting any excess batter drip off, then gently lower into the hot oil, being careful to separate the pieces to ensure they don't stick together (you can also spread them apart in the oil using chopsticks). Deep-fry for 3 minutes until crisp but not brown. Remove with a slotted spoon, drain on paper towels and leave to cool.

Just before you want to serve them, reheat the oil to 190°C/375°F and deep-fry the chips (fries) a second time for 45 seconds (this ensures they have a nice crunch and texture). Serve the chips with 1 teaspoon of the ketchup per person.

Taiwanese Fried Chicken

Taiwanese fried chicken! I have so many childhood memories of eating this with friends at night markets, and it was one of the three items we sold when we first started BAO as a market stall, along with the Classic Pork BAO (see page 51) and the Daikon BAO (see page 54). These memories of fried chicken have now been replaced with memories and stories involving our pursuit of perfecting BAO's fried chicken over the years. Right from the beginning we had spreadsheets full of marinade timings and frying stages that we tested to get the juiciness and crispiness we wanted. We discovered that there was a certain amount of time you could keep the flour on the meat and a specific way to coat the chicken with the flour using a flick of your palm. This journey made us very protective of the recipe.

So many people would quiz us, trying to find out the flour and the spice mix we used, especially in our market days. There weren't many Taiwanese restaurants back then, so it wasn't readily available information. The lengths we went to keep the fried chicken coating a secret ... we would have the flour delivered to another location or beat the staff to the delivery so we could hide it and empty the small packets into clear containers when everyone had left. The spice and marinade mix were the hardest to keep doing in secret – it was only a couple of years ago that we had that moment, looking at each other, lab coats on, rubber gloves on, masks on, on a hot summer day in an unventilated office, when we asked ourselves, Why are we still doing this every week? That powder in large volumes really gets up your nose! At that, we decided we had had enough and eventually moved the process to an external producer with a signed NDA. But now, after all that secrecy, it is here for you to see.

Serves 2–3

vegetable oil, for deep-frying
Hot Sauce (see page 231), to serve

For the marinated chicken:
200 ml soy milk, plus extra if needed
1 clove garlic, grated
2.5 cm (1 inch) piece of fresh ginger, peeled and grated
2 teaspoons cornflour (cornstarch)
1 teaspoon ground cumin
1 teaspoon five spice powder
1 tablespoon soy sauce
1 teaspoon rice vinegar
300 g skinless, boneless chicken thighs, cut into 10 equal pieces

For the spiced flour mix:
200 g tapioca flour (starch)
1 teaspoon red Sichuan peppercorns, ground to a powder
1 teaspoon cayenne pepper
¼ teaspoon garlic powder
½ teaspoon five spice powder
1 tablespoon salt

Tip
The double-fry technique for the chicken pieces gives the coating extra crispiness while ensuring that the centre remains incredibly juicy. If you are feeling lazy, then just deep-fry the chicken once for 4 minutes at 180°C/350°F, or until a cube of ginger sizzles and browns in 10 seconds. It won't have quite the same super-crispy texture but it will still be juicy.

Marinated chicken

In a large non-reactive bowl, mix together all the ingredients except the chicken. Add the chicken pieces, stir to coat, cover and leave to marinate in the refrigerator overnight. If you are in a hurry, marinate for 1 hour at room temperature.

When ready to cook, run your fingers through the chicken mixture to moisten any overlapping pieces. If it requires more soy milk, add some now so all the chicken pieces are submerged in the marinade.

Spiced flour mix

In a bowl, mix together all the ingredients, making sure the spices are evenly distributed.

To assemble

Toss a piece of chicken straight from the marinade into the flour mix. Roll it around lightly with your fingers to form a nugget shape. Do not flatten it or try to press more of the mix onto it. If you want more spiced flour on the chicken, roll it in the bowl of flour mix a few times and dust extra spiced flour mix on top. Make sure the piece is fully coated, then transfer to a plate or tray. Repeat the process with the remaining chicken pieces.

Heat the oil in a deep, heavy-based saucepan to 160°C/325°F, or until a cube of ginger sizzles and browns in 20 seconds. Very lightly shake off any excess flour mix, then – in 2 batches – carefully hold the chicken and slowly drop it away from you into the hot oil and deep-fry for 3 minutes until cooked through, lightly golden and crisp. Remove with the tongs or slotted spoon, drain on paper towels and leave to cool completely.

When cool, reheat the oil to 190°C/375°F and deep-fry again for 2 minutes. Place the chicken pieces in a shallow bowl and drizzle with hot sauce to serve.

小吃 — 包蘇活店

Pig's Blood Cake with Soy-cured Egg Yolk

Shortly after I moved to the UK from Taipei, I went on a school trip with my class to the countryside and we stayed at a proper British bed and breakfast that served a full English breakfast in the morning. Our teacher kept going on and on about this 'thing' that we were about to eat, and how we would all be so scared. He wouldn't even tell us what it was until it arrived. When he finally described what turned out to be black pudding (blood sausage), I just thought, 'Oh it's just like pig's blood cake without the rice!'

In Taiwan, pig's blood cake is served on a stick like a lollipop and is topped with a popular Taiwanese flavour combination of peanut powder and coriander. It's made with pig's blood, salt and glutinous rice, which is then steamed so it is soft and chewy. Unlike other street food vendors, where you can see the food constantly being prepared, you would often just walk past a discreet metal box written 'pig blood cake' that can be easily missed in the hustle and bustle of a nightmarket. When you order, the vendor, wearing a thick cotton glove, would take a glistening black lollipop out of the box, with a waft of steam floating upwards like a magic trick.

I loved the idea of introducing this dish to London, as it is so Taiwanese but so British, too. When we were developing the recipe, I wanted to get lots of flavour into the pig's blood cake by adding cubes of pork fat and caramelized onions, but it results in a much softer texture than the classic Taiwanese style, so we pan-fried our blood cake after steaming to give it a crisp, crunchy exterior. The bonus is the fat on the surface starts to release its fragrance, which is salivating. We serve it with a soy-cured egg yolk, as a nod to the British breakfast of black pudding and fried egg.

Serves 3

100 g glutinous (sticky) rice, rinsed
rapeseed (canola) oil, for pan-frying
260 g diced onions (about 2 onions)
80 g pork fat, cut into 8 mm (⅜ inch) cubes
120 ml fresh pig's blood (ask your butcher if they have this)
3 Soy-cured Egg Yolks (see page 228), to serve

For the spice mix:
1 teaspoon salt
½ teaspoon ground white pepper
½ teaspoon ground cumin
¼ teaspoon ground ginger

Tip
This recipe makes three portions, but the pig's blood cake can be frozen for up to 3 months. Just defrost it gently in the refrigerator overnight before pan-frying it – perfect for breakfast whenever you need a Taiwanese pick-me-up. And the cake trimmings are great for tossing through fried rice, so don't let them go to waste. You could also mash them into a baking ring and bake for about 10 minutes at 180°C/350°F/Gas Mark 4 to serve alongside fried eggs and bacon for a Taiwanese accompaniment to a full English.

Put the rice into a bowl, cover with cold water and leave to soak overnight.

The next day, mix together all the ingredients for the spice mix in a small bowl. Set aside.

Heat a splash of oil in a frying pan (skillet) over a low heat, add the onions and caramelize until they are very soft and have taken on a jammy consistency. This can take 30–40 minutes, but make sure to check them regularly so they don't burn. If they look like they are catching, add a splash of water. Remove from the heat and leave to cool.

Drain the rice, then transfer to a large bowl. Add the pork fat, pig's blood, caramelized onions and the spice mix and mix together.

Prepare a large steamer (see page 47) and line an 18 × 11 × 2.5 cm (7 × 4¼ × 1 inch) baking pan with 2 layers of cling film (plastic wrap). Pour the mixture into the pan, then rake the mixture with a fork, as you might fluff couscous or a rice pilaf (this helps the blood to get between the grains of rice and will also make sure that not too much blood is at the top or at the bottom of the pan). Put the pan into the prepared steamer, and steam, uncovered, over a low-medium heat for 1 hour until it solidifies and sets, making sure that the water does not boil dry. Remove the pig's blood cake from the steamer and leave to cool.

To assemble

Turn the cake out of the pan and cut into three 11 × 6 cm (4¼ × 2½ inch) rectangles. The sides that were flush to the edge of the pan should be nice and flat, but if the tops are not smooth, trim off any excess and reserve (see Tip, left).

Heat a splash of oil in a frying pan over a medium heat until it starts to shimmer, then fry the flattest side of the blood cake pieces until crispy, 1–2 minutes. Flip and fry on the other side until crispy. Using a pair of tongs, gently turn each piece on its side to crisp the edges. Transfer to a plate with the neatest sides facing upwards.

Push the back of a spoon into the centre of each piece to make a small indentation, then gently place a cured egg yolk on top of each. They should sit neatly in the indentations without falling off.

Trotter Nuggets with Burnt Chilli Sauce

Full of natural collagen, which is purported to soften and plump the skin, trotters (pig's feet) are a really popular dish for women all over Asia. They are an ingredient that is often overlooked, but I love them, with their delicious gelatinous stickiness when done right. One of my favourite trotter dishes is from Zhu Jiao Fan in Tainan. It consists of a soy-braised trotter on steamed short-grain rice, served with stewed bamboo shoots and *meigan* fermented greens. At BAO Soho we braise the trotters overnight with some yellow bean paste and then roll the meat in their unctuous reduced juices to bind into nuggets. The burnt chilli sauce we serve with them is a bright mustard-green colour that beautifully offsets the deep golden hue of the nuggets. The combination of spicy sauce with the fatty rich trotter and flecks of flaky salt is a holy trinity of flavour.

Serves 6

splash of rapeseed (canola) oil, plus extra for deep-frying
3 cloves garlic, smashed
2 banana shallots, halved
3 large trotters (pig's feet)
1 tablespoon yellow bean paste
1 x 400-g pork belly (side)
200 ml Shaoxing rice wine
pinch of salt

For the panko coating:
50 g plain (all-purpose) flour
2 eggs, beaten
100 g panko breadcrumbs

To serve:
flaky sea salt
Burnt Chilli Sauce (see page 230), to taste

Heat a splash of oil in a wide, deep saucepan, over medium heat, add the garlic and shallots and fry for 2 minutes.

Rub the trotters (pig's feet) with the yellow bean paste and place them in the pan, then lay the pork belly (side) alongside. Pour in the wine and top up with water to cover and bring to the boil. Reduce the heat to low, cover and cook for 3 hours until the trotter meat is falling off the bones. Carefully lift the trotters and pork belly out onto a chopping (cutting) board and leave until it cools to a temperature that hands can handle. Reserve the cooking liquid.

Remove all the trotter meat from the bones. Trotters have many small joint bones. To make sure you have removed them all, run the trotter meat through your fingers and thumbs. Cartilage is good, though, so don't throw those bits away! Don't be intimidated; bone is significantly harder than cartilage so even if this is your first time doing it you will be able to tell the difference. Chop the picked trotter and pork belly into 8 cm (3 inch) cubes, then put into a large heatproof bowl. Season with a pinch of salt.

Pass the cooking liquid through a fine-mesh sieve into a deep saucepan. Set the pan over a high heat and reduce the liquid by just over half, then pour over the chopped meat and mix well.

Lay a large sheet of cling film (plastic wrap) on the work counter, place the meat mixture into the centre of the cling film. Roll into a 4.5-cm (1¾-inch) diameter sausage shape using the cling film. Chill the rolled trotter sausage in the refrigerator for 3–4 hours until set. It needs to be really firm.

Panko coating

Remove the sausage from the cling film and cut in half lengthways. Place the halves flat side down on a chopping board and cut into 1.25 cm (½ inch) semicircles (about 24). In a large bowl, toss the trotter pieces in the flour.

Put the eggs into a shallow dish and put the panko breadcrumbs into a separate shallow dish. Position the bowl of floured trotter nuggets on your left, followed by the eggs and the breadcrumbs. Working from left to right, toss the nuggets in the egg and then in the breadcrumbs. Gently press the breadcrumbs into the nuggets until covered. If they are not fully coated, the juicy fat will leak out when deep-frying and you might end up with a hollow nugget. Transfer the coated nuggets to a baking sheet. The nuggets can be frozen for up to 3 months (defrost them before deep-frying).

To assemble

Heat the oil in a deep, heavy-based saucepan to 180°C/350°F, or until a cube of ginger sizzles and browns in 10 seconds. Carefully place the nuggets, a few at a time, in the hot oil and deep-fry for 1–2 minutes until golden brown, then remove with a slotted spoon and drain on paper towels.

Place 3 nuggets in each bowl, then place another one on top. Crush flaky sea salt over the nuggets and serve with burnt chilli sauce.

小吃 — 包蘇活店

Scallops with Yellow Bean Garlic

Using good-quality scallops is essential for this dish. We source ours from Henderson Seafood, who provide us with hand-dived scallops picked from the seabed off the Isle of Mull or Brixham, Devon.

Eating scallops in the shell like this brings back memories of eating my mother-in-law's classic Cantonese steamed scallops topped with garlic and vermicelli noodles. The best bit was slurping the scallop juice mixed with the dressing from the shell while trying to scoop up the last bits of vermicelli. When we first opened BAO Soho, lonely diners would come in and order one scallop, slurp it up, then order another straight away.

Serves 4

4 scallops in their shell
vegetable oil, for pan-frying
salt

For the yellow bean garlic:
75 g garlic, finely chopped
50 ml rapeseed (canola) oil
1 tablespoon yellow bean paste
1 teaspoon caster (superfine) sugar
1 teaspoon salt

For the scallop dressing:
120 ml Sichuan Chilli Oil (see page 229), strained
80 ml light soy sauce
32 ml Chinkiang black rice vinegar
35 ml lemon juice
1½ teaspoons caster (superfine) sugar

For the nori powder:
2 sheets nori seaweed

Tip
Yellow bean garlic goes well with so many dishes, so make more if you like. If kept in oil, it will keep for up to 1 month. We often make six times the quantity given here to keep on hand for eating with stir-fried vegetables.

Yellow bean garlic

Rinse the chopped garlic in a fine-mesh sieve, then dry on paper towels and leave it to air for a few hours (this removes the bitterness from the garlic).

Put the oil and garlic into a small saucepan and cook gently over a very low heat for 15–20 minutes until the garlic is fragrant and cooked. You want to see small bubbles rising from around the garlic, but you don't want it to brown or fry (it is similar to making confit garlic). Remove the garlic from the heat, then while still hot, stir in the yellow bean paste, sugar and salt.

There will be more yellow bean garlic than is needed for this recipe, but it can be stored in a sterilized glass jar (see page 89) in the refrigerator for up to 1 month.

Scallop dressing

Put all the ingredients into a bowl or jar and mix together with 250 ml water. There will be more dressing than is needed for this recipe, but it can be stored in a sterilized glass jar (see page 89) in the refrigerator for up to 1 week.

Nori powder

Preheat the oven to 160°C/325°F/Gas Mark 3. Put the nori sheets onto a baking sheet and toast in the oven for 5 minutes until completely dry, then tear into pieces. Put into a blender and blend at high speed to a powder. There will be more nori powder than is needed for this recipe, but it can be stored in an airtight container somewhere cool and dry for up to 1 month.

To assemble

Delicately remove the scallops from their shells by lifting each one with your thumb and running a knife through the muscle to release it, being careful not to cut the surface of the scallop itself. Let the scallops come to room temperature before cooking.

Keep the shells to serve – wash them thoroughly and then put them into the oven at 160°C/325°F/Gas Mark 3 for 15 minutes until they dry out.

Salt both sides of the scallops. Heat a frying pan (skillet) over a medium heat until it is quite hot. Pour a small circle of oil into the centre of the pan and lay the scallops in the oil with the orange coral facing away from you. Pan-fry for 1–2 minutes until the surface is brown and starting to char, then flip them over and cook for another 30 seconds until there is a nice bounce when you touch them. Remove from the pan.

Put the cooked scallops back into their shells and pour in some of the dressing until the shell is one-third full. Put ½ teaspoon of the yellow bean garlic on top of each scallop and dust the scallop through to the edge of the shell with the nori powder.

To eat, lift the scallop shell up to your lips and slurp the scallop down with all the dressing, then exhale with satisfaction.

Guinea Fowl Rice

This dish is inspired by the turkey rice bowls from Chiayi City in Taiwan and uses the most amazing rice from the Chishang township. There is so much that goes on behind the scenes for this dish, all to create a bowl that is, for me, a perfect example of that moment in solitude we so often refer to. At BAO Soho, our Long Day single-dining menu consists of this rice bowl, a Classic Pork BAO (see page 51) and a small glass of Peanut Milk (see page 214). I get emotional thinking about this trio. There are a lot of memories centred around this dish, but the combination of these three dishes really captures the menu we first opened with.

The bowls we use to serve this in are the perfect size for one: smaller than the rice bowls you usually get in the UK, but the same size as those back in Taiwan. It's a small portion but packs a lot of punch in terms of flavour. We worked with Owen Wall to create straight-edged rice bowls that neatly show off each ingredient.

For some of our rice bowls, we coat the rice with rice dressing, while others we keep plain. The guinea fowl rice bowl is one in which we do dress the rice. We also blacken the rice with a blowtorch to create a smoky flavour, like you would have with clay-pot rice (only here the burnt rice is on the surface, rather than on the bottom of the pot). The acidic and sweet nature of the blowtorched, dressed rice balances well with the savouriness of the braised guinea fowl and the sauce made with goose fat dripping. We used to import the goose dripping from a roast goose shop in Taipei, but unfortunately it has now closed due to the pandemic, so we infuse our own fat with shallots and spring onions (scallions). My mother used to think we were crazy, but she stuck to our silly requests (there were many) and would queue up and fight for the precious goose fat and send it to us every few months.

Serves 4

For the guinea fowl:
4 guinea fowl legs, boned but with skin left on (ask your butcher to do this for you)
2 cloves garlic, crushed
2 spring onions (scallions)
2 star anise
300 ml light soy sauce
60 ml dark soy sauce
90 ml Shaoxing rice wine
20 g rock sugar

For the rice:
300 g short-grain rice (preferably Chishang or Japanese sushi rice)
300 ml filtered water

For the infused goose fat:
200 g goose fat
200 g shallots, sliced
1 clove garlic, crushed
1 cm (½ inch) piece of fresh ginger, crushed
1 spring onion (scallion), halved
1 star anise

For the guinea fowl rice dressing:
100 ml guinea fowl braising liquid
50 ml infused goose fat (see above)
1 teaspoon rice vinegar

To serve:
4 tablespoons Rice Dressing (see page 229)
4 Soy-cured Egg Yolks (see page 228)
8 Soy-pickled Cucumber sticks (see page 89)
25 g Crispy Shallots (see page 228)
4 teaspoons Ginger Spring Onion Oil (see page 229)

Shout out to the pregnant woman whose water broke in BAO Soho, but who demanded to wait for her Guinea Fowl Rice to come before heading to the hospital.

Guinea fowl

Trim any excess skin from the edges of the boned legs, feeling for any leftover bones or cartilage and carefully removing without piercing the skin. Lay the boned legs out flat, with the thigh meat at the top and the shin meat closest to you. For each leg, fold up the bottom edge and pinch, then carefully roll up as tight as you can until the leg is tightly rolled.

Combine the remaining ingredients in a saucepan with 360 ml water and bring to the boil. Add the guinea fowl legs (the liquid should just about cover the meat) and braise gently, covered, over a low heat for 1 hour until cooked through. Keep the meat warm in the braising liquid.

Rice

While the guinea fowl is cooking, wash the rice thoroughly, 3 times. After the final rinse, tip the rice into a bowl, cover with cold water and leave to soak for 30 minutes.

Pour the filtered water into a saucepan and bring to the boil. Drain the soaked rice and add to the boiling water. When the water is boiling again, put a lid on, reduce the heat to low and cook for 18 minutes. Open the lid to check that the rice is cooked and ever-so-slightly glistening but not wet. Put the lid back on, remove from the heat and let the rice stand for 10 minutes before serving (this process allows the remaining steam to absorb back into the grains, resulting in fluffy and bouncy rice). At no point remove the lid from the pan.

Infused goose fat

Heat the goose fat in a small saucepan until it reaches 110°C/230°F, then reduce the heat to medium-low, add the rest of the ingredients and let it simmer for 5 minutes, or until the shallots turn golden. Strain through a fine-mesh sieve into a measuring jug (large measuring cup) and discard the solids.

This makes more infused goose fat than is required for this recipe, but it can be stored in an airtight container in the refrigerator for up to 1 month.

Guinea fowl rice dressing

Whisk together 100 ml of the warm guinea fowl braising liquid, 50 ml of the infused goose fat and the vinegar in a small bowl until the dressing is emulsified and creamy beige in colour.

To assemble

Drizzle the 4 tablespoons of rice dressing over the steamed rice. Wet a rice paddle or wooden spoon with a little water, then fluff the rice using a scoring gesture (this mixes the dressing through the rice while ensuring the rice grains are not crushed). Scoop the rice into 4 shallow bowls and very gently smooth the surface. Do not press or compact the rice down. Using a cook's blowtorch, lightly blacken the top of the rice, then pour 2 tablespoons of the guinea fowl rice dressing over each bowl.

Take the guinea fowl legs out of the braising liquid and place them skin side up on a chopping (cutting) board, then cut into 5-mm (¼-inch)-thick slices. Fan out the slices a little, then divide them over the rice in the bowls.

For each bowl, pour 1 tablespoon of the guinea fowl braising liquid over the sliced guinea fowl. Gently place 1 soy-cured egg yolk on the opposite side, then place 2 pickled cucumber sticks between the guinea fowl and the egg yolk (they should run parallel to the guinea fowl). In the remaining blank patch of rice, add a three-finger pinch of crispy shallots. The rice should now be completely covered. Finish with 1 teaspoon of ginger spring onion oil on top of the guinea fowl.

40-day Aged Beef Rump Cap with Aged White Soy

The beauty in this dish lies in its simplicity – it's the pairing of two amazing products from different sides of the world that makes it perfect. We're privileged to work with Philip Warren & Son who age our beef for 40–50 days. Similarly, we label the 400-day aged white soy sauce (see page 233) we use as 'liquid gold' to ensure the team in our restaurants use it sparingly. Most people don't know that soy sauces have first presses, like olive oils. The soy is light, sweet and deep in umami and brings the best out of our aged beef, along with just a pinch of sea salt added at the end. We like to serve this on our Ozu plate (see page 33).

Serves 4

1 × 500-g 40-day aged beef rump (top sirloin) cap
2½ tablespoons aged white soy sauce (see page 233)
flaky sea salt

Season the beef all over with sea salt and leave to rest at room temperature for 30 minutes.

Preheat the oven to 110°C/225°F/Gas Mark ¼.

Heat a dry frying pan (skillet) over a high heat. When the pan starts to smoke, carefully put the rump (top sirloin) cap, fat side down, into the pan. You want to render the fat before searing off the sides in the beef fat. When a pool of fat forms around the meat, tip the rump cap and sear all sides until brown.

Transfer to a roasting pan and cook in the oven for 25 minutes until medium-rare. If you have a meat thermometer, the internal temperature should be 57°C/135°F. Transfer the beef to paper towels and pat dry. Leave to rest for 10 minutes, then slice thinly.

To assemble

Divide the thinly sliced rump cap among 4 plates and layer it so that the fat lines up and the pieces slightly overlap. Sprinkle with a pinch of salt and pour over the aged soy sauce.

The Bar
BAO Fitz

Perched on the corner of a leafy street in Fitzrovia, central London, the scene at BAO Fitz was inspired by Edward Hopper's 1942 painting *Nighthawks*. This painting is a bit of an overused reference, and nods to it can feel cheesy, but if there is one thing we try to stick to, it is our gut instinct when we first visit a site. It's the first blood and spark of inspiration that pumps through our veins and into our brains, getting us excited about a space and our imaginations flowing.

We not only felt this architecturally, but we also felt a connection to the solitude in Hopper's paintings. Whilst the solitude here is a different type of solitude and comes from the world war era, the melancholy is the same feeling that connects to the *Rules to Be a Lonely Man* (see page 20). And so, it made so much sense to take that inspiration and connect it physically and emotionally to the site.

The restaurant is tucked away on a quiet street that has a neighbourhood vibe despite being minutes away from the commotion of Oxford Street. A wooden-clad U-shaped bar dominates the room and can be seen through the expansive windows from the corner of the street. The bar is perfect for the Lonely Man to linger at, sipping his Taiwanese-inspired cocktails or Taiwanese tea among the oak panelling, with a ribbed bar on which he can itch his knee with ease.

We opened BAO Fitz one year after our first restaurant. When we opened BAO Soho, it was incredibly busy, with a now-infamous queue that wound down the street. As a result, our 'bakery' lived in a 2 × 3 metre (6½ × 10 foot) prep room in the basement with no proper ventilation. There was one summer that we had a heatwave, and it was so hot that the cold room broke down, chefs were in wet T-shirt competitions (no joke) and the tiny basement bakery was at full steam (literally). We knew we had to get the bakery out of there, and that's when we came across the Fitzrovia site, just over ten minutes' walk away. It's a beautiful corner site, close to the Slade School of Fine Art, where Shing and I graduated from. It was like a secret neighbourhood spot but only a street away from London's West End. It felt private and secluded – just like Edward Hopper's paintings – and we immediately knew we wanted to create the type of vibe that felt like an escape.

FITZ'S U BAR ON THE CORNER OF WINDMILL STREET.

THE 6M² BASEMENT BAKERY IN BAO SOHO BEFORE WE MOVED TO FITZ.

ERCHEN AND HER MOTHER SAMPLING TEA FROM THE TEAHOUSE THAT HER GRANDFATHER FREQUENTED.

Another thing we wanted to do at BAO Fitz was to focus on tea. I always wanted to bring a fast-casual approach to tea, as an effort to promote Taiwanese tea culture, retain a connection to my upbringing and celebrate the provenance of the tea we use at BAO. I grew up with tea culture as part of my daily life. My grandfather had an obsessive love of Taiwanese tea – he would take me to dance classes and, while he waited, he would sit and drink in the local teahouse, chatting to friends and acquaintances. I wanted to bring the tea my grandpa had drunk to BAO, so it was quite touching when I returned all those years later to buy tea for our restaurant from the very same teahouse he sat in, to find that the shopkeeper also remembered those moments that live so strongly in my childhood memory. My grandfather would go on about Taiwanese tea competitions and why Taiwanese oolong tea is the best and that more people should know about it. It means a lot to me to be able to have that connection with him and with the teahouse. At Fitz, you can have a fast-casual tea moment, watching the therapeutic brewing of the tea, which includes washing the teapot (which means it wears down beautifully), then 'brightening' it by warming it, putting the tea leaves in and filling it with water, then finally pouring hot water over the teapot to keep it warm. During this last phase, the water flows down the sides of the pot and through a specially designed perforated tray.

The food at BAO Fitz also marks a moment of our journey in which we dived further into my Taiwanese heritage. While BAO Soho was very much inspired by the street food culture in Taiwan, at Fitz it was about taking classic, home-style flavours and translating them to fit our setting. One vision we had was of the Lonely Man perched at the bar, watching couples on dates sitting at the opposite side of the bar. (When coming up with the brief for the food, we once joked that the dishes should be Taiwanese refined date-night food with cocktails – it's funny that a lot of our friends now say this is where they take people on dates.) As BAO Fitz was modelled around that U-shaped bar, we decided to focus on pairing classic Taiwanese flavours with drinks. Taiwanese drinking (alcohol) culture is quite hard to pin down. Similar to a lot of Asian countries, drinking is often combined with eating. I have memories of my grandfather eating cold poached goose and drinking crisp Taiwan Beer. He would have his gentlemen friends over and they would share a large bottle of the beer, pouring it into each other's mini beer glasses. When I was a child, I would picture this as 'adult eating'. So, our aim was to create a similar ambience, with dishes inspired by those that you might eat while drinking with large groups, but distilled into a bar environment that would also be perfect for dates.

Before opening BAO Fitz, we travelled around Taiwan visiting traditional restaurants and more casual eateries. One place we particularly love going to when we are back is Luo Ji Xiao Chao, off the Tong Hua night market in Taipei – just one man and his wok with a limited menu of perfect little plates of clams in basil or lamb, delicious with a cold beer. Another of my favourite forms of eating in Taiwan is 'quick-fry', also known as *kuai chao* or *re chao*. Quick-fry restaurants are places you might go with a group of friends or colleagues to eat wok-fried dishes and fresh seafood and drink Taiwan Beer. You sit around laminated round tables with lazy Susans in the middle and enjoy typical Taiwanese flavours such as *san bei* (a 'three cup' sauce of soy, rice wine and sesame oil; see page 147), salt and pepper dishes, *yu shiang* (a 'fish fragrant' sauce; see page 137), deep-fried dishes, broths and basil stir-fries. The establishments are often named 'quick-fry 100' because everything is 100NT (equivalent to £2.70) or less! The dishes we have at BAO Fitz are reminiscent of these classic flavours – the *san bei* tofu balls, the salt and pepper fried cheese – that would often be eaten with alcohol, but with those little added touches that make us who we are.

When eating with my large family in Taiwan, however, we mostly choose the classic Taiwanese eating houses, where banqueting is the norm. One chicken restaurant I would frequent often with my family when I was little is Ji Jia Zhuang in Taipei. They specialize in wild mountain chicken and take great pride in it. In Taiwan, UK chickens are known as broiler chickens – white chickens with thin skins. The key to really delicious chicken is thick skin, which shows they have had space to run around. When we visited restaurants in the mountains that cook indigenous Taiwanese-style food, there were huge chickens with strong legs roaming next to us. The Taiwanese love their chicken – from these pumped-up wild chickens to the smaller, tighter birds. Shing also has vivid childhood memories of chicken served at a restaurant in Yuen Long in Hong Kong. They serve a seemingly simple chicken fat rice that is decadently good. So good we imported a box of the fat to put on as a special at BAO. At Fitz, the Chilli Chicken was one of the first larger dishes we ever served and one of the best components of that dish was the drippings from cooking the marinated chicken, when combined with a dash of aged soy sauce. It was the best eaten over rice. I could eat just the rice and that sauce without anything else – it's that good.

While Taiwan is all about the love of chicken, in England we have a special love for beef. There is one cult dish we have at BAO Fitz, which is a side dish of Bone Marrow Rice (see page 122). There is something I love about sneaking great dishes in as sides because they are unexpected and often overlooked. This dish says so much about the Taiwanese approach to animal fat and soy and it feels like the perfect example of the kind of culinary translation a London Taiwanese restaurant should produce. The dishes we serve at Fitz are meant to hint at these classic Taiwanese flavours while still having their own identity.

LUO JI XIAO CHAO, TAIPEI.

TOM, ANAIS AND WEI TING AT A LONG TURTLE ISLAND FRESH SEAFOOD.

Braised Pork Skin Sushi

We call this dish the 'One-bite Bento' as it is reminiscent of the popular bento boxes in Taiwan that serve up braised pork belly (side) or trotter (pig's foot) and bamboo shoots on rice. You'll find bento box vendors on every street in Taiwan serving the boxes all day long, but mainly for lunch. There is an amazing trotter rice shop in Tainan, and if I close my eyes and eat this dish, the memories of eating it there come flooding back. Pork skin is soft and unctuous when braised – some would say it's the best part of braised pork belly. So why not just serve the best part as one bite? Perfect little morsels for the start of a meal.

Makes 4 sushi

120 g pork skin (ask your butcher)
splash of rapeseed (canola) oil
2 cloves garlic, crushed
40 g fresh ginger, peeled, sliced and crushed
100 ml light soy sauce
80 ml dark soy sauce
120 ml Shaoxing rice wine
40 g spring onions (scallions)
2 star anise
40 g rock sugar
pinch of garlic powder
6 dried red chillies
1 cinnamon stick

To serve:
60 g cooked short-grain rice (preferably Chishang or Japanese sushi rice, see page 234)
4 slices preserved bamboo shoots in chilli oil
4 teaspoons Ginger Spring Onion Oil (see page 229)

Remove any hair from the pork skin, either by singeing it with a cook's blowtorch or plucking it, then cut the skin into four 8 × 3.5 cm (3¼ × 1½ inch) rectangular pieces.

Heat a splash of oil in a saucepan over a low heat, add the garlic and ginger and lightly cook for a few minutes to release their flavours, then add the remaining ingredients except the pork skin and increase the heat to medium to dissolve the sugar.

Add the skin to the soy braising liquid and simmer over a low heat for at least 3 hours until the skin is a glossy dark brown colour, being careful not to let the pork skin or sauce catch on the bottom of the pan.

To assemble

Wet your hands, then take 15 g of the cooked rice and shape it into a long, oval rice ball. Carefully lay a slice of bamboo shoot on the rice, then top with a piece of pork skin. Finish with 1 teaspoon of the ginger spring onion oil, making sure to include both ginger and green spring onion (scallion). Repeat with the remaining ingredients.

Whipped Tofu with Century Eggs

We've come across quite a few chopped or whipped tofu dishes on our travels, from Chengdu to Kyoto. For this dish, we crumble the tofu to create a meaty, mince texture that takes on flavour very well. Combining the tofu with century eggs (eggs preserved in a mixture of clay, ash and salt for several months) and *zha cai* (a fermented mustard green root) gives the dish both the creaminess from the egg and the extra texture and bite from the savoury *zha cai*.

Serves 5

1 x 500-g block firm tofu
2 century eggs, peeled cut into 1.5 cm (⅝ inch) cubes
20 g spring onion (scallion), white parts only, thinly sliced
20 g caster (superfine) sugar
1 tablespoon light soy sauce
60 ml sesame oil
1 teaspoon salt
20 g toasted sesame seeds
100 g *zha cai* (Chinese preserved vegetables), cut into 1 cm (½ inch) cubes
20 ml Sichuan Chilli Oil (see page 229)
50 g coriander (cilantro), coarsely chopped, plus extra to garnish

To serve:
2 teaspoons Ginger Spring Onion Oil (see page 229)
1 *cong zhua bing* or *paratha* (shop-bought is fine)
50 ml Sichuan Chilli Oil (see page 229)
Chinkiang vinegar, to taste

Put the tofu into a large plastic container and put something heavy on top, for example, a smaller plastic container full of water. Leave to stand for 1 hour to press out excess water.

Drain and pat dry the pressed tofu, then transfer to a bowl and use your hands or a fork to crumble it into a cottage cheese texture (be careful not to make it too smooth—we are not making mashed potato). Add the remaining ingredients except the coriander (cilantro) and mix together. Stir through the coriander, transfer to the refrigerator and leave to marinate for 1 hour.

To assemble

Heat the ginger spring onion oil in a frying pan (skillet) over a medium heat, add the *cong zhua bing* or *paratha* and cook on both sides until golden brown and crispy. Remove the *cong zhua bing* or *paratha* from the pan and cut into 2 × 1 cm (¾ × ½ inch) pieces, then mix with the tofu. Divide among 5 bowls, drizzle over the chilli oil and vinegar, and garnish with more coriander.

Raw Oyster in Mee Shua Broth

Having not been back to Taiwan for a couple of years due to the pandemic, Shing asked me what the first dish that I would want to eat would be when I finally get there. Of course, it took me a couple of minutes to think, but I decided that it was oyster vermicelli noodles. In the UK, people love raw oysters; however, in Taiwan we mainly cook them – we grill them, cook them in omelettes or toss them through vermicelli noodles. We hardly ever eat them raw. So, we combined the spirit of both in this dish, keeping the oyster raw and serving it in a fresh *mee shua* (thin noodle) broth with a few strands of vermicelli on the bottom to give added texture. The essence of this dish brings me straight back home.

Serves 5

100 g vermicelli noodles
5 freshly shucked oysters
35 ml Chinkiang black rice vinegar
5 teaspoons finely chopped coriander (cilantro), to serve

For the mee shua broth:
3 g *katsuobushi* (bonito flakes)
½ teaspoon premium soy sauce
25 ml Chinkiang black rice vinegar
½ teaspoon caster (superfine) sugar
½ teaspoon salt
½ clove garlic, minced

Mee shua broth

Pour 200 ml water into a saucepan and bring to the boil. Add the *katsuobushi* (bonito flakes), then remove from the heat straight away. Leave to infuse for 10–15 minutes, then strain through a fine-mesh sieve into a measuring jug (large measuring cup). Mix with the remaining ingredients, then chill in the refrigerator for 1 hour.

To assemble

Bring a large saucepan of water to the boil, add the noodles and cook for 3 minutes, then drain. Using scissors, cut the noodles into about 2 cm (¾ inch) lengths and divide them among 5 bowls, then place an oyster in the centre of each followed by 1½ teaspoons Chinkiang black rice vinegar. Carefully pour in some of the chilled broth until it almost covers the oysters. Sprinkle 1 teaspoon of the chopped coriander (cilantro) around each oyster.

Beef Cheek and Tendon Nuggets

Shing and Wai Ting were brought up eating beef brisket and tendon; a classic Hong Kong dish that my mother in law has continued to cook for us. The beef cheek and tendon nugget is a deep-fried morsel that recreates those flavours.

Just like the trotters (pig's feet) in our Trotter Nuggets (see page 96), the tendon in these nuggets is the star of the dish. Combined with the reduced, Bovril-like liquor, it makes these nuggets the holy grail of unctuousness. Be ready to chop the tendon quickly once it's out of the oven, as the tendons become resistant once they cool down. It's quite a wet mix so it's a handful when trying to roll it into a ballotine. Zoltan, who was our sous chef at Fitz at the time this dish was conceived, mastered it so well he became our Head of Production in the kitchen. Rumour is he can make this with one hand.

Serves 5

330 g beef cheeks
120 g beef tendon (ask your butcher)
1 shallot, halved
20 g *doubanjiang* (fermented chilli bean paste)
50 ml Shaoxing rice wine
1 clove garlic, crushed
10 ml light soy sauce
10 ml Chinese red vinegar
½ teaspoon rice vinegar
vegetable oil, for deep-frying
salt

For the panko coating:
50 g plain (all-purpose) flour
2 eggs, beaten
100 g panko breadcrumbs

To serve:
flaky sea salt
Burnt Chilli Sauce (see page 230), to taste

Preheat the oven to 200°C/400°F/Gas Mark 6. Put all the ingredients except the vinegars and oil into a deep roasting pan and cover with water, ensuring there are at least a few centimetres of water above the ingredients. Roast in the oven for 30 minutes, then turn the heat down to 90°C/195°F/Gas Mark ¼ and cook for 8 hours, covered.

Pass the braising liquid through a fine-mesh sieve into a saucepan to remove any solids. Transfer the meat to a large heatproof bowl, discarding the shallot and garlic. Cut the beef cheeks into about 1 cm (½ inch) pieces, and the tendon into 5 mm (¼ inch) pieces.

Reduce the braising liquid over a medium heat, stirring regularly so that the sauce does not catch on the bottom of the pan, until it has a very sticky, gelatinous texture and is about a quarter of the original volume. Pour into the bowl with the meat and mix together. Season with both the vinegars. Taste and check for seasoning and add salt if needed.

Lay a large sheet of cling film (plastic wrap) on the work counter, then place the meat mixture in the centre of the cling film. Roll into a 6-cm (2½-inch) thick sausage shape using the cling film. Transfer to the refrigerator to chill for 3–4 hours.

Panko coating

Remove the beef and tendon sausage from the cling film, place it on a chopping (cutting) board and cut into 1.5 cm (¾ inch) circles (about 10). In a large bowl, toss the pieces in the flour.

Put the eggs into a shallow dish and put the panko breadcrumbs into a separate shallow dish. Position the bowl of floured nuggets on your left, followed by the eggs and the breadcrumbs. Working from left to right, toss the nuggets in the egg and then in the breadcrumbs. Gently press the breadcrumbs into the nuggets to ensure all the sides are covered. If they are not fully coated, the juicy fat will leak out when deep-frying and you might end up with a hollow nugget. Transfer the coated nuggets to a baking sheet.

The nuggets can be frozen for up to 3 months (you will need to defrost them before deep-frying).

To assemble

Heat the oil in a deep, heavy-based saucepan to 180°C/350°F, or until a cube of ginger sizzles and browns in 10 seconds. Carefully place the nuggets in the hot oil and deep-fry for 2½ minutes until golden brown, then remove with a slotted spoon and drain on paper towels.

Place 2 nuggets in each bowl, crush flaky sea salt over them and serve with burnt chilli sauce.

Half Roasted Chilli Chicken with Aged White Soy

This recipe is a legacy left by one of our ex-research and development chefs, Eryk. It has an amazing marinade that is used in all of our restaurants but in different forms. At BAO Fitz, we use it to marinate a boned half chicken. The trick for this one is blasting the chicken briefly in a hot oven, turning it once and then letting it rest. Make sure you sprinkle the chicken liberally with oil and salt just before cooking as it helps bring out the natural juices – when combined with the marinade, this is one of the best things about this dish. We take the juice and fat and emulsify them with aged white soy sauce (see page 233) to make a magical sauce.

Serves 2

½ small chicken, boned (ask your butcher to do this for you)
120 ml Yellow Chilli Marinade (see page 145)
1 teaspoon flaky sea salt
40 ml vegetable oil, plus extra for pan-frying
20 ml aged white soy sauce (see page 233)
2 *kow choi* (Chinese chives), finely sliced

Put the chicken into a non-reactive bowl or dish and rub with 50 ml of the yellow chilli marinade. Cover and leave to marinate in the refrigerator overnight, or for 8 hours.

Preheat the oven to 210°C/410°F/Gas Mark 6½. Transfer the chicken to a baking pan and sprinkle with the sea salt and oil, then smear the chicken with the remaining marinade. Roast in the oven for 20 minutes, or until the juices run clear when the thickest part of the chicken is pierced with a knife. Turn the chicken once midway through cooking.

Remove from the oven and leave the chicken to rest for 5 minutes. Collect the cooking juices in a small mixing bowl and whisk together with the aged soy sauce until well incorporated.

Heat a frying pan (skillet) over a medium heat, add a splash of oil and the *kow choi* (Chinese chives) and briefly pan-fry until they are a vibrant glossy green and have softened slightly, being careful not to overcook them. Spread them over the chicken and serve with the chicken juice sauce.

XO Sweetcorn and Ox Heart with Beef Butter

Whenever I go to my mother-in-law, Hop Mui's, home, she seems to be cooking up a big batch of XO sauce (a popular condiment in Hong Kong made with dried scallops and Jinhua ham, making it a luxury). You would have to put goggles on because of the number of shallots she fries, which she cooks over a medium–high heat to make them crispy – something I've grown to love. A common treat is to dip poached ham hock (from the Chinese medicinal soup she makes) into this XO sauce, then top it with soy. At BAO we cook our XO sauce at a much lower and slower simmer that yields a softer sauce. We cheekily add a slab of Spanish *jamón*, too, but you can use anything from dried scallops to shrimp to give it that all-important savouriness. XO sauce is a great condiment that can be used for almost everything, from rice or noodle dishes to a dip for meats, so any leftovers won't go to waste. You can also use shop-bought XO sauce if you don't have time to make your own. In this dish, we quickly fry the XO sauce with sweetcorn in spiced beef butter and top it off with ox heart cooked over charcoal.

Serves 4

500 g (about 2) corn cobs
500 g (about ¼) ox heart, cleaned and sliced into 1 cm (½ inch) thick strips
salt and black pepper

For the XO sauce:
25 g jamón trimmings (or dried scallops)
15 g dried shrimps
5 g dried red chillies
250 ml vegetable oil
40 g shallots, finely chopped
40 g garlic, finely chopped
1½ teaspoons caster (superfine) sugar
1 teaspoon fish sauce
¼ teaspoon chilli powder
¼ teaspoon salt

For the spiced beef butter:
100 g beef fat
1 star anise
1½ teaspoons *doubanjiang* (fermented chilli bean paste)
½ teaspoon red Sichuan peppercorns
½ teaspoon chilli powder
¾ teaspoon salt

XO sauce

Put the jamón, dried shrimps and chillies into a blender and blend on a medium speed for 1 minute until the ingredients start to become incorporated, then scrape them into a bowl and set aside.

Heat the oil in a saucepan over a medium heat to 120°C/250°F. Add the jamón mixture and the shallot and garlic, reduce the heat to low and cook gently for 20 minutes (this cooks the sauce at somewhere between confit and deep-frying). Add the remaining ingredients and cook for another 10 minutes. Remove from the heat and leave to cool.

Transfer to a sterilized jar (see page 89), leaving a 1 cm (½ inch) head space, and seal. The sauce can be stored in the refrigerator for up to 1 month.

Spiced beef butter

Melt the beef fat in a deep saucepan over a medium heat, add the remaining ingredients and cook for 10 minutes until everything is very fragrant. Remove from the heat and leave to cool.

Using a fine-mesh sieve to remove the solids, strain the fat into a sterilized jar (see page 89), leaving a 1 cm (½ inch) head space, and seal. The beef butter can be stored in the refrigerator for up to 1 month.

To assemble

Prepare a barbecue or a robata grill, if you have one, then grill the corn cobs over white-hot coals for 5–10 minutes, turning regularly to ensure an even char. If you don't have a barbecue, grill (broil) the corn under a preheated hot grill (broiler). You want to get a smoky and slightly burned flavour. When the corn is cool enough to handle, cut the corn kernels from the cobs.

Season the ox heart slices with salt and pepper, then grill for about 1 minute on each side until the pieces have started to colour. Leave to cool before cutting into cubes.

Melt 4 tablespoons of the beef butter in a wok or frying pan (skillet) over a medium heat, add the corn kernels and the ox heart and pan-fry for 4–5 minutes. Add 120 g of the XO sauce and cook for another 1 minute until all the flavours combine. Divide among 4 bowls and serve.

Bone Marrow Rice with Fermented Daikon

We like to hide a few of our favourite dishes in the sides section of the menu. They're the kind of thing you order without thinking about it too much, and then when it comes it's a nice surprise. Tucked away on the side menu at BAO Fitz is a dish inspired by St. JOHN's classic roast bone marrow on toast with parsley salad. It brings back memories of our student years, when we would eat at the legendary bar. Here we place the bone marrow on torched, dressed rice, which we match with the umami flavour of aged white soy sauce (see page 233) and balance with fermented daikon and soy-cured egg yolk. The daikon gives the dish the acidity it needs similar to the freshness of the parsley salad at St. JOHN. When our BAO OG Alice's mum came to visit us from Taiwan, she said our bone marrow rice tasted like an upgraded version of Lu Rou Fan, which brought a tear to my eye. I cannot think of a better compliment.

The daikon and bone marrow need to be prepared in advance of making this dish.

Serves 2

For the spicy pickled daikon:
85 ml rice vinegar
20 g caster (superfine) sugar
1 teaspoon salt
160 g daikon, peeled and diced
15 g garlic, peeled and crushed whole
½ bird's eye chilli, left whole
½ red chilli
½ jalapeño
12 g fresh ginger, sliced
50 g onion, sliced

For the bone marrow rice:
170 g canoe-cut marrow bones (ask your butcher to do this for you)
150 g short-grain rice (preferably Chishang or Japanese sushi rice)
150 ml filtered water

To serve:
2 Soy-cured Egg Yolks (see page 228)
10 ml aged white soy sauce (see page 233)

Spicy pickled daikon

Combine the vinegar with sugar and salt in a bowl, until fully dissolved. Add all the remaining ingredients and transfer to a 500 ml sterilized jar (see page 89), leaving a 1 cm (½ inch) head space, and seal. Leave to pickle in the refrigerator or a cool, dark place for 1 day before using. The pickled daikon can be stored in the refrigerator or a cool, dark place for up to 1 week (the daikon will start to lose its texture and colour after 2 days but will still be tasty). Once opened, keep in the refrigerator.

Bone marrow rice

Soak the marrow bones in cold water for 48 hours, changing the water each evening.

Preheat the oven to 180°C/350°F/Gas Mark 4. Drain the bones and pat dry, then put onto a baking sheet and roast in the oven for 20–25 minutes until blistered. Remove from the oven and scoop out the marrow into a small saucepan. Keep warm.

Meanwhile, wash the rice thoroughly, 3 times. After the final rinse, tip the rice into a bowl, cover with cold water and leave to soak for 30 minutes.

Pour the filtered water into a saucepan and bring to the boil. Drain the soaked rice and add to the boiling water. When the water is boiling again, put a lid on, reduce the heat to low and cook for 18 minutes. Open the lid to check that the rice is cooked and ever-so-slightly glistening but not wet. Put the lid back on, remove from the heat and let the rice stand for 10 minutes before serving (this process allows the remaining steam to absorb back into the grains, resulting in fluffy and bouncy rice). At no point remove the lid from the pan.

To assemble

Scoop the cooked rice into 2 bowls using a rice paddle or wooden spoon and very gently smooth the surface. Do not press or compact the rice down. Using a cook's blowtorch, lightly blacken the top of the rice, then roughly score. Scoop the bone marrow into a saucepan and mix with the aged white soy. Give it a good swirl then spoon half into the middle of each bowl of rice. For each serving, create a depression in the marrow with the back of a spoon, top with a soy-cured egg yolk. Finish with 1 tablespoon of the spicy pickled daikon, set to one side of the yolk.

Peanut Ice Cream Roon Bing with Coriander

Coriander (cilantro), peanut brittle and ice cream in a wrap – most people would shudder at the thought but what a magical combination it is. When Shing and Wai Ting came to Taiwan, there were so many amazing dishes to introduce them to, but there were only a handful that really surprised them. Ice cream *roon bing* (Taiwanese pancakes) was one of them – strange, surprising and absolutely delicious.

Serves 2

For the peanut brittle:
250 g skinned peanuts (groundnuts)
200 g caster (superfine) sugar
100 g maltose

For the roon bing:
130 g strong white bread flour
½ teaspoon salt
1 teaspoon caster (superfine) sugar
340 ml filtered water
2 tablespoons vegetable oil, plus extra to grease the pan

To serve:
2 teaspoons coarsely chopped coriander (cilantro)
4 scoops peanut ice cream (shop-bought is fine – you can also use a simple vanilla ice cream as the combination of peanut powder and coriander is already pretty special)

Tip
The quantity of peanut brittle powder made is more than is needed for this recipe, but it will keep for months if stored in an airtight container in the refrigerator and is great sprinkled over ice cream or with other desserts.

Peanut brittle

Preheat the oven to 170°C/340°F/Gas Mark 3½. Spread out the peanuts (groundnuts) on a baking sheet and toast in the oven for 7 minutes until golden brown and fragrant, being careful they don't burn. Set aside.

Line a tray with greaseproof (wax) paper. Melt the sugar and maltose in a wide, high-sided frying pan (skillet) over a very low heat without stirring for about 20 minutes or until it turns into a golden-brown caramel. You can occasionally swirl the pan as if making a wet caramel, but, as much as possible, try not to move it. Add the toasted peanuts, but do not stir. When the peanuts have settled into the melted mixture, carefully pour out onto the prepared tray and leave to cool and set firm.

Break the brittle into a blender and blend to a coarse powder – you don't want the powder to be too fine, it should still have some crunchy bits. Transfer to an airtight container and store in the refrigerator.

Roon bing

Combine the flour, salt and sugar in a bowl. Whisk in the filtered water until combined and smooth (you can use a hand held blender if desired). Add the oil, then pass the batter through a sieve into a clean bowl to ensure there are no lumps.

Heat a non-stick frying pan (skillet) over a low-medium heat. Grease the pan with a little vegetable oil and use paper towels to remove excess oil. Pour in the batter and pour out any excess batter straight away, leaving a thin layer of the batter to cook in the pan. Cook for 90 seconds until the edges start to lift and the middle is set, then flip the pan upside down onto greaseproof paper to release the pancake. The thickness of the *roon bing* should be so thin that it's translucent. It may take a few goes to get it right. This recipe makes 3–4 pancakes in case of any failures. Repeat to make a second *roon bing*.

To assemble

For each serving, lay a *roon bing* flat on a plate, sprinkle over 1 tablespoon of the coriander (cilantro) followed by 1 tablespoon of the peanut brittle and top with 2 scoops of ice cream, then roll up and eat like a burrito.

Grill House
BAO Borough

BAO BOROUGH, BOROUGH MARKET, STONEY STREET.

Nestled between a railway track and the outer edges of Borough Market in South London, is our interpretation of a late-night Asian grill house. So many of our favourite grill houses have been under a railway, as if they are strategically placed to emit a subliminal message that you must stop off for a skewer and a drink on the way home from work. I have one particularly perfect memory of sitting in a twelve-seater bar while on a trip to Osaka in Japan with Shing. A lone man came in, sat down next to us and quickly ordered and drank a crisp, cold beer before moving on to a *chuhai* (a highball drink made with shochu and soda water/club soda). As there was no menu, halfway through our meal we sheepishly showed the grill chef a photo of a chicken liver and ovaries skewer from its location tag on Instagram, which we wanted to try. He laughed and had a conversation with our neighbour. The next thing we knew, the dish was served to the rosy-cheeked man next to us, who gestured his hand towards us, offering us his skewer. It turned out it was the last one available – that was a kindness we will never forget.

This is what Borough means to us – these little everyday occurrences of joy. There is joy in the ritualistic daily happiness of having a skewer, a beer and a BAO HI (our version of the *chuhai*, see page 213), while trains tremor past every five minutes and BAOs fly out the hatch to passers-by, city workers or those making their way home. It is wonderful to have had the opportunity to create this atmosphere in a market that has such a rich heritage and history reaching back thousands of years. We're proud that we were able to design a place that fits so well within its surroundings.

When we first approached the site for BAO Borough, with the railway track above and the openness and buzz of the market all around, we were immediately compelled to create a restaurant that reflected that feeling. We decided to break down the divide between interior and exterior by having a fully open shop front hung with plastic draught-excluding curtains and opting for cheaper terracotta tiles that flowed in from the pavement outside. It is a no-frills interior that is accessible for all – one where you can drop in on your way home, just as we envisioned.

In Taiwan, the grill culture is dominated by Japanese *yakiniku* or Korean barbecue houses. Taiwanese barbecue is often more home-style, sold in night markets and eaten during the Mid-autumn (fall) Festival. Because of this, I must admit that the initial inspiration for BAO Borough came more from our travels in Japan and Korea than from Taiwan. But as we started delving into and investigating Taiwanese grill culture, we uncovered its richness.

The Mid-autumn Festival is a time when people gather together and celebrate with a barbecue. Like eating KFC at Christmas in Japan, it actually evolved from a marketing campaign by a Taiwanese shacha sauce company (shacha is a Taiwanese barbecue sauce made from dried shrimp and fish). The company encouraged consumers to eat barbecue and appreciate the moon with family and friends – it's funny how this has now become integrated into our culture. When I was young, I spent a lot of time tagging along on my parents' company Mid-autumn outings. We would celebrate by having a grill party anywhere – from outside the house, kerbside, to car parks and camping sites. We would lay down newspaper and sit on the floor, tending a communal grill. This is something we re-created for our team party to celebrate the Mid-autumn Festival in London. Our development chef Hsuan arranged all the classic Taiwanese must-haves to grill and we took over a park, spread newspaper on the floor, scattered small metal grills around, and brushed shacha sauce on everything. My favourite is grilled meat brushed with the sauce and eaten with a cheap slice of white bread that has also been grilled on the barbecue. Not only is there something really down-to-earth about it, but it is also an indicator of how young this grill-culture phenomenon is.

There are other times that Taiwanese barbecue is enjoyed outside of the Mid-autumn Festival, though. When I was younger, I often used to visit Kenting, a town in the south of Taiwan where my auntie lived. We stopped at roadside stalls on the way to the beach and ate huge, whole grilled squid brushed with shacha. It was perfect with a beer while sitting by the seaside, listening to music. There was also Taiwanese sausage served by a man on a motorcycle with a grill attached to the back of his bike. He would drive up and park on the roadside to trade. Quite often, Taiwanese sausage vendors had a sausage gambling game, where you would roll dice and bet against them (if you win, you win the sausage). I love these nomadic sellers who serve their specialities in the middle of nowhere, usually in smaller towns or roadside stops. Of course, you can also find skewers of all sorts in most night markets. When Shing, Wai Ting and I visited the more famous ones, such as Hua Yuan (Garden) Night Market in Tainan, we were able to try all the classics, from the famous Taiwanese sausage with rice and pickles to grilled oyster mushrooms with Xinjiang spices.

TEAM MID-AUTUMN BARBECUE IN RUSSELL SQUARE.

BAO Borough represents stories of our travels and our desire to dive deeper into my Taiwanese heritage. In Japan, *yakiniku* (grilled meat) and *yakitori* (grilled meat skewers) are very much about the meat and seasoning – often simply seasoned with either a specific salt or in a *tare* (a beautiful fortified soy concoction). At Borough, there is less purity, and the dishes are seasoned with a mix of ingredients that tell the stories of our upbringings, all washed down with a highball-focused drinks menu that complements the strong flavours.

Because of the location and the connection to celebratory and casual Taiwanese grill culture, we wanted to create an ambience at BAO Borough that was fun and a little 'dirtier' than our two preceding restaurants, Soho and Fitz. This was the place where we wanted to go a bit wild. We designed tongue-in-cheek posters to dot around the room and different shades of timber to give an eclectic feel. The experience is gritty but still smooth – perfect for a single diner who arrives, knows what they want and can sit at the bar and watch the chef at work, losing themselves in the noise of cooking and chatter. We pictured the Lonely Man disappearing into the lively ambience, and even designed a peep window on the way down to the cloakrooms inspired by one in the film *Paris, Texas*. Through the window, he can glimpse drunk parties singing in the karaoke room.

When we knew we would have a spare space downstairs at Borough, there were lots of ideas of what we could do with it, including a School of BAO (see page 27) classroom. We eventually chose karaoke, and now it feels as if karaoke has been part of us since the beginning. I grew up going to karaoke (known as KTV in Taiwan) with my friends, with some KTVs even secretly famous for their food. So it married my two favourite things: eating and going wild while singing. It's so intriguing seeing how different people treat karaoke – from those who just sing their hearts out to the people who treat it like a profession, taking turns to sing as well as they can. That's BAO Borough – a no-frills ambience, karaoke craziness in the basement and chefs grilling away.

SHRIMP SKEWERS, HUAYUAN NIGHT MARKET.

THE GRILL SIDE COUNTER AT BAO BOROUGH.

MARINATED BEEF FROM THE WET MARKET READY TO BE BARBECUED.

GRILL HOUSE – BAO BOROUGH

Borough House Pickles

Makes 1 × 500 ml jar per pickle

For the soy-pickled shiitakes:
100 g dried shiitake mushrooms
10 g fresh ginger, cut into 1-cm (½-inch)
wide strips
50 ml light soy sauce
50 ml Chinkiang black rice vinegar
10 g dark brown sugar
½ star anise
½ cinnamon stick
1 dried red chillies

For the Taiwanese pickled cabbage:
125 ml rice vinegar
100 g rock sugar (if using larger sized
rocks, smash lightly with a rolling pin)
1 teaspoon salt
125 g Taiwanese (flat) cabbage, coarsely
chopped

For the yellow pickled daikon:
175 g daikon, peeled, halved and cut into
5-mm (¼-inch) thick semicircles
½ tablespoon salt, plus extra as needed
(see method)
65 g caster (superfine) sugar, plus extra as
needed (see method)
200 ml rice vinegar
1 cloves garlic
½ teaspoon green Sichuan peppercorns
½ teaspoon ground turmeric
½ cinnamon stick
5 black peppercorns
1 bay leaf
1 jalapeño, halved lengthways and seeded

Soy-pickled shiitakes

Rinse the dried shiitakes under water, put into a large heatproof bowl, cover with boiling water and leave to soak for an hour until they are fully hydrated.

Put the soaked shiitakes into a saucepan with 250 ml of their soaking liquid and the remaining ingredients. Bring to a simmer and cook for 20–30 minutes until soft. Remove from the heat and leave to cool to room temperature.

Transfer the shiitakes and their pickling liquid to a 500 ml sterilized jar (see page 89), leaving a 1 cm (½ inch) head space, and seal. To serve, remove the shiitake stems and slice each mushroom into 5–6 slices. The pickled shiitakes are ready to eat straight away but can also be stored in the refrigerator for up to 3 months.

Taiwanese pickled cabbage

Put the vinegar, sugar and salt into a metal saucepan and leave overnight to dissolve the sugar. The next day, place the pan over a low heat and whisk until the sugar has completely dissolved. The liquid must not boil or reduce. Remove from the heat and leave to cool.

Put the cabbage into a 500 ml sterilized jar (see page 89), then pour over the pickling liquid, leaving a 1 cm (½ inch) head space, and seal. Leave to pickle in the refrigerator for 5 days before using. The pickled cabbage can be stored in the refrigerator for up to 1 month.

Yellow pickled daikon

Weigh the prepared daikon, then put into a bowl and toss with 2.5 per cent of its weight in sugar and 2.5 per cent of its weight in salt. Leave to stand for 20–30 minutes.

Meanwhile, bring the remaining ingredients to the boil in a saucepan. Drain the daikon, then rinse under cold running water and add to the hot pickling liquid. Remove from the heat and leave to cool to room temperature.

Transfer the daikon and its pickling liquid to a 500 ml sterilized jar (see page 89), leaving a 1 cm (½ inch) head space, and seal. Leave to pickle in the refrigerator for 5–7 days before using. The pickled daikon can be stored in the refrigerator for up to 1 month.

Cold 'Self-serve' Dishes

In Taiwan, it is quite common to find refrigerated self-serve dishes in restaurants, chilled and ready for you to grab and bring back to your table. It feels so good to have food straight away, as soon as you sit down. Two cold dishes like this that I particularly love are chilled, marinated clams and shredded tofu. It's such a nice way to start your meal.

One of the great things about London is the Turkish grill culture, which also prizes cold dishes, either as mezes in Turkish restaurants or via the canteen-style refrigerators you can find at casual *lokantalar*. That London influence seeped into our cold dishes at BAO Borough – they are the quick, no-frills snacking items that complement the grilled dishes so well.

Taiwanese (flat) cabbage can be found in Turkish or Asian shops as Flat Cabbage. Alternatively, Hispi cabbage can be used instead.

Yu Shiang Boiled Eggs

When we were opening Borough, we were obsessed with the idea of serving a platter of soy boiled eggs. But we didn't think it would go down well. So instead we landed on our Yu Shiang Eggs. *Yu shiang* means 'fish fragrant', although this sauce in fact has no fish in it – the name comes from the fact that the flavour imitates that used to cook fish in Sichuan cuisine. It's salty, sweet, sour, spicy, fresh and fragrant. We make a yu shiang base and mix the paste through our mayonnaise.

Serves 4

For the yu shiang base:
75 g cloves garlic
20 g caster (superfine) sugar
20 g *doubanjiang* (fermented chilli bean paste)
20 g Fermented Red Chillies (see page 228)
rapeseed (canola) oil, to cover
pinch of chilli powder

For the yu shiang mayonnaise:
90 g yu shiang base (see above)
1 egg yolk
25 ml Chinkiang black rice vinegar
300 ml rapeseed (canola) oil
1½ teaspoons yu shiang cooking oil (see above)
½ teaspoon salt
¼ teaspoon caster (superfine) sugar

To serve:
4 eggs
200 g Lincolnshire Poacher cheese or Cheddar

Yu shiang base

Bring a saucepan of water to the boil, add the garlic cloves and blanch for 10 seconds to remove their spicy raw flavour. Drain, then transfer to a food processor and pulse until coarsely chopped.

Put the garlic, sugar, *doubanjiang* (fermented chilli bean paste) and fermented chillies into a saucepan, then pour in oil until the ingredients are just covered. Cook slowly over a low heat until the garlic is soft and caramelized, about 15 minutes. Remove from the heat and leave to cool.

Reserve 1½ teaspoons of the cooking oil, then transfer the rest of the mixture to a sterilized jar (see page 89), stir in the chilli powder and seal. The base can be used straight away or stored in the refrigerator for up to 1 week.

Yu shiang mayonnaise

Put 90 g of the cold yu shiang base into a food processor or blender with the egg yolk and vinegar and blend until combined. With the motor running, slowly pour in the rapeseed (canola) oil through the lid, making sure it is incorporated before adding more. Blend until all the oil is fully incorporated. If the mayonnaise is too thick, add a little water. Add the reserved yu shiang cooking oil, salt and sugar.

To assemble

Put the eggs into a saucepan of cold water and bring to the boil, then cook for 6 minutes. Drain, then refresh in cold water. Peel and slice the eggs in half.

For each serving, spoon 1 tablespoon of the yu shiang mayo into a shallow bowl and place 2 egg halves, yolk sides up, on top. Dab a teaspoon of the yu shiang base on each yolk and grate over a generous amount of the cheese to serve.

Cold Smoked Aubergine with Panko BAO

When we first opened BAO, we used to have menu hacks where the customer could choose to have their BAO deep fried. People used to go crazy over that customisable element, but as time went on, it was soon forgotten. You could argue that the introduction of deep-fried BAO (see page 73) was the cause. The panko-fried BAO in this dish takes it to another level. It feels a bit silly to panko bread, but we have a Taiwanese dish called the Nutritious Sandwich, a roll that is panko fried and filled with ham, tomato mayonnaise and cucumber. The panko on the BAO creates a super crust that works really well when scooping the aubergine mix.

The key to the smokiness of the aubergine (eggplant), is to further dry the skins, blitz and reintroduce as an ash. We pop it in a warm place, on top of our hot oven, but you can put it on a radiator. Just make sure it's not touching your socks.

Serves 4

For the smoked aubergine:
600 g (about 2) aubergine (eggplant)
2 cloves garlic, grated
40 ml Sichuan Chilli Oil (see page 229), plus extra to serve
2 teaspoons flaky sea salt
1 teaspoon caster (superfine) sugar
2 tablespoons vegetable oil
½ teaspoon aubergine ash

For the nori peanut powder:
50 g Peanut Powder (see page 228)
1¼ teaspoons toasted black sesame seeds (see page 49)
5 g Nori Powder (see page 99)
¼ teaspoon salt
pinch of citric acid

For the panko-crumbed fried BAO:
vegetable oil, for deep-frying
2 eggs, beaten
250 g panko breadcrumbs
4 unsteamed Round BAO (see page 46), cut in half

Smoked aubergine

Over a high heat on a barbecue or gas burner (or on the hottest setting of your grill/broiler), char the aubergines (eggplants) all over and until soft, then transfer to a large container with a lid. Cover and leave to steam in the container.

When cool enough to handle, peel away the charred skins, reserving the skins, and chop the aubergine flesh. Put the flesh into an airtight container and place in the refrigerator. Drain off any excess liquid when ready to use.

Leave the skins to dehydrate overnight (make sure you have peeled off all the flesh). You can do this by placing them either on a baking sheet in the oven at 50°C/120°F or on a fine-mesh grill on top of a radiator (be careful that they don't fall through and make a mess). When the skins are dry, transfer to a blender and blend to a fine powder to make 'aubergine ash'.

Put ½ teaspoon of the aubergine ash into a bowl with the aubergine, then whisk in the remaining ingredients. Chill until ready to serve or for up to 3 days.

Nori peanut powder

Mix together all the ingredients in a bowl, then transfer to a jar and seal.

Panko-crumbed fried BAO

When ready to serve, heat the oil in a deep, heavy-based saucepan to 180°C/350°F, or until a cube of ginger sizzles and browns in 10 seconds.

Put the beaten eggs into a shallow bowl and the breadcrumbs into a separate shallow bowl. Position the dishes in front of you so you can move easily between them, from left to right. Using your left hand, dunk one of the round BAO halves in the egg mixture before placing it into the breadcrumbs (be careful that your left hand does not touch the panko itself). Using your right hand, coat the BAO in the breadcrumbs, making sure all the sides are covered, then transfer to a plate. (This method allows you to work as efficiently as possible, and means the breadcrumbs won't become clumpy.) Repeat with the remaining BAO halves.

Working in batches, carefully place the BAO halves in the hot oil and deep-fry for 1 minute on each side until golden, then remove with a slotted spoon and drain on paper towels.

To assemble

Spoon 4 generous tablespoons of the cold smoked aubergine onto each of 4 flat bowls, drizzle with chilli oil and dust with 1 tablespoon of the nori peanut powder. Serve with the warm BAO.

燒烤屋 一 包博羅店

Homestyle Pork Jowl

Inspired by the culture of o *bei che* (black and white) chopped meat dishes in Taiwan, this dish uses cold, thinly sliced smoked and brined pork jowl, which can be purchased from your butcher. 'Black and white' in this context means coarsely chopped, which suggests a sense of casualness, but there is so much elegance in that coarse chop.

Serves 6

For the pork jowl:
½ smoked and brined pork jowl (about 350–500 g)
10 g black peppercorns
10 g star anise
10 g coriander seeds
1 small cinnamon stick
100 g spring onions (scallions), white parts only
150 g fresh ginger, peeled and sliced

For the pork jowl dressing:
1 tablespoon caster (superfine) sugar
pinch of five spice powder
50 ml pork jowl cooking liquid
2 teaspoons sesame oil
2 tablespoons vegetarian oyster sauce
20 ml light soy sauce
1½ teaspoons Chinkiang black rice vinegar
2 teaspoons cornflour (cornstarch) optional

For the leek and spring onion garnish:
120 g leek, white parts only, cut into 7-cm (2¾-inch) long strips
60 g spring onion (scallion), green parts only, finely sliced into rings
4 tablespoons Sichuan Chilli Oil (see page 229)

Pork jowl

Preheat the oven to 110°C/225°F/Gas Mark ¼. Put all the ingredients into a casserole dish (Dutch oven) and cover with water. Wet a piece of baking (parchment) paper and place on top of the meat to ensure it doesn't dry out while cooking. Put the lid on the dish and cook in the oven for 2 hours, then turn off the oven but leave the dish inside for another hour.

Transfer the jowl to a container with a lid and leave to cool. Reserve and chill the cooking liquid. Cover the jowl and store in the refrigerator overnight or until thoroughly chilled, about 8 hours. (The pork jowl dressing can be made in advance once the cooking liquid has chilled.)

The next day, slice the jowl as thinly as possible using a sharp knife or meat slicer.

Pork jowl dressing

Put the sugar and five spice powder into a small saucepan and add 50 ml of the pork jowl cooking liquid and 2 teaspoons water. Heat gently to dissolve the sugar and spice in the sauce. Add the remaining ingredients and stir to combine. The consistency of the dressing should be slightly thick, so if you feel it is too liquid, add some cornflour (cornstarch) slurry: cornflour mixed with 2 teaspoons water. Leave the dressing to cool.

Leek and spring onion garnish

Put the leek and spring onion (scallion) into a bowl. In a separate, small bowl, combine 2 tablespoons of the chilli oil with 5 teaspoons of the jowl dressing, then lightly dress the leek and spring onion.

To assemble

Divide the leek and spring onion garnish and pork jowl dressing among 6 plates, then arrange strips of pork jowl on top, with the fat side lined up and drizzle 1 teaspoon of chilli oil around the edge.

燒烤屋 — 包博羅店

Glazed Tofu and Taiwanese Pickles

We've always wanted to work with Clean Bean, an organic tofu maker from Brick Lane in the East End of London. It's so great to see someone using traditional techniques for this craft in London. For this recipe, the tofu is brined for 24 hours, which is the first step in making stinky tofu (a type of fermented tofu with a strong smell). Although not quite the same thing, our finished dish closely resembles deep-fried stinky tofu, which is the most friendly way to eat this form of tofu! This is where our Black Garlic Glaze (see page 229) was born, which we now love to use in everything – it is a complex and savoury sauce, and one of the favourites in the BAO pantry.

Serves 2

For the tofu:
100 ml rice vinegar
1 tablespoon salt
1 x 325-g block firm tofu
vegetable oil, for deep-frying

For the coriander relish:
5 g coriander (cilantro), finely chopped
2½ teaspoons Taiwanese red vinegar
1½ teaspoons sesame oil
¾ teaspoon rapeseed (canola) oil
pinch of caster (superfine) sugar
pinch of salt
pinch of ground red Sichuan peppercorns

To serve:
4 teaspoons Black Garlic Glaze (see page 229)
60 g Taiwanese Pickled Cabbage (see page 135)

Tofu

Combine the vinegar, salt and 500 ml water in a non-reactive bowl, then add the tofu block. Cover loosely with a tea towel, transfer to the refrigerator and leave to brine for 24 hours.

Coriander relish

Just before you're ready to assemble the dish, mix together all the ingredients in a small bowl.

To assemble

Take the tofu out of the brining liquid and cut into four 1-cm (½-inch) thick slices along the shorter side of the rectangle, then cut the slices in half into triangles and pat dry.

Heat the oil in a deep, heavy-based saucepan to 180°C/350°F, or until a cube of ginger sizzles and browns in 10 seconds. Carefully place the tofu pieces into the hot oil and deep-fry for 2–3 minutes until crispy and lightly golden, then remove with a slotted spoon and drain on paper towels.

For each serving, line up 4 tofu triangles on a plate with the points facing upwards. Drizzle with 2 teaspoons of the black garlic glaze, letting it run off the long edges onto the plate. Place 1 tablespoon of the coriander relish over the tofu followed by 30 g Taiwanese pickled cabbage on top of the tofu.

Grill Dishes

At BAO Borough, we focus on using Taiwanese seasoning for our grill dishes, from the important brushing of shacha sauce on the ox heart to the *san bei* (a traditional Taiwanese quick-fry sauce; see page 147) used to glaze the chicken butts.

We use an imported yakitori grill from Tokyo to cook the skewers as it focuses and channels the direction of the heat. Make sure you soak the skewers overnight in water, and when grilling, dab the part of the skewer that touches the grill with water to stop it from burning through.

Chilli Chicken Wings

Grilled, deep fried, braised, whatever the process, I find the best part of the wing is the two bone or flat wing. The two bones keep the middle flesh nice and moist. (Whenever I order KFC I leave a note saying I'm allergic to the one bone wing...) Here we use the same chilli marinade used on the half chicken (see page 118) for the wings. If you have time, use scissors and nip between the two bones on both ends of the wing. This will allow you to fan out the wing over the skewer.

Makes 4 skewers

12 chicken wingettes (also called flats, these are the half of the wing with 2 bones)

For the yellow chilli marinade:
30 g carrot, coarsely chopped
1 cloves garlic
17 ml lemon juice
½ teaspoon lemon zest
40 ml rapeseed (canola) oil
5 g lemongrass stalks, thinly sliced
15 g tamarind paste
50 g mild yellow chillies, stems removed

To serve:
aged white soy sauce (see page 233)
Urfa chilli flakes, to taste

First make the yellow chilli marinade by hand blending all the ingredients except the chillies and flaky sea salt until smooth. Add the chillies and continue blending until you have a smooth paste. If you want to pre-make the marinade, it can be stored in an airtight container in the refrigerator for up to 3 days.

Put the chicken wingettes into a non-reactive bowl and cover with the yellow chilli marinade. Stir to coat, then cover and leave to marinate in the refrigerator overnight.

To assemble

The next day, thread 3 of the chicken wings horizontally onto 2 wooden skewers, making sure they are flat when skewered so that they will cook evenly. Repeat with the remaining wings to make 4 skewers, then season the wings generously with flaky sea salt.

Prepare a barbecue, then grill the skewers over a medium heat (not too close to the charcoal) for 15–20 minutes, turning them frequently, until nicely charred and cooked through. If indoors, use the grill setting on your oven set to 250°C/480°F. Drizzle with a dash of aged soy sauce and sprinkle with chilli flakes.

燒烤屋 — 包博羅店

San Bei Chicken Butt Skewers

The chicken butt, a.k.a. the parson's nose, is my all-time favourite part of the chicken alongside the chicken oyster. It is oily, juicy and fatty with a soft bite of bone – perfect washed down with an ice-cold beer. If you aren't a fan of the chew of soft bone, you can cut it out. The larger the chicken butt, the harder the bone will be. In Taiwan, the contrast of cartilage against a fatty cut of meat is considered a delicacy.

Makes 4 skewers

16 chicken butts (parson's noses), ask your butcher
Thai basil, to garnish

For the san bei sauce:
1 teaspoon vegetable oil
1½ teaspoons sesame oil
1 cm (½ inch) piece of fresh ginger, peeled and sliced
3 cloves garlic, sliced
½ spring onion (scallion), coarsely sliced
½ red chilli, seeded
10 g rock sugar
75 ml Shaoxing rice wine
25 ml dark soy sauce
50 ml light soy sauce
20 ml mirin

San bei sauce

Heat the vegetable and sesame oils in a frying pan (skillet) over a low heat, add the ginger and cook for 10–15 minutes until lightly golden. Add the garlic, spring onion (scallion) and red chilli and cook for another 5 minutes, then add the rock sugar and cook until the sugar has dissolved.

Pour in the Shaoxing wine and stir to deglaze the pan, scraping up any residue from the bottom of the pan. Cook for 1 minute, then add the remaining ingredients and 65 ml water and bring to the boil. Boil for 3 minutes, then remove from the heat and leave to infuse at room temperature for 1 hour.

To assemble

Put the chicken butts (parson's noses) into a saucepan and cover with the san bei sauce. Bring to the boil, then remove from the heat and cover. Leave to poach in the residual heat for 20 minutes, then remove the butts and leave to cool. Reserve the sauce.

If the butts are different sizes, cut any oversized ones in half. The soft bone in the butt is a delicacy so keep it in (it gives this fatty cut a little crunch, like eating cartilage). Thread 4 chicken butts onto a wooden skewer. Repeat with the remaining butts to make 4 skewers.

Prepare a barbecue, then grill the skewers over high heat for 2 minutes on each side until nicely charred. If indoors, use the grill setting on your oven set to 250°C/480°F. As the chicken butts are already cooked, you just want to get a nice colour on them. Dip the skewers into the san bei sauce midway through cooking or brush it on the skewers, whichever is easier. Garnish with the Thai basil to serve.

Shacha Ox Heart Skewers

Makes 7 skewers

¼ ox heart, cleaned and cut into bite-size slices
Crispy Shallots (see page 228), to serve

For the shacha marinade:
50 ml spicy shacha sauce (we use Bull Head Barbecue
Sauce)
40 ml vegetarian oyster sauce
40 ml Taiwanese red rice vinegar
40 ml light soy sauce
50 ml mirin
25 g Greek yogurt

Shacha marinade

Mix together all the ingredients in a non-reactive bowl. The marinade can be used straight away or stored in an airtight container in the refrigerator for up to 1 week. Place the ox heart slices in the non-reactive bowl, stir to coat and marinate overnight.

To assemble

Thread 5–6 pieces of the marinated ox heart onto a wooden skewer, folding the slices over so that each end is skewered. Repeat with the remaining ox heart to make 7 skewers (depending on the size of the ox heart).

Prepare a barbecue, then grill the skewers over a high heat for 6 minutes, turning regularly and basting with the marinade, until the ox heart is medium-rare. If indoors, use the grill setting on your oven set to 250°C/450°F. Transfer the skewers to a plate.

Gently warm some of the shacha marinade in a small saucepan, then spoon over the ox heart skewers and sprinkle with the crispy shallots.

Ox Tongue Skewers

Makes 6 skewers

¼ smoked and brined ox tongue (ask your butcher)
35 ml Black Garlic Glaze (see page 229)
15 ml Coriander Relish (see page 143)
Dijon mustard, to serve

Put the ox tongue into a large saucepan and cover with cold water. Bring to the boil, then reduce the heat and simmer for 4 hours, topping up the water as needed so that the tongue is fully submerged at all times. The ox tongue is cooked when a chopstick easily pierces the flesh. Leave to cool in the cooking liquid. When cool enough to handle, peel the skin off the tongue and chop into 2 cm (¾ inch) cubes.

Mix together the black garlic glaze and coriander relish in a small bowl.

To assemble

Thread 4–5 cubes of tongue onto a wooden skewer. Repeat with the remaining cubes to make 6 skewers.

Prepare a barbecue, then grill the skewers over a high heat for 2 minutes on each side until nicely charred. If indoors, use the grill setting on your oven set to 250°C/450°F. As the ox tongue is already cooked, you just want to get a nice colour on it. Transfer the skewers to a plate, brush with the mixed glaze relish and serve with a dollop of Dijon mustard on the side.

40-day Aged Beef and Taipei Butter Rice

For a while, I was obsessed with steak served with café de Paris butter, so Shing and I frequented Le Relais de Venise l'Entrecote when we used to live in Soho. If you had to close your eyes and picture what a 'French bistro' would look like, this would be the place: waitresses in classic outfits, tables too close to each other, a simple menu with just steak, fries and salads. I loved the sauce so much I took Anais there, too, to dissect their delicious house sauce. After having it, Anais came up with the idea of creating our Taipei butter made with our spiced beef butter (see page 230) as a base.

We wanted to use a cut of beef that was super tender when flash-grilled and had a good marbling of fat running through it. Working with Philip Warren & Son in Cornwall, we picked out the Denver cut, which is an often-overlooked cut of beef from the shoulder. The beef is aged for 40 days in a vacuum-packed bag, meaning no moisture can enter but simultaneously the meat is able to breathe. The ageing allows the enzymes in the meat to break down, so that when flash-grilling, the meat is soft and not chewy.

As well as going through many different beef cuts, the beginnings of the dish took many different forms – a skewer, a dish that was supposed to be in a BAO, and a bowl of rice. Sometimes the best dishes come from that last bit of sweat. At the eleventh hour, when the pressure hit, this dish was created and is now what we consider a classic.

The rice is slathered with the Taipei butter before the beef is precisely fanned out in a spiral pattern on top, with the golden soy-cured egg yolk sitting in the middle.

Serves 2

For the beef:
80 g onion, diced
2 cloves garlic
80 g vegetarian oyster sauce
2 tablespoons honey
4 teaspoons Chinkiang black rice vinegar
4 teaspoons rapeseed (canola) oil
2 teaspoons premium soy sauce
1 x 200-g 40-day aged Denver steak
splash of vegetable oil
flaky sea salt

For the Taipei butter:
110 g Spiced Beef Butter (see page 230)
90 g butter, at room temperature
30 g shallot, very finely chopped
40 ml light soy sauce
½ teaspoon chilli powder
2 cloves garlic, finely chopped
½ teaspoon ground star anise
pinch of ground white pepper
7 g basil, finely chopped
15 g coriander (cilantro), finely chopped
7 g curly parsley, finely chopped

For the rice:
150 g short-grain rice (preferably Chishang or Japanese sushi rice)
150 ml filtered water

To serve:
60 ml Rice Dressing (see page 229)
2 Soy-cured Egg Yolks (see page 228)
Urfa chilli flakes, to taste

I wanted to create a bowl that could be filled perfectly to the rim. We worked with Anna Hodgson, a close friend and one of the ceramicists we often collaborate with, to achieve this. With this bowl, the beef slices look as if they are overflowing – an extremely enticing prospect for the hungry Lonely Man on his way home from work.

Beef

A day in advance, put the onion and garlic into a blender and blend until they form a smooth paste. Tip into a bowl and whisk with the vegetarian oyster sauce, honey, vinegar, rapeseed (canola) oil and soy sauce. Add the steak and stir to coat, then cover and leave to marinate in the refrigerator overnight.

Taipei butter

Put all the ingredients except the herbs into a bowl and blend using a hand held blender. If the blending makes the butter mixture warm, leave it to cool. When cool, stir in the herbs and chill. There will be more butter than is needed for this recipe, but it can be stored in an airtight container in the refrigerator for up to 1 month or in the freezer for up to 3 months.

Rice

Half an hour before you want to eat, take the beef and Taipei butter out of the refrigerator.

Wash the rice thoroughly, 3 times. After the final rinse, tip the rice into a bowl, cover with cold water and leave to soak for 30 minutes.

Pour the filtered water into a saucepan and bring to the boil. Drain the soaked rice and add to the pan. When the water is boiling again, put a lid on, reduce the heat to low and cook for 18 minutes. Open the lid to check that the rice is cooked and glistening but not wet. Put the lid back on, remove from the heat and leave the rice to rest for 10 minutes before serving (this process allows the remaining steam to absorb back into the grains, resulting in fluffy and bouncy rice). At no point remove the lid from the pan.

To assemble

While the rice is resting, preheat the oven to 150°C/300°F/Gas Mark 2 and place 2 shallow bowls in the oven to warm.

Heat a heavy-based frying pan (skillet) over a medium-high heat. Add a splash of oil to ensure the beef does not stick, but not too much. Remove the beef from the marinade and place it in the hot pan. Season with flaky sea salt, then cook for 2–3 minutes on each side until medium-rare. Remove from the pan and leave to rest in a warm place for 5 minutes. If you have a meat thermometer, the internal temperature of the beef should reach 57°C/135°F. Slice the beef to a thickness of 5 mm (¼ inch).

Drizzle the rice dressing over the steamed rice. Using a rice paddle or wooden spoon, fluff the rice using a scoring gesture (this mixes the dressing through the rice while ensuring the rice grains are not crushed). Scoop the rice into the warmed bowls and gently smooth the surface. Do not press or compact the rice down.

Spread 1 tablespoon of the Taipei butter over the rice in each bowl, then using the back of a spoon, make a small indentation in the middle of each bowl. Layer the beef in a rose pattern around the indentation, then gently place a soy-cured egg yolk in the middle of each beef rose. Sprinkle with chilli flakes and some more flaky sea salt.

Taiwanese Café
BAO King's Cross

Set among the leafy walkways behind King's Cross sits our exploration into the nostalgic, often forgotten parts of Taiwan: the old-fashioned foam tea rooms (*pao muo hong cha dian*, which serve foam teas and all-round Taiwanese dishes) and café-style rice houses that our grandparents frequented on dates and where schoolkids do their homework or loiter in gangs. If BAO had a 'non-space' (the types of spaces that sit between other spaces) it would be this – you can come just to sit and lose yourself in the old-world architecture and atmosphere. The restaurant floor is sandwiched between double-height windows and the busy kitchen counter, with a mezzanine space looming over it all that houses our workshops and office, from where I can peer through the blinds at the scene below. Akari lampshades designed by Isamu Noguchi light up the space and reflect off the Bauhaus-red floor.

We all have nostalgic moments in our lives that we can reconnect to through food. Shing stores emergency fish fingers (sticks) in the freezer because that's what he was brought up on in Nottingham. For Wai Ting, it's frankfurters with macaroni soup. And for me it's the everyday meals in those restaurants that seem to transport you back in time.

BAO King's Cross is our connection to the Taiwan of the past, seen through the lens of a modern café. While in Taiwan there are no 'cafés' per se, there are plenty of eateries that share that same atmosphere – eclectic in the sense that they serve a mix of casual all-rounder dishes in a space that feels neither here or there. BAO King's Cross draws from these places – from the nostalgia of the old-fashioned foam tea shops and the pork chop rice 'disco' restaurants as well as the Taiwanese breakfast houses.

BAO KING'S CROSS ON PANCRAS ROAD.

ERCHEN PEERING DOWN INTO THE KING'S CROSS DINING ROOM.

ALICE AND ANAIS AT CAFÉ ASTORIA, TAIPEI.

I remember asking my close friend Alice what was one of her favourite places in Taiwan. Alice has been with us since day one, from helping us steam BAO in our flat for markets to her role as general manager now. She mentioned an old Taiwanese disco restaurant specializing in pork chop rice called Dong Yi in Ximending district in Taipei that her dad used to take her to. It's an eclectic place with crazy decor that's a little lost in time, but it's this kind of history that I love. The big TV screens, the jazzy lights and the materials used in the decor make it feel like a retro disco. The menu is broken up into *xiao tsai* ('small plates' – not to be confused with *xiao chi*, which is street food) and a collection of rice dishes, which includes their speciality pork chop rice. This club like vibe suddenly made me see pork chop rice in a different light! While not comparable to the old pie and mash shops in London, due to Taiwan having a shorter history, these Taiwanese disco restaurants are a perfect example of a heritage Taiwanese 'café', where you can drop in on any day for a little bit of happiness. In Taiwan, breakfast is also a huge part of our food culture – the amazing congee (rice porridge), soy milk and *dan bing* (egg pancakes) or *fan tuan* (stuffed sticky rice rolls). Taiwanese breakfast shops are iconic and were a big part of my upbringing. Just downstairs from where I was brought up in Muzha in Taipei was a local breakfast store, and my daily order was egg, bacon, sweet mayo and grated cucumber sandwiched in white bread with *dan bing*. I love that when I introduced this to Shing his first reaction was 'That's gross!', but suffice to say he's addicted to it now.

DONG YI SPARE RIB RESTAURANT, TAIPEI.

My fascination with these kinds of places means you'll definitely always find me in an old restaurant rather than the hot new place in town. During our travels around Asia over the past ten years we would search out similar eateries wherever we went – for example, the *kissatens* in Japan, which are all-day teahouses that were once popular from the 1920s to the 1980s but are now slowly disappearing. They are very kitsch and often serve *yoshuku* cuisine, which merges Japanese and Western influences. One of my favourite *kissaten* memories is of eating a simple piece of sweet buttered Japanese toast with a hard-boiled egg and drip coffee while sitting next to an old man smoking a cigarette. Whenever we travel, or when Shing and I go back to Taiwan together, we love visiting places like these and we have a few in certain countries that we must revisit whenever we're there. Of course, we take in new experiences, too, but some rituals we just have to stick to! In Hong Kong, we always eat the goose noodles at Yat Lok and then we move on for a small bowl of wonton noodles down the street. In Taiwan, after the first night with jet lag we never miss a trip to the breakfast shop Fu Hang in Taipei, which invariably has a queue of locals and tourists extending all the way down the staircase, onto the street and around the corner. They will be waiting for their *dan bing* with a dollop of fermented chilli sauce and soy or curdled savoury milk with a fried dough stick to dip, while office workers take away boxes of freshly made sealed soy milk for colleagues. It's these scenes and ritual traditions we find comfort in.

What nostalgia means to me will be different for someone else. For my grand-parents' generation, the Bolero – the equivalent of a western style restaurant in Taipei – was the 'it' place. When we last visited the Bolero, we sat next to an old couple who were eating a simple lettuce salad before their steak. They were probably reminiscing of times gone by. For me, the old-fashioned foam tea shops, which serve snacks, rice bowls and noodles alongside a tea-focused drinks list, is my childhood nostalgia. Taiwan's foam tea shops had a bit of a bad reputation back in the day as they would crop up in the news for being the locations of gang fights and where the misfits hung out. They were the places your parents would advise you not to go. But fast-forward to today and they're more polished and well presented. The shop that claimed it invented bubble tea was a foam tea shop, too. Bubble tea is a craze that will never go away – my friends and I would queue for it after school and teachers would even reward good behaviour with bubble tea. These foam tea shops are a source of inspiration for our tea-focused cold drinks at Kings Cross and across BAO (see pages 224 and 225).

The common theme with all the places we've been on our travels that has inspired King's Cross is that you are able to slip into these spaces and be with yourself. A true non-space is not your home, not your workplace but a space that you glide into both physically and architecturally as well as nostalgically transporting you through time.

CHEN SAN DING BUBBLE MILK, GONGGUAN NIGHT MARKET, TAIPEI.

BOLERO WESTERN RESTAURANT, TAIPEI.

Savoury Soy Milk with Fried Youtiao

We have a tradition that on the first morning after a flight to Taipei, we take advantage of our heavy jet lag and go to Fu Hang for breakfast at 5.30 a.m., where the quintessential Taiwanese breakfast is served. We always order the same thing: egg *dan bing* (see page 163), hot soy milk and savoury soy milk. Shing wasn't a fan when he first tried it, but now he's a convert.

Vinegar is used to curdle the soy milk, creating a texture similar to very softly set custard that has been stirred and broken up into pieces. The joy of this dish comes from the pickles, soy sauce and chilli oil toppings, which inject the soy milk with flavour, as well as the fried youtiao (dough stick), which provides crunch. If you don't want to make the dough sticks yourself, you can buy them ready-made from Chinese bakeries or supermarkets.

Zha cai is a type of fermented mustard stem that is salted, pressed and dried before being rubbed with spices and left to ferment. We haven't come across the fresh mustard green stem variety here in the UK, so we make our own version using what is widely available here, kohlrabi, for a similar texture. Most Chinese supermarkets sell ready-made *zha cai*, we would normally rinse it under water to wash away the heavy salt. You will need to make the kohlrabi *zha cai* and spicy daikon in advance.

Serves 4

For the kohlrabi zha cai:
1 kohlrabi (about 300 g), peeled and sliced into 5-mm
(¼-inch) wide sticks
salt, as needed (see method)
2 teaspoons chilli powder
¼ teaspoon five spice powder
½ teaspoon caster (superfine) sugar
2 teaspoons sesame oil

For the spicy daikon:
1 large daikon (about 1 kg), peeled and sliced into 5 x 1.5 cm
(2 x ⅝ inch) sticks
salt, as needed (see method)
2 tablespoons whole-bean soy sauce
1–2 red mild red chillies, seeded and coarsely chopped
1 tablespoon sesame oil
50 g caster (superfine) sugar

For the fried youtiao (dough sticks):
300 g plain (all-purpose) flour, plus extra for dusting
1 small egg
1 teaspoon salt
2 tablespoons caster (superfine) sugar
1 teaspoon baking powder
½ teaspoon bicarbonate of soda (baking soda)
2 teaspoons vegetable oil, plus extra for deep-frying

To serve:
4 pinches of salt
4 teaspoons rice vinegar
1 litre unsweetened soy milk
32 g pickled bamboo shoots (from a jar)
20 g coriander (cilantro), coarsely chopped
20 g spring onion (scallion), coarsely chopped
20 ml Sichuan Chilli Oil (see page 229)
2½ tablespoons premium soy sauce

Tip
Try to find freshly made, local soy milk that uses only soybeans and
water – the richer and creamier the better. It is very important that
it is unsweetened.

Kohlrabi zha cai

Weigh the kohlrabi, then put it into a colander. Measure out 3 per cent of its weight in salt, then sprinkle over the kohlrabi sticks and leave to draw out the moisture for 1–2 hours. Drain well, then transfer to muslin (cheesecloth), wrap and squeeze out as much water as you can. Remove the kohlrabi from the muslin, put back into the colander and place a heavy weight on top. Leave to draw out more liquid overnight.

The next day, tip the drained kohlrabi into a large bowl and mix with the remaining ingredients. Pack into a 500 ml sterilized jar (see page 89), leaving a 1 cm (½ inch) head space, and seal. Leave to ferment at room temperature for 1 week before using. Be sure to 'burp' the jar every night by opening the lid momentarily – this will release the gasses and ensure that the jar doesn't explode! The kohlrabi *zha cai* can be stored in the refrigerator for up to 1 month.

Spicy daikon

Weigh the daikon, then put it into a colander. Measure out 3 per cent of its weight in salt, then sprinkle over the daikon sticks and leave for 1–2 hours. Drain well, then wrap in muslin (cheesecloth) and squeeze out as much water as you can. Remove the daikon from the muslin, put back into the colander and place a heavy weight on top. Leave to draw out more liquid overnight.

The next day, preheat the oven to 60°C/140°F, or as low as your oven will go. Spread out the daikon sticks on a baking sheet and leave to dehydrate in the oven for 3 hours, or until the sticks curl up and the outer sides have dried out.

Put the semi-dried daikon into a bowl and mix together with the remaining ingredients to season (taste and adjust the seasonings as needed). Pack into a 500 ml sterilized jar (see page 89) as tightly as possible leaving a 1 cm (½ inch) head space, and seal. Leave to marinate in the refrigerator for 2 days before using. (It can be stored for up to 2 weeks in the refrigerator.)

Fried youtiao (dough sticks)

Put all the ingredients except the oil into a bowl, add 140 ml water and mix together until you have a smooth, soft dough. Drizzle the oil over the dough, cover and leave to rest overnight in the refrigerator, or for 4 hours at room temperature. Remove the dough from the refrigerator 30 minutes before you want to cook, to allow it to come to room temperature.

Dust the surface of the dough with flour, then roll out into a 40 x 12-cm (15¾ x 4-inches) long rectangle and cut into twenty 2-cm (¾-inch) wide strips. Gently place 1 strip on top of another to create 10 double strips.

Heat the oil in a deep, heavy-based saucepan to 190°C/375°F. Use a chopstick to press the centre of each double strip together so they form 1 dough stick. Carefully lower 2 or 3 dough sticks into the hot oil, stretching the dough out as you place it in. Fry for about 2 minutes until crisp and golden, using a pair of chopsticks to turn the dough in the oil, to ensure all surfaces puff up nicely. Drain on paper towels and repeat with the remaining *youtiao*. There will be more dough sticks than are needed for this recipe, but they can be stored in an airtight container in the freezer for up to 1 month. To reheat them, place in the oven at 220°C/425°F for 2 minutes and serve.

To assemble

Divide the salt, vinegar and 40 g of the kohlrabi *zha cai* among 4 bowls.

Heat the soy milk in a saucepan over a low heat until it reaches 90°C/195°F (you should see small bubbles but it should not boil). Pour into the prepared bowls (the soy milk will curdle once it interacts with the vinegar) and add a dough stick. Divide 32 g of the spicy daikon, the pickled bamboo shoots, coriander (cilantro) and spring onion (scallion) among the bowls. Drizzle with the Sichuan chilli oil and 2 teaspoons of the soy sauce per bowl.

台灣咖啡廳 — 包國王十字店

Dan Bing

I could eat endless amounts of these – soft, waxy, slightly oily pancakes filled with egg (or whatever you want), topped with a slick of soy and fermented red bean chilli and served with a warm, freshly made soy milk to wash it down. So good. This recipe is our version of the ones we eat on our travels.

There are two styles of dan bing: the old style which is soft and has a slightly QQ chewiness and the modern style which is crispy. Most modern breakfast shops in Taiwan do the crispy version, which I grew up eating. One summer I discovered Fu Hung's dan bing (a famous breakfast place in Taipei) – my world turned upside down! And I never looked back. The soft chew with the fluffy fried egg provided two different types of gentle texture. The warmth and the bouncy softness feel like a gentle hug.

Makes 5 dan bing

4 eggs
140 ml warm water
70 g strong white bread flour
20 g cornflour (cornstarch)
vegetable oil, for cooking the dan bing
5 spring onions (scallions), green parts finely sliced and white parts finely sliced
5 tablespoons Black Garlic Glaze (see page 229)
5 cooked bacon rashers (slices) and/or grated Cheddar (optional)
salt and black pepper

In a small bowl or jug (pitcher), whisk 1 of the eggs with the warm water until smooth and homogeneous.

Put the flour and cornflour (cornstarch) into a bowl and stir together, then make a well in the middle and add the water and egg mixture. Whisk thoroughly until no clumps remain, then pass through a fine-mesh sieve into a clean bowl. Leave to rest, uncovered, at room temperature for 45 minutes.

Heat a thin layer of oil in a small frying pan (skillet) over a medium heat. Pour a thin layer of the batter into the pan, tilting the pan to make sure it is evenly covered, as if you were making a crêpe. When the middle of the dan bing is starting to set, after 1–2 minutes, gently ease a metal spatula under a corner, being careful not to tear it. Flip it over and cook on the other side. Slide the dan bing onto some greaseproof (wax) paper. Repeat with the remaining batter to make 5 pancakes.

To assemble

Lightly season the spring onion (scallion) greens with salt and pepper and leave for about 10 minutes or until wilted. In a small bowl, whisk together the remaining eggs and add the wilted spring onion greens.

Heat a non-stick frying pan over a medium-high heat and add a fifth of the egg mixture, tilting the pan to cover the bottom. The egg will start to bubble. When the edges are set but the middle is still liquid, place a dan bing on top and cook for 30 seconds until the dan bing has stuck to the egg. When you can see the egg has properly set, flip it over and add a line of the spring onion whites across the middle. Drizzle with 1 tablespoon of the black garlic glaze and add a slice of bacon and/or some grated cheese, if using. Fold the edges of the dan bing into the middle to form a neat rectangle, then flip it again and cook for another 20 seconds. Carefully transfer the dan bing to a chopping (cutting) board and cut it into 4 equal sections to serve. Repeat with the remaining dan bing and fillings.

Fried Prawn Roll

This is our version of a traditional Taiwanese snack that consists of minced (ground) prawns (shrimp) wrapped in caul fat. Caul fat is most famous for its use as a wrapping for faggots – I love how it is a very rarely used ingredient but is so deeply British. It adds a light meaty flavour to the prawn roll and keeps the prawns juicy. In Taiwanese cooking, pork and prawns is a classic combination; the pork carries the prawn flavour further, rounding it off and giving it more fragrance. We pair the rolls with a dip made with the delicious honey from local producers The London Honey Company. It is our version of a sweet chilli sauce.

Serves 5

For the ancho chilli honey dip:
1½ dried ancho chillies
250 g local honey
1¼ teaspoons salt
75 ml rice vinegar

For the pickled rhubarb:
50 g caster (superfine) sugar
½ teaspoon salt
100 ml rice vinegar
200 g rhubarb, cut into 6 cm (2½ inch) pieces
on the diagonal

For the prawn rolls:
75 g caul (lace) fat
30 g lard
pinch of ground white pepper
½ teaspoon caster (superfine) sugar
½ teaspoon salt
½ clove garlic, very finely chopped
1 teaspoon sesame oil
½ teaspoon cornflour (cornstarch)
1 green chilli, seeded and finely chopped
345 g uncooked prawns (shrimp), shelled and cut half
of them into 1 cm (½ inch) pieces
vegetable oil, for deep-frying

For the beer batter:
60 g plain (all-purpose) flour
25 g rice flour
1 teaspoon baking powder
pinch of salt
125 ml lager

Ancho chilli honey dip

Soak the ancho chillies in warm water for 20 minutes, then drain and finely chop. Put into a small saucepan with the remaining ingredients, stir well and bring to a gentle boil. Reduce the heat and simmer gently for 5 minutes. Remove from the heat and leave to cool.

Once cool, the dip can be used straight away, or be stored in an sterilized glass jar (see page 89) in a cool, dark place for up to 3 months.

Pickled rhubarb

Combine the sugar, salt and vinegar in a saucepan, then bring to the boil. Add the rhubarb and cook for 20 seconds (no longer!). Remove from the heat and leave to cool. The rhubarb can be used straight away or stored in an airtight container in the refrigerator for up to 1 month.

Prawn rolls

Soak the caul fat in cold water for 20 minutes until it becomes malleable.

Put all the remaining ingredients except the green chilli, prawns (shrimp) and oil into a blender and blend until a paste forms. Scrape out into a bowl, then mix in the green chilli and prawns.

Drain the caul fat and rinse under water, then cut out an 8-cm (3¼-inch) wide strip that is as long as the caul fat piece allows. Place it on the work counter. Put 40 g of the prawn mix towards a clean edge end and roll up like a spring (egg) roll. Repeat with the remaining caul fat and prawn mix to make 10 rolls. Set aside until ready to cook.

Beer batter

Whisk together all the ingredients in a bowl, making sure the batter stays cool.

To assemble

Heat the oil in a deep, heavy-based saucepan to 180°C/350°F, or until a cube of ginger sizzles and browns in 10 seconds. Working in batches, dip the prawn rolls into the beer batter, then carefully place in the hot oil and deep-fry for 2 minutes until crisp and golden. Remove with a slotted spoon and drain on paper towels.

Chop each prawn roll into 3 pieces. Divide the pieces among 5 shallow bowls, filling side up, and add some of the pickled rhubarb on the side. Serve with the ancho chilli honey dip in a small dish.

台灣咖啡廳 一 包國王十字店

台灣咖啡廳 — 包國王十字店

Taro Congee with Crispy Shallot Rings

When I was growing up in Taiwan, Sunday was the day when all the family would gather together. My grandma would often cook taro congee in the afternoon as it's an easy, lazy option for feeding a mass of people. She would add whatever she felt like to the congee, but usually she would include pork and dried shrimp along with the taro. Congee is often eaten with a classic crispy shallot flavour, so when developing this dish for BAO we decided to make shallot rings. England seems to have a fondness for onion rings and I have developed a soft spot for them, too.

Taro is a root vegetable similar to a yam with a mild sweet taste and a purple flesh with flecks. *Jujube* are an Asian red date typically used in broths and desserts. Both can be found in most Asian supermarkets.

Serves 4

For the lovage oil:
50 g lovage
100 ml vegetable oil

For the vegetable stock (broth), makes 1.3 litres:
135 g daikon, peeled and coarsely chopped
70 g carrot, peeled and coarsely chopped
100 g corn cobs (about ½ a cob), cut into quarters
120 g leeks, coarsely chopped
45 g celery, coarsely chopped
4 *jujubes* (red dates), halved
2.5 cm (1 inch) piece of fresh ginger, crushed
3 dried shiitake mushrooms
1 star anise
1.5 litres filtered water

For the taro congee:
16 g dried shiitake mushrooms
4 tablespoons vegetable oil
60 g shallots, cut into 3 mm (⅛ inch) slices using a mandoline
100 g short-grain rice (preferably Chishang or Japanese sushi rice)
1.2 litres vegetable stock (broth), see above
120 g peeled and cubed taro root (1 cm/½ inch cubes)
1½ teaspoons flaky sea salt
pinch of ground white pepper

For the crispy shallot rings:
vegetable oil, for deep-frying
80 g shallots, sliced into 5-mm (¼-inch) thick rings
80 g Beer Batter (see page 164)
salt and white pepper

To serve:
handful of coriander (cilantro), chopped
handful of chives, chopped
20 g fried sun-dried daikon or other preserved vegetables

Lovage oil

Prepare two ice baths. Bring a saucepan of water to the boil, add the lovage and blanch for 10 seconds. Drain, then refresh immediately in one of the ice baths. Drain well. Transfer the lovage to a blender, add the oil and blend at high speed for 5 minutes, then strain through muslin (cheesecloth) hung over a bowl. Once strained, transfer the bowl to the ice bath to cool down any residual heat from the blending.

The oil can be stored in an airtight container in the refrigerator for up to 3 days, or frozen for up to 1 month. It is great for dressing salads or vegetables.

Vegetable stock (broth)

Put all the ingredients into a large saucepan and bring to the boil, then reduce the heat to medium and simmer for 1 hour. Strain through a fine-mesh sieve into a measuring jug (large measuring cup), discarding the solids, then leave to cool. The stock can be stored in an airtight container in the refrigerator for up to 3 days or frozen for up to 1 month.

Taro congee

Put the dried shiitake mushrooms into a heatproof bowl, cover with boiling water and leave to soak for 20 minutes. Drain, then slice thinly.

Heat the oil in a saucepan over a medium heat, add the mushrooms and shallots and pan-fry until fragrant. Add the rice and cook for another 1 minute, then pour in 1.2 litres of the vegetable stock. Reduce the heat to low and cook for at least 45 minutes, until the rice has broken down. Stir occasionally, making sure the rice doesn't catch on the bottom of the pan. A tip I learned from my mother in law is to use a whisk, mid way through cooking, to help break down the grains – it works a treat!

While the congee is cooking, prepare a steamer (see page 47) and steam the taro cubes for 15 minutes. Add the taro cubes to the congee towards the end of cooking (when the rice has broken down) and cook for another 15–20 minutes until the taro is tender. Season with the salt and pepper.

Crispy shallot rings

Just before serving, heat the oil in a deep, heavy-based saucepan to 180°C/350°F, or until a cube of ginger sizzles and browns in 10 seconds. Dip the shallot rings into the beer batter, then carefully place in the oil, in batches, and deep-fry for 90 seconds, or until golden and crisp. Remove with a slotted spoon and drain on paper towels. Season with salt and pepper.

To assemble

Pour the congee into 4 bowls. Dress the chopped herbs with lovage oil, then add to the bowls with some fried sun-dried daikon and crispy shallot rings.

Jiang Shao Beef Short Rib Pancake with Bone Marrow

If you walk the streets of Taiwan, you're likely to stumble past a street vendor selling a flaky spring onion (scallion) pancake called *cong zhua bing* topped with anything from cheese, egg, basil or ham. The pancakes are cooked in lard on a flat griddle and 'flaked' up through some vigorous spatula action. We've always wanted this on our menus, and at BAO King's Cross we serve it with *jiang shao* (reduced red braise) beef short rib, with the option of roasted bone marrow for extra unctuousness.

Makes 10 pancakes

For the jiang shao beef short ribs:
500 g beef short ribs
1 teaspoon salt
3 cloves garlic
1 bunch spring onions (scallions), roots trimmed
60 g honey
50 g *doubanjiang* (fermented chilli bean paste)
25 g chilli powder
80 g smooth peanut butter

For the bone marrow:
10 x 250-g pieces marrow bone
3½ tablespoons aged white soy sauce (see page 233)
salt

For the cong zhua bing
600 g plain (all-purpose) flour, plus extra for dusting
30 g caster (superfine) sugar
10 g salt
350 g lukewarm water
lard, melted
50 g spring onion(scallion), finely sliced into rings
5 g white pepper
rapeseed (canola) oil, for frying

For the salad:
80 g leek, white parts only, cut into very fine 7-cm (2¾-inch) long strips
80 g daikon, peeled and cut into very fine 7-cm (2¾-inch) long strips
160 g cucumber, cut into very fine 7-cm (2¾-inch) long strips
160 g coriander (cilantro), leaves and stems
1 clove garlic, minced
70 ml mirin
2 teaspoons soy sauce
70 ml rice vinegar
1 teaspoon sesame oil
1 tablespoon caster (superfine) sugar
½ teaspoon salt

Tip
You can buy ready-made cong zhua bing at most Asian supermarkets, or use shop-bought paratha as an alternative.

Jiang shao beef short ribs

Preheat the oven to 180°C/350°F/Gas Mark 4. Season the short ribs with the salt and place in a flameproof casserole dish (Dutch oven) with the garlic. Cook in the oven for 15–20 minutes until browned, then remove the dish, cover the ribs with water and stir in the remaining ingredients except the peanut butter. Put the lid on the dish, turn down the oven to 90°C/195°F/Gas Mark ¼ and cook in the oven overnight, or for 8 hours. While the short ribs are cooking, you can start soaking the bone marrow.

Remove the short ribs from the braising liquid, reserving the liquid, and shred the meat from the bones. In a pan over medium–high heat, reduce the braising liquid down to about 130 ml. Strain through a fine-mesh sieve into a clean saucepan, then whisk together with the peanut butter, and add the meat. Keep warm until needed.

Bone marrow

Soak the marrow bone pieces in cold water with approximately 10 per cent salt for 3–4 hours to remove the blood. When ready to cook, preheat the oven to 180°C/350°F/Gas Mark 4. Drain the marrow bone pieces and pat dry, then put onto a baking sheet and roast in the oven for 25 minutes.

Cong zhua bing

Mix the plain flour, sugar and half of the salt in a non-reactive mixing bowl, pour in the lukewarm water and mix with chopsticks until combined. Using your hands knead the dough for 5–10 minutes until smooth, cover with cling film (plastic wrap) and let it rest for 30 minutes.

Once the dough has proved, knead it again until smooth, roll into a long log and divide into 10 pieces. Dust the surface with flour and roll out the pieces very thinly to rectangle shapes, cover with a wet cloth to prevent them from drying out. Brush the rectangles with melted lard and sprinkle the spring onion (scallion), white pepper and remaining salt over evenly. Fold each end of the dough horizontally, so the lengths of the dough meet in the middle. Brush with more lard and fold each end again, horizontally, towards the middle, then fold over to form a long strip. Starting with one end of the strip, roll into to a ball. Let rest for 15 minutes, then press and roll out into flat pancakes.

Salad

Toss the vegetables and coriander (cilantro) in a bowl. In a separate bowl, whisk the remaining ingredients with 1 teaspoon water to create the dressing.

To assemble

Just before serving, drizzle the bone marrow with the aged soy sauce and toss the salad with the dressing.

Heat a splash of oil in a frying pan (skillet) and cook the pancakes, one at a time, until crispy on the outside but still soft on the inside, 1½–2 minutes. Brush each pancake with 1 tablespoon of the braising sauce, then pile 35 g braised short rib in the middle of each one. Top with the salad. Serve each with a piece of bone marrow to spoon onto the pancake.

Chilli Chicken Rice with Meinong Daikon

The main star of this dish is the sun-dried daikon, which we source from the Meinong district of Taiwan. It provides crunch and a slight chewy savouriness to the dish while also flavouring the rice without taking away from the chicken. The daikon is the 'Bai Yu' variety, which is small and sweet. The best examples are grown in the Meinong area – it's a speciality of the Hakka (a Chinese ethnic group from Southern China), which is harvested in November when the winter sun is perfect for sun-drying it. It has an incredibly thin skin, meaning the daikon can be dried whole with the skin on under the tropical Taiwanese sun. Sun-dried daikon can be found in most Asian supermarkets and needs to be soaked for 1–2 hours before using.

The other star of the dish is the chicken roasting juices, which are emulsified with soy sauce and poured over the rice so the mixture slowly seeps through and coats each grain.

Serves 4

For the yellow chilli chicken thighs:
4 boneless skin-on chicken thighs
120 g Yellow Chilli Marinade (see page 145)
4 teaspoons flaky sea salt
4 tablespoons vegetable oil

For the rice:
300 g short-grain rice (preferably Chishang or Japanese sushi rice)
300 ml filtered water

For the crispy chicken skin:
400 g chicken skin
flaky sea salt

For the black-bean fried Meinong daikon:
1½ teaspoons preserved black beans
300 g sun-dried daikon, soaked in cold water for 1–2 hours
25 ml vegetable oil
3 cloves garlic, finely diced
½ mild red chilli, seeded and chopped
1 tablespoon caster (superfine) sugar

To serve:
1 tablespoon aged white soy
4 teaspoons Ginger Spring Onion Oil (see page 229)
120 g Soy-pickled Cucumber (see page 89)
4 Soy-cured Egg Yolks (see page 228)
Urfa chilli flakes, to taste

Yellow chilli chicken thighs

Put the chicken thighs into a non-reactive bowl and coat with the marinade. Cover and leave to marinate in the refrigerator for 8 hours (the longer the better).

Rice

Wash the rice thoroughly, 3 times. After the final rinse, tip the rice into a bowl, cover with cold water and leave to soak for 30 minutes.

Pour the filtered water into a saucepan and bring to the boil. Drain the soaked rice and add to the boiling water. When the water is boiling again, put a lid on, reduce the heat to low and cook for 18 minutes. Open the lid to check that the rice is cooked and ever-so-slightly glistening but not wet. Put the lid back on, remove from the heat and let the rice rest for 10 minutes before serving. This process allows the remaining steam to absorb back into the grains, resulting in fluffy and bouncy rice. At no point remove the lid from the pan.

Yellow chilli chicken thighs (cont.)

When ready to cook the dish, preheat the oven to 200°C/400°F/Gas Mark 6. Remove the chicken from the refrigerator and season with salt, then put into a baking pan lined with aluminium foil with a raised edge of about 1 cm (½ inch) on each side. This will help retain moisture while allowing the chicken skin to brown and crisp up. Drizzle with the oil and roast in the oven for 12–15 minutes until cooked through and the juices run clear when pierced with a sharp knife, then remove and set aside, reserving the roasting juices. Keep warm.

Crispy chicken skin

Line a baking sheet with baking (parchment) paper. Spread out the chicken skin thinly and in a single layer across on the sheet, sprinkle with salt and bake in the oven at 200°C/400°F/Gas Mark 6 for 20–30 minutes until totally crisp. Remove from the oven, pat dry, and allow to cool, then finely chop the chicken skin to create a crumb.

Black-bean fried Meinong daikon

Place the preserved black beans in a bowl, cover with water and soak for 5 minutes, then drain. Drain the soaked daikon, then cut into 1 cm (½ inch) cubes.

Heat the oil in a wok or frying pan (skillet) over a medium heat, add the garlic, red chilli and preserved black beans and cook for 5 minutes until fragrant and the garlic is soft and coloured. Add the daikon, reduce the heat to low and cook for up to 5 minutes, or until fragrant. Stir in the sugar.

To assemble

Pour the chicken roasting juices into a small bowl and whisk in the aged white soy until it combines and emulsifies. Divide the rice among 4 bowls and gently smooth the surface. Do not press or compact the rice down. Using a cook's blowtorch, lightly blister the top of the rice. Spread 1 teaspoon of the ginger spring onion oil over the rice in each bowl. Chop the chicken into 2 x 2 cm (¾ x ¾ inch) cubes and place around the rice, pushing it to the edges of the bowls and leaving a space in the centre. Pour the emulsified chicken juices over the chicken and rice.

For each serving, add a few soy-pickled cucumber sticks, some of the crispy chicken skin crumb and 1 teaspoon of the fried Meinong daikon at the side of the bowl. Gently place a soy-cured egg yolk in the centre and sprinkle with the chilli flakes.

'Pork Chop' Lard Rice

I have specific associations with pork chop rice, in that I see it as a 'work lunch'. I used to spend a lot of time at my parents' workplace when I was growing up, and the staff would routinely place group orders of *bian dang* (rice boxes) with a local vendor, where pork chop rice was always the most popular option. It's those boxes that inspired us to create Rice Error (see page 11), but the flavour of the pork chop rice specifically that inspired this version in our restaurant. There are lots of different variations of pork chop rice – we marinate the pork in red fermented tofu, which is our interpretation of the traditional dish where the pork is marinated in *hong tsao* (red wine yeast), and serve it on top of lard rice, a dish that was served at our beloved restaurant XU (see page 11). Although modelled on pork chop rice, we actually use pork belly (side) as the cut, as it is fattier, and, to my mind, tastier.

You can find red fermented tofu (often sold as 'red bean curd' in jars or cans) and tapioca starch at Asian supermarkets. It is best to scoop out the tofu without draining the liquid, until it weighs 200 g.

Serves 5

For the 'pork chop':
1 teaspoon ground white pepper
200 g red fermented tofu and liquid
5 teaspoons soy sauce
5 cloves garlic, minced
5 teaspoons caster (superfine) sugar
5 teaspoons five spice powder
5 teaspoons bicarbonate of soda (baking soda)
1 x 350-g pork belly (side)
50 g coarse tapioca starch
vegetable oil, for deep-frying

For the compressed cucumber:
1 cucumber
1 teaspoon salt
¾ teaspoon caster (superfine) sugar

For the compressed cucumber pickle:
20 g table salt
40 g caster (superfine) sugar
200 ml rice wine vinegar
2 green bird's eye chillies
2 teaspoons sesame oil
30 g garlic, grated

For the rice:
375 g short-grain rice (preferably Chishang or Japanese sushi rice)
375 ml filtered water

For the soft-boiled soy eggs:
5 eggs
500 ml soy cure (see page 228, about 6½ quantities)

For the lard dressing:
100 g lard
25 ml premium soy sauce
1 tablespoon mirin

To serve:
5 teaspoons Black Garlic Glaze (see page 229)
75 g Pickled Daikon (see page 192)
5 teaspoons English mustard
25 g Crispy Shallots (see page 228)

'Pork chop'

For the marinade, whisk together all the ingredients except the pork, tapioca starch and oil in a small bowl with 2 teaspoons water.

Remove the skin from the pork belly (side), then cut the meat into five 1-cm (½-inch) thick slabs, each 12 cm (4½ inches) long. Put the slabs into a non-reactive bowl, then coat with the marinade. Cover and leave to marinate in the refrigerator overnight, or for 8 hours. Remove the pork from the refrigerator and set aside while you prepare everything else.

Compressed cucumber

Peel the cucumber and cut off the ends. Put the skin and end trimmings into a blender, add 2 teaspoons water and the remaining ingredients and blend until smooth. Pass the mixture through a chinois sieve.

Dice the cucumber flesh into 1.2 cm (½ inch) cubes, then put the cubes into a vacuum-pack bag with the liquid, seal and compress. Leave in the bag overnight, or for 8 hours. If you don't have a vacuum-pack machine you can skip this compression step.

Compressed cucumber pickle

Dissolve the salt and sugar in the vinegar. Add the chopped chilli, sesame oil, grated garlic to the pickling liquor. Remove the compressed cucumber from the vacuum-pack bag and place in the pickling liquor. It just requires a quick pickle of at least 20 minutes.

Rice

Wash the rice thoroughly, 3 times. After the final rinse, tip the rice into a bowl, cover with cold water and leave to soak for 30 minutes. Pour the filtered water into a saucepan and bring to the boil. Drain the soaked rice and add to the boiling water. When the water is boiling again, put a lid on, reduce the heat to low and cook for 18 minutes. Open the lid to check that the rice is cooked and ever-so-slightly glistening but not wet. Put the lid back on, remove from the heat and let the rice rest for 10 minutes before serving. This process allows the remaining steam to absorb back into the grains, resulting in fluffy and bouncy rice. At no point remove the lid from the pan.

Soft-boiled soy eggs

While the rice is cooking, put the eggs into a saucepan of cold water, bring to the boil, and boil for 3 minutes. Drain, then refresh in cold water. Peel the eggs and put into a bowl. Add the soy cure and leave to marinate for 6–12 hours.

Lard dressing

Melt the lard in a saucepan, then emulsify with the soy sauce and mirin.

To assemble

When ready to serve, coat the pork in the tapioca starch. Heat the oil in a deep, heavy-based saucepan to 180°C/350°F, or until a cube of ginger sizzles and browns in 10 seconds. Working in batches, carefully place the pork slabs in the hot oil and deep-fry for 2½ minutes until cooked through, crisp and golden, then remove with a slotted spoon or tongs and drain on paper towels.

Divide the rice among 5 bowls and very gently smooth the surface. Do not press or compact the rice down. Use a cook's blowtorch to blacken the top of the rice. Drizzle the lard dressing generously over the rice. Brush each pork slab with 1 teaspoon of the black garlic glaze, then cut into 1 cm (½-inch) slices and lay on top of the rice. Top with the pickled daikon, compressed cucumber and the halved eggs. Finish with the mustard and crispy shallots.

40-day Aged Beef Rump Rice

When walking through a night market, it's hard to miss the beef sizzler vendors as they normally take up a larger footprint than their other market counterparts. The smoke from the sizzlers hits your nostrils as they fly past, being handed to diners at their tables in the middle of the market, all adding to the excitement and atmosphere. The steaks at the market are served with a fried egg, black pepper sauce and either a side of noodles or rice. We serve ours on a dome of rice with a soy-cured egg yolk.

Serves 5

For the black pepper sauce:
50 ml vegetable oil
130 g fresh ginger, peeled and sliced
500 g onions, sliced
200 g shallots, sliced
40 g garlic, sliced
30 g tomato purée (paste)
40 ml vegetarian oyster sauce
2 tablespoons Worcestershire sauce
1 tablespoon dark soy sauce
90 ml light soy sauce
120 ml red wine
95 ml Shaoxing rice wine
570 ml beef stock (broth) or water
1 star anise
65 g butter
10 g freshly cracked black pepper, plus extra to serve
1 teaspoon caster (superfine) sugar

For the rump cap:
1 x 300-g 40-day aged beef rump (top sirloin) cap
flaky sea salt

For the rice:
325 g short-grain rice (preferably Chishang or Japanese sushi rice)
325 ml filtered water

For the soy onions:
340 ml rapeseed (canola) oil
200 g onions, finely diced
65 ml light soy sauce

To serve:
vegetable oil, to drizzle
300 g onions, thinly sliced
50 ml Sichuan Chilli Oil (see page 229)
5 Soy-cured Egg Yolks (see page 228)

Black pepper sauce

Heat the oil in a deep saucepan over a low-medium heat, add the ginger, onions and shallots and cook for 15 minutes, adding the garlic just before the end of the cooking time. Add the tomato purée (paste) and vegetarian oyster sauce, mix thoroughly and cook for 2 minutes. Add the Worcestershire sauce, both soy sauces, the red wine, Shaoxing wine, beef stock (broth) or water and the star anise and simmer over a low heat for 1½ hours. Strain the sauce through a fine-mesh sieve into a bowl, letting the solids drain into the sauce for as long as you can.

Rump cap

Season the beef all over with sea salt and leave to rest at room temperature for 30 minutes.

Preheat the oven to 110°C/225°F/Gas Mark ¼.

Heat a dry frying pan (skillet) over a high heat. When the pan starts to smoke, carefully put the rump (top sirloin) cap, fat side down, into the pan. When a pool of fat forms around the meat, sear all sides until brown. Transfer to a roasting pan and cook in the oven for 25 minutes until medium-rare. If you have a meat thermometer, the internal temperature should be 57°C/135°F. Transfer the beef to paper towels and pat dry. Leave to rest for 10 minutes, then slice thinly.

Rice

Meanwhile, wash the rice thoroughly, 3 times. After the final rinse, tip the rice into a bowl, cover with cold water and leave to soak for 30 minutes.

Pour the filtered water into a saucepan and bring to the boil. Drain the soaked rice and add to the pan. When the water is boiling again, put a lid on, reduce the heat to low and cook for 18 minutes. Open the lid to check that the rice is cooked and glistening but not wet. Put the lid back on, remove from the heat and leave the rice to rest for 10 minutes before serving. This process allows the remaining steam to absorb back into the grains, resulting in fluffy and bouncy rice. At no point permanently remove the lid from the pan.

Soy onions

While the rice is resting, heat the oil in a small, deep frying pan over a medium-high heat (to 150°C/300°F), add the onions and cook for 5–10 minutes until browned and caramelized. Remove the onions from the oil with a slotted spoon, transfer to a bowl and add the soy sauce.

To assemble

Increase the oven to 200°C/400°F/Gas Mark 6. Place 5 cast-iron dishes in the oven to heat for 20 minutes.

Mix the rice with the soy onions. Line five 10 cm (4 inch) bowls or deep round dishes with the thinly sliced beef, followed by the rice, pushing it down firmly.

To finish the black pepper sauce, transfer the sauce to a clean pan and warm it over a low-medium heat, then add the butter, cracked black pepper and sugar and thicken to a nice glossy and thick consistency, so it coats the back of a spoon. Bring to the boil, then set aside in the pan.

When the cast-iron dishes are smoking, remove from the oven very carefully using thick oven gloves (mitts) and drizzle with vegetable oil. Divide the thinly sliced onions among the dishes, then turn out the beef and rice domes onto them. Pour over the hot black pepper sauce, ensuring the beef is totally covered, then top each dome with 2 teaspoons of the chilli oil. Make an indent in the top of the domes with the back of a spoon and gently place a soy-cured egg yolk on top of each. Finish with more freshly ground black pepper.

BAO Noodle Shop

The famous Taiwanese beef noodles are a symbol of Taiwanese cuisine with annual beef noodle festivals held every year in Taipei. Everyone has their favourite beef noodle shop and their own perception of how this dish should be – thick or thin noodles, and spicy and rich or clear and delicate broth. When noodle-shop-hopping in Taiwan with Shing and Wai Ting one time, travelling in a taxi to our next noodle destination, we ended up in a deep conversation with the driver about the nuances of beef noodles and which noodle shop was the best. He diverted our plan and took us to a 24-hour noodle shop. From the taxi-driver's dream all-night noodle shop haven (see below) to the 'old man' noodle shops (see opposite), there is a place for everyone.

In a world in which we are all searching for our inner Lonely Man, this is the dish that can help restore our souls. A dish to sip and let out a sigh of contentment in solitude. It's not a bowl to share. You slurp, you eat, you don't talk. On the back of the menu at BAO Noodle Shop we share our rules on how you should treat your bowl of noodles. It's like Juzo Itami's 1985 film *Tampopo*, which illustrates so beautifully the art involved in approaching and eating a bowl of ramen. From tapping the beef into the broth and holding the spoon in your non-writing hand to how you should take a sip from the flared lip of the bowl (designed to allow the noodles to peep out when you tip the bowl so there's less chance of your nose saying 'Hi' to the broth) and the way in which slurping to finish the broth shows respect to the chefs, there's an art to it. That's how you master your own noodle – the bowl that sits in front of you, with your hands reached out on either side, protecting it.

Going back to Taiwan once or twice a year is important to us and when we do, we always visit a beef noodle shop. I might be a little out of touch now, but back in the day Yong Kang Beef Noodle and Lin Dong Fan in Taipei were our two favourite spots, and Shing, Wai Ting and I visited them when they first travelled to Taiwan. Yong Kang Beef Noodle serves a much spicier, oilier and richer soup with a thinner and less lively noodle. They also do an amazing side dish there: spare rib steamed rice. The key here is to load up your bowl with the tableside fermented greens and coriander (cilantro). Lin Dong Fan, on the other hand, serve a much thicker and bouncier noodle with an elegant, clear soup broth. They have a spiced beef butter that is skimmed off the top of the braising beef and you can add it back into the soup to make it 'red'. It comes in a jar with a spoon on the table so you are able to help yourself.

THE TAXI DRIVER'S RECOMMENDED 24 HOUR BEEF NOODLE PITSTOP.

刈包麵店

JAPANESE BEEF UDON AT CHITOSE, OSAKA.

A CLEAR BEEF SOUP VERSION AT LIU SAN DONG BEEF NOODLE, TAIPEI.

It's weird but I have quite vivid memories of those 'aah' sipping the broth moments, attached to specific noodle houses. Two particular memories stick out. One is from my more recent travels back to Taiwan with Shing, when we visited Liu San Dong, which we call the 'old man noodle shop'. It has more old-fashioned, classic-style condiments that sit tableside – a choice of black beans and raw garlic to crush into the clear soup. I can clearly remember sitting in that restaurant, staring at the white tiles, metal interior and open kitchen, and drifting off to the sound of fans buzzing away in the background and old men spooning black beans into their soup, coupled with them peeling the raw garlic and taking a bite before slurping in noodles. Wild. My other vivid memory is of a perfect moment in Osaka in Japan, at a restaurant that my good friend and mentor Junya Yamasaki recommended I visit, which serves only two dishes: beef udon or a beef and tofu broth. The restaurant is small and can fit only twenty guests, so naturally the queue is long. We queued as usual, but as we walked in the whole room was silent. It was quite strange to begin with – until the bowl of noodles arrived, and then you realize why it is silent: there is no time to speak, just head down, slurp and reflect on your inner self; feel that bead of sweat form on your forehead and bathe in the steam of beef and bonito like a spa treatment. It's moments like these that really do make you feel like your soul has been restored and all is well with the world. That is what I believe beef noodles can do for you and the reason why we wanted to bring a translation of those moments to London, focusing once more on the purity of a moment.

Broths and tonics are so important to the way of life in Taiwan and a lot of other South and East Asian countries. At home, the Chinese tonic broth has always been an important mainstay at the large family dinners my grandma would cook for us every day. The nutrients in the tonic broth are absorbed into your blood very quickly and this increases your *qi* (energy flow). It's like the tonic levels you up, and even more so if you are feeling under the weather. It's that *qi* that runs through your veins when you eat a bowl of noodles. A lot of time and different processes go into our broth to achieve that harmony.

Since that first trip to Taiwan with Shing and Wai Ting, opening a beef noodle shop was always on our minds. Why it took us six years, who knows – maybe it was the fear of not doing it the justice it required or the barrier of importing huge amounts of flour to London (more on that later). In hindsight, it was a blessing in disguise because it would take us years of research to get it even remotely close to right.

Several years ago, when travelling around Taiwan (and eating lots of noodles), my good friend Evelyn took me to her local noodle master in Taipei to pay a visit to the place she had grown up eating in. His place is tucked away on the edge of a food market, and when I was introduced to him, I thought he looked more like a Taiwanese gangster in a tank top than a noodle master. His workshop was a very simple set-up and his noodle machine looked like it was part of a nineteenth-century steam train. It was painted a vintage khaki colour and was robust and elegant. This noodle shop supplies many well-known noodle houses in Taipei. It's discreet, with no name; just quietly providing for the masses. The master was silent, sceptically sizing me up – I always look like a naive tourist, so I don't blame him for not taking me seriously, I blame my plump cheeks and the Nikon F100 film camera hanging around my neck.

He made the noodles swiftly, talking us through his process at the same speed. He took pride in his great ingredients and his skills, telling us that 'All you need is good flour and good water.' Nothing else is needed – forget about alkaline water or anything else, the secret to a bouncy wheat noodle lies in the strength of the gluten, how many times you press it and how long you rest the noodles before you serve them. Work with the weather, observe the humidity and adjust. The noodle master climbed up to the top of the mixer, took a tin out from next to the hanging lights (his secret spot) and sprinkled something into the mixer. I asked what it was and he replied, 'Salt, nothing special.' I'm not sure if he was being entirely honest with me, but he seemed to be openly showing me everything.

Much like when we first started the arduous process of perfecting the BAO, the process of perfecting the noodle took a long time and a lot of effort. Searching for the perfect flour with the right protein level, for example. In London, we made multiple attempts with different types of specialist local flour, but nothing worked. To get liveliness and spring into the noodle, we tried using alkaline or lye water and even part-dried the noodles, but it was never right. After a long search, we finally found the flour that was perfect for us back in Taiwan, and we now import it. This was another item that we originally had to persuade my mum to ship over – to the detriment of her living room. Imagine 1,000 kg of flour sitting in my mum's living room. No normal mum would do that for their daughter! Thanks Mum!

So, in the end, what the noodle master told me was exactly right – all you need is good flour and good water (and salt). However, the specialist ingredients for the beef noodles weren't just limited to the flour. Our journey continued in finding the right fermented chilli paste, the right soy sauce, the right machine... Sourcing recipes and techniques from masters is so difficult in Chinese cuisines. In Taiwan, the culture is very much about hiding recipes and skills and keeping them to hand down to apprentices or family. I was actually quite surprised and appreciative that the noodle master was so open and transparent about his process. You hear many stories about apprentices from famous noodle shops falling out with their boss and then opening their own noodle shop next door, staging a mini war against each other, with each bragging about who was the first or the best. When something is popular, everyone starts doing the same thing – the struggle is real. But we were the same. We spent a long time keeping recipes hidden from our staff, yet here we are now sharing everything. I have learned a lesson from the noodle master to be more open, take pride in other people's skills, respect their specialisms and continually try to improve. In any case, if someone opens a beef noodle shop next door to us, it will push us harder to do it better! But please don't.

OLD-SCHOOL NOODLE MACHINE FROM THE NOODLE MASTER.

Plain Wheat Noodles

Just as the master in Taipei said, 'All you need is good water and good flour.' Our noodle recipe is just as simple because the flavour and texture are down to the quality flour that we import directly from Taiwan, which has the right protein level (12–13 per cent) and is finely milled to process the innermost part of the wheat grain.

You will need a noodle machine or pasta machine to make your own noodles.

Serves 4

300 g 12–13% protein noodle flour
pinch of salt
100 ml filtered water
cornflour (cornstarch), for dusting

For the Lonely Man:
Skip making your own noodles and instead purchase our plain Emergency Noodles (see page 233). Freeze them, so when you need a noodle fix, your emergency noodles will be ready and waiting for you.

Sift the noodle flour and salt into a large bowl, then gradually pour in the filtered water, using a pair of chopsticks to mix. The mixture will be very dry. Scrape all the bits of flour stuck on the bowl back into the mix and start kneading with your hands and pressing the flour together until it binds together. Put a clean, damp cloth over the bowl and leave to rest at room temperature for 1 hour.

Tip the dough out onto the work counter and knead it again by folding it in on itself. Using a noodle or pasta machine, roll out the dough on the thickest setting. Fold the rolled dough and pass it through the machine. Repeat this folding and rolling 8 more times, until the dough becomes smooth. While rolling, reduce the thickness setting bit by bit until the dough is 2 mm (1/16 inch) thick. It might be useful to split the dough in half and work each batch at a time. Dust the dough with cornflour (cornstarch) on both sides and gently fold onto a baking sheet. Wrap in cling film (plastic wrap) and leave to rest overnight in the refrigerator or for a few hours at room temperature.

Using the noodle machine, roll out the dough again to a thickness of 2 mm (1/16 inch), then cut into 2-mm (1/16-inch) wide noodles using the noodle attachment.

Slow-cooked Beef Cheek and Short Rib Noodles in a Rich Beef Soup with Beef Butter (Taipei Style)

The main event – rich beef noodles, based on the traditional version you'll find in Taiwan. With this dish, you're not expected to finish drinking the broth as it's so highly seasoned, adding richness and oil to the noodles (but you can). When I eat this dish in Taiwan, I always garnish it lavishly with fermented greens and coriander (cilantro). It's what makes the dish in my eyes.

It takes a while to prepare this dish as the stock (broth) is cooked slowly with 40-day aged beef bones and a selection of spices. Usually, these beef noodles are served with slices of beef shin that have cartilage and veins running through them. Controversially, I've never been a fan, so at BAO we use cheek and short rib instead. We cook the meat slow and then keep it warm in beef butter so it stays meltingly soft.

This recipe makes more beef soup than you need for the recipe. While I recommend you drink it fresh, it will keep in the refrigerator for a few days. You can reheat it and drink it whenever you need an energy boost, or if you want to make another portion of noodles. You will need to make the master stock one night in advance.

刈包麵店

Serves 4

For the beef cheek and short ribs:
240 ml vegetarian oyster sauce
120 g onion, finely diced
35 g garlic, crushed
20 g ground star anise
60 ml Chinkiang black rice vinegar
50 ml rapeseed (canola) oil
30 ml light soy sauce
300–400 g beef short ribs
300–400 g beef cheek, trimmed
1 quantity Spiced Beef Butter (see page 230)

For the rich beef soup:
1 star anise
1 cinnamon stick
pinch of red Sichuan peppercorns
pinch of fennel seeds
1 teaspoon Spiced Beef Butter (see above)
1 tablespoon vegetable oil
400 g lean beef trimmings (ask your butcher)
75 g onion, halved
40 g carrot, coarsely chopped
25 g shallots, halved
25 g spring onions (scallions), coarsely chopped
25 g fresh ginger, peeled and smashed
1 red chilli, halved
3 cloves garlic, coarsely chopped
½ tomato
75 g *doubanjiang* (fermented chilli bean paste)
45 ml whole bean soy sauce
10 g rock sugar
1.35 litres Master Stock (see page 232)

To serve:
1 teaspoon grated garlic
1 quantity (400 g) Plain Wheat Noodles (see page 183,
or use our ready-made noodles, see page 233)
4 tablespoons chopped coriander (cilantro)
4 tablespoons Fermented Mustard Greens
(see page 231)

Beef cheek and short ribs

Combine all the ingredients except the meat and spiced beef butter in a large non-reactive bowl to form the marinade. Add the meat and coat with the marinade, then cover and leave to marinate in the refrigerator overnight, or for 8 hours.

Preheat the oven to 150°C/300°F/Gas Mark 2. Transfer the meat to a roasting pan, pour in about 2 cm (¾ inch) water (it should come about halfway up the meat), cover with aluminium foil and braise in the oven for about 3 hours until tender. Leave the meat to cool. Melt half the spiced beef butter in a saucepan, then slice the beef into 1-cm (½-inch) thick slices. Place the sliced beef in the beef butter, cover with foil, and put in the oven at 60°C/140°F, to keep warm until ready to serve.

Rich beef soup

Make the soup while the beef cheek and short ribs are braising. Put the star anise, cinnamon stick, Sichuan peppercorns and fennel seeds onto a piece of muslin (cheesecloth) or into a spice bag and tie shut.

Heat the teaspoon of spiced beef butter and the oil in a large wok or a deep frying pan over a medium heat. Add the beef trimmings and pan-fry until golden brown, then remove and set aside. Add the onion, carrot, shallots, spring onions (scallions), ginger, chilli, garlic and tomato to the pan and pan-fry over a medium heat for 5 minutes. Reduce the heat to low and add the *doubanjiang*. Cook for 5 minutes until it smells very fragrant (but do not allow it to burn), then add the soy sauce and the rock sugar and cook for another minute.

Pour in the beef master stock and return the browned beef trimmings. Put the spice bag into the braising liquid, increase the heat to medium and bring to the boil. Reduce the heat to low and cover (if your pan does not have a lid, place a piece of baking (parchment) paper directly on the braising liquid and then cover the pan with aluminium foil). Simmer for 1 hour.

Taste the soup. It should be rich and deep in flavour. If it's not, continue cooking for up to another 1 hour. Leave the soup to cool slightly, then strain into a heatproof bowl, discarding all the solids. Leave the soup to cool, then skim the fat from the top with a spoon.

To assemble

Preheat the oven to 150°C/300°F/Gas Mark 2 and place 4 heatproof bowls in the oven to warm.

Pour 1 litre of the soup into a saucepan and bring to a gentle boil over a medium heat. Keep warm until needed.

Bring a large saucepan of salted water to the boil. While the water is coming to the boil, add ¼ teaspoon of grated garlic to each warmed bowl.

Cook the noodles in two batches. Place half of the noodles in the boiling salted water and give them a stir with chopsticks to separate the strands. Once the water comes to the boil again, cook for 1 minute and 10 seconds. (If the noodles aren't freshly prepared, it may require longer cooking time. Have a test bite before straining.) Drain and immediately divide between 2 of the prepared warmed bowls by picking up half of the noodles with a pair of chopsticks. Gently lay the ends of the strands into the bowl and fold them over so the noodles are all uniformly sitting snug next to each other. Repeat for the second batch of noodles.

Pour the soup over the noodles and top each bowl with a slice of beef cheek, a slice of beef rib and 1 teaspoon of the spiced beef butter. Finish with the coriander (cilantro) and 1 tablespoon of fermented mustard greens. Slurp away.

刈包麵店

Rare Beef Rump Noodles in a Light Beef Soup (Tainan Style)

This is a restorative bowl of noodles that is much lighter and more elegant than our rich Taipei-style broth (see page 184). If you are feeling under the weather, this is the bowl you need to warm your soul and get that *qi* coursing through your veins. We based it on the lighter beef noodles you get all over Taiwan, but also on the famous shops in Tainan that serve a gentle beef broth with lightly poached beef, which we eat every time we visit the city.

The soup is delicate because it's made for you to drink rather than for seasoning the noodles. It's slightly less rich and salty than the standard beef noodles. We layer thin slices of 40-day aged raw beef rump (sirloin) on top of the noodles, which add complexity to the broth as they slowly submerge and are poached. This beef is then perfect for dipping into a soy-cured egg yolk.

Do not cook the master stock (broth) too early, otherwise the flavour will be lost.

Serves 4

For the beef:
1 x 180-g piece beef rump cap (sirloin)

For the light beef soup:
1.4 litres Master Stock (Broth), see page 232
4 teaspoons light soy sauce
4 teaspoons salt
4 teaspoons caster (superfine) sugar
8 teaspoons *doubanjiang* (fermented chilli bean paste)

To serve:
4 Soy-cured Eggs (see page 228)
8 teaspoons aged white soy (see page 233)
2 cloves garlic
4 teaspoons rice vinegar
1 quantity (400 g) Plain Wheat Noodles (see page 183, or use our ready-made noodles, see page 233)
pinch of flaky sea salt
4.5 cm (1 inch) piece of fresh ginger, cut into 7-mm (¾-inch) long strips
40 g garlic shoots (or leek), green parts only, cut into 5-mm (¼-inch) long strips
40 g spring onions (scallions), green parts only, cut into 5-mm (¼-inch) long strips

Beef

Wrap the beef up in baking (parchment) paper and freeze for 1–2 hours until it is part-frozen and feels hard enough to slice but not fully frozen. Using a sharp knife, slice or shave off thin slices of the part-frozen beef. Refrigerate the slices until ready to use.

Light beef soup

Bring the master stock (broth) to the boil in a saucepan. Add the remaining ingredients and stir well, then pass the stock through a sieve into a clean pan and keep warm (you want the soup to be piping hot when served).

To assemble

Prepare the soy-cured eggs by placing each egg into a shallow dipping saucer with 1 teaspoon of aged white soy.

Preheat the oven to 150°C/300°F/Gas Mark 2 and place 4 heatproof bowls in the oven to warm. In each of the warmed bowls, grate half a clove of garlic, and add 1 teaspoon of rice vinegar.

Cook the noodles in two batches. Bring a large saucepan of salted water to the boil, add half the noodles and give it a stir with chopsticks to separate the strands. Once the water comes to the boil again, cook for 1 minute and 10 seconds. (If the noodles aren't freshly prepared, it may require longer cooking time. Have a test bite before straining.) Drain and immediately divide into 2 bowls by picking up half of the noodles with a pair of chopsticks. Gently lay the ends of the strands into the bowl and fold them over so the noodles are all uniformly sitting snug next to each other. Repeat for the second batch of noodles.

Arrange the slices of beef on top of the noodles in each of the 4 bowls. Pour over the hot soup, drizzle over 1 teaspoon aged soy sauce and sprinkle the salt over the beef. Garnish with the ginger, chopped garlic shoots and spring onions (scallions). When eating the beef, make sure you dip it into the soy-cured egg on the dipping saucer.

Dan Dan Tofu Noodles

When we were travelling around Chengdu, China, we tried so many different bowls of dan dan noodles, and it was there we learned that dan dan is a style of noodle, rather than just referring to spicy minced (ground) meat noodles as we often suppose. There's such elegance in each noodle house's perfectly balanced flavours, with the small bowls topped with everything from *yu shiang* ('fish fragrant') ribs to fermented cowpeas (black-eyed beans/peas). The balance of seasoning is crucial, so make sure you measure these to a T when making your own. I particularly like to appreciate the oily residue and bits of fermented vegetables left at the edge of the bowl at the end. Finishing a bowl is the ultimate way to show my respect to the chefs and restaurant owners.

The method of cooking the tofu is the same as how you would cook the minced meat, confiting it in rapeseed (canola) oil to fluff up the tofu pieces. I love using tofu in this way as it acts like a sponge and soaks up all the flavour of the spiced oil.

Serves 4

For the dan dan tofu:
250 ml cold-pressed rapeseed (canola) oil
1 x 200-g block firm tofu, crumbled into coarse 1 cm
(½ inch) pieces
2 cm (¾ inch) piece of fresh ginger, peeled and finely diced
2 teaspoons chilli powder
1½ teaspoons ground white pepper
1½ teaspoons caster (superfine) sugar
2½ tablespoons whole bean soy sauce
pinch of salt

For the dan dan tofu dressing:
3 teaspoons mirin
8 teaspoons whole bean soy sauce
2 cloves garlic, grated
4 tablespoons Fermented Mustard Greens (see page 231)
2 teaspoons Tung Choi Preserved Vegetable (you can find in most Asian Supermarkets)
4 teaspoons Chinkiang vinegar
8 teaspoons Sichuan Chilli Oil (see page 229)

To serve:
400 g Plain Wheat Noodles (see page 183, or use our ready-made noodles, see page 233)
4 generous handfuls of coriander (cilantro), finely sliced

Dan dan tofu

Heat the oil in a frying pan (skillet) over a medium heat. Add the tofu and ginger and pan-fry for 2 minutes, then add the remaining ingredients and cook gently for 10 minutes. The tofu should soak up all the flavours, and the texture will be very tender and fluffy. Remove from the heat and set aside.

Dan dan tofu dressing

While the tofu is cooking, preheat the oven to 150°C/300°F/Gas Mark 2 and place 4 bowls in the oven to warm.

Put ¾ teaspoon mirin, 2 teaspoons soy sauce, grated ½ clove garlic, 1 tablespoon fermented mustard greens, ½ teaspoon preserved vegetable, 1 teaspoon Chinkiang vinegar and 2 teaspoons chilli oil, including some pulp, into each bowl. It's important to measure into each warmed bowl rather than make a batch of dressing because the flavour balance is key to this dish.

To assemble

Cook the noodles in two batches. Bring a large saucepan of salted water to the boil, add half the noodles, then give it a stir with chopsticks to separate the strands. Once the water comes to the boil again, cook for 1 minute and 10 seconds. (If the noodles aren't freshly prepared, it may require longer cooking time. Have a test bite before straining.) Drain and immediately divide into 2 bowls by picking up half of the noodles with a pair of chopsticks. Gently lay the ends of the strands into the bowl and fold them over so the noodles are all uniformly sitting snug next to each other. Repeat for the second batch of noodles.

Top each bowl of noodles with 4 tablespoons of the dan dan tofu. Be sure to include the oil as it will give it extra flavour. Top each bowl with a generous handful of the coriander (cilantro). Mix the noodles thoroughly before eating.

刈包麵店

Kelp Soup Noodles with Aubergine Tempura

We use three types of kelp to add complexity and depth of flavour to this broth. Just like the Tainan-style beef soup, this is the type of broth you crave when feeling unwell: clear, fragrant and light. After eating and drinking too many beef noodle soups, this has become my go to noodle. The chefs get super annoyed because every time I visit Noodle Shop, I ask for a box of noodles and kelp soup vacuum packed to take home. (That's why we call it Emergency Noodles on our packaging!)

Serves 4

For the kombu stock (broth), makes 1.2 litres:
12 g kombu
4 dried shiitake mushrooms
1.1 litres filtered water
55 ml light soy sauce
55 ml whole bean soy sauce
40 ml mirin
1 star anise
1 cm (½ inch) piece of fresh ginger, peeled and crushed

For the ribbon seaweeds:
20 g fresh dulse, washed (if you can't get hold of any, using wakame only is fine)
1 teaspoon dried wakame

For the aubergine tempura:
1 aubergine (eggplant), cut into twelve half moon pieces
1.5 cm (¾ inch) thick
140 g cornflour (cornstarch)
120 g plain (all-purpose) flour
330 ml Taiwan Beer (or light lager)
400 ml rapeseed (canola) oil, plus extra for deep-frying
salt

To serve:
1 quantity (400 g) Plain Wheat Noodles (see page 183, or use our ready-made noodles, see page 233)
few pinches of toasted white sesame seeds
2 teaspoons sesame oil
8 teaspoons finely diced celery

Tip
Sometimes I hack the dish and swap the aubergine (eggplant) with elegant long strips of rare beef rump. Do not make the batter for the aubergine too early or it will lose its magic.

Kombu stock (broth)

Put the kombu and mushrooms into a saucepan, add the filtered water and leave to soak for 2–3 hours, or in the refrigerator overnight.

Add the rest of the ingredients to the pan and bring to a very gentle simmer for 10 minutes, making sure not to let the water come to the boil. Remove from the heat, remove only the star anise and leave to cool. It's important not to boil kombu or it releases bitterness. If you have time, chill the broth overnight. When ready to serve, strain through a fine-mesh sieve into another saucepan and heat gently over a low heat.

Ribbon seaweeds

If using fresh dulse, it's important to wash it thoroughly as it comes with salt on it. After washing, cut the dulse into 10 cm (4 inch) ribbons and discard the stems from the dulse. Place into a large bowl, cover with cold water and leave until serving.

In a separate bowl, soak the dried wakame in cold water for 5 minutes. When you are ready to serve, drain both and add the dulse and wakame to the heated broth.

Preheat the oven to 150°C/300°F/Gas Mark 2 and place 4 bowls in the oven to warm.

Aubergine tempura

Season the aubergine (eggplant) pieces with salt and set aside.

Mix together the cornflour (cornstarch) and flour in a large bowl, then whisk in the beer. Add the oil, whisking constantly, until a smooth batter forms. Dip the aubergine pieces into the batter, making sure they are fully covered.

Heat the oil in a deep, heavy-based saucepan to 180°C/350°F, or until a cube of ginger sizzles and browns in 10 seconds. Working in batches, carefully place the aubergine pieces in the hot oil and deep-fry for 2 minutes until crisp and golden, then remove with a slotted spoon and drain on paper towels.

To assemble

Gently heat up the kombu stock over low heat with the dulse and wakame seaweed for 5 minutes, keep it on a low heat while preparing your noodles.

Cook the noodles in two batches. Bring a large saucepan of salted water to the boil and place half of the noodles in, giving them a stir with chopsticks to separate the strands. Once the water comes to boil again, cook for 1 minute and 10 seconds. Drain and immediately divide into 2 bowls by picking up half of the noodles with a pair of chopsticks. Gently lay the ends of the strands into the bowl and fold them over so the noodles are all uniformly sitting snug next to each other. Repeat for the second batch of noodles.

Decorate the outer edge with the ribbon seaweeds. Pour over the hot kombu broth. Garnish with a sprinkling of toasted white sesame seeds, ½ teaspoon sesame oil and 2 teaspoons diced celery then gently place 3 pieces of aubergine tempura in the middle of each bowl.

Pao Tsai Pickles

Pao tsai literally translates as 'vegetable submerged in liquid' and is also known as water kimchi. The trio of *pao tsai* pickles we serve at Noodle Shop are diverse but naturally complement each other, working in harmony by providing different flavour profiles of acidic, sweet and spicy. With pickles it is so important that the flavour is light and clean, and the texture should be crunchy and crisp.

Makes 1 × 500 ml jar per pickle

For the yellow pickled fennel:
200 ml rice vinegar
½ tablespoon salt
65 g caster (superfine) sugar
1 cloves garlic, crushed
¼ teaspoon green Sichuan peppercorns
pinch of ground turmeric
½ cinnamon stick
5 black peppercorns
1 bay leaf
½ jalapeño, seeded
225 g fennel, thinly sliced

For the red-vinegar pickled radish:
65 ml Chinese red vinegar
25 g caster (superfine) sugar
5 g salt
200 g long red radishes, halved lengthways
½ long red chilli, deseeded

For the spicy pickled daikon:
85 ml rice vinegar
20 g caster (superfine) sugar
1 teaspoon salt
160 g daikon, peeled and diced
15 g garlic, peeled and crushed whole
½ bird's eye chilli, left whole
½ red chilli
½ jalapeño
12 g fresh ginger, sliced
50 g onion, sliced

Yellow pickled fennel

Combine all the ingredients except the fennel in a saucepan and bring to the boil, then remove from the heat and add the fennel. Leave to cool to room temperature.

Transfer the fennel and the pickling liquid to a 500 ml sterilized jar (see page 89), leaving a 1 cm (½ inch) head space, and seal.

The pickled fennel is ready to eat straight away but can also be transferred to the refrigerator and will taste even better after 2 days. It can be stored in the refrigerator or in a cool, dark place for up to 1 month. Once opened, keep in the refrigerator.

Red-vinegar pickled radish

Combine the vinegar, sugar and salt in a bowl, and stir until the sugar and salt have fully dissolved. Add all the remaining ingredients and transfer to a 500 ml sterilized jar (see page 89), leaving a 1 cm (½ inch) head space, and seal. Leave to pickle in the refrigerator or a cool, dark place for 1 day before using.

The pickled radish can be stored in the refrigerator or a cool, dark place for up to 1 month. Once opened, keep in the refrigerator.

Spicy pickled daikon

Combine the vinegar, sugar and salt in a bowl, and stir until the sugar and salt have fully dissolved. Add all the remaining ingredients and transfer to a 500 ml sterilized jar (see page 89), leaving a 1 cm (½ inch) head space, and seal. Leave to pickle in the refrigerator or a cool, dark place for 1 day before using.

The pickled daikon can be stored in the refrigerator or a cool, dark place for up to 1 week (the daikon will start to lose its texture and colour after 2 days but will still be really tasty). Once opened, keep in the refrigerator.

To assemble

Arrange a trio of pickles on a small dish, admiring the colours. Drizzle over a little of the pickled daikon liquor to finish.

Spinach with Tofu Sauce

A simple, light dish that is all about the balance – if you get this slightly off, it can taste either too bland or too strong. Beware, you'll need a lot of spinach as it shrinks when blanched. Blanched green leaves, *tang ching tsai*, are one of the most common side dishes in Taiwanese noodle shops. My favourite greens are sweet potato leaves, which while commonly eaten in Taiwan, unfortunately can't be found in England. Each noodle house makes their own unique dressing. Our dressing recipe is a combination of grassy olive oil, sesame oil, soy sauce and lemon juice. The silky mixture coats the delicate spinach, and the dish is finished with a creamy, salty tofu sauce.

Serves 4

For the spinach dressing:
3 tablespoons extra virgin olive oil (preferably a green and grassy one)
3 tablespoons whole bean soy sauce
5¼ teaspoons lemon juice
2¾ teaspoons sesame oil
25 g caster (superfine) sugar

For the sour tofu sauce:
30 g firm tofu, drained
15 g fermented white beancurd, drained
2 teaspoons lemon juice
4 teaspoons soy milk
pinch of salt
2 tablespoons rapeseed (canola) oil

To serve:
400 g baby spinach
120 ml spinach dressing
40 ml sour tofu sauce

Tip
Keeping the spinach dressing in a bottle in the refrigerator will help to keep it at the right consistency for the finished dish.

Spinach dressing

Whisk together all the ingredients in a small bowl until fully emulsified. Transfer to a sterilized glass bottle (see page 89) and store in the refrigerator for up to 3 days.

Sour tofu sauce

Put all the ingredients except the oil into a blender and blend to a smooth consistency. Gradually pour in the oil while the blender is still running, until all the oil is incorporated and the sauce is emulsified, shiny and has a similar thickness to yogurt.

There will be more sauce than is needed for this recipe, but it can be stored in an airtight container in the refrigerator for up to 3 days. It can be used as a sauce to eat with blanched vegetables, like asparagus.

To assemble

Bring a large saucepan of water to the boil and blanch the baby spinach for 10 seconds, then drain thoroughly.

Using a pair of chopsticks, arrange the blanched baby spinach in piles in 4 small, shallow bowls, then generously spoon over each serving 2 tablespoons of the spinach dressing and 1 teaspoon of the sour tofu sauce, so they drip gracefully from the top and down one side. Eat straight away.

Eel and Smacked Cucumber

Whenever I think of smacked cucumber salad, my mouth salivates. The perfect smacked cucumber is salted so that the moisture is drawn out from the cucumber, giving it a refreshing crunch. The secret of the dish lies in the garlic, which is rubbed onto the flesh. Make sure you crush the garlic well so the inside is exposed when you rub it over the cucumber – it definitely takes this simple dish to the next level.

We are always inspired by the produce we have in England and our twist on this refreshing classic is to pair it with a very British ingredient: smoked eel. The smoked eel has a creamy and salty quality similar to cured fat. You can usually find it at your local fishmonger.

Put the cucumber, cut sides down, onto a chopping (cutting) board and crush with the flat part of your knife. Rub the flesh side of the smacked cucumber with a generous sprinkle of salt and sugar and leave to macerate for 1 hour until the moisture is drawn out.

Rinse the salt and sugar off the cucumber and pat dry with paper towels. If you have the time, transfer to an airtight container and leave to sit in the refrigerator overnight, to draw more moisture out.

Rub the smashed garlic onto the flesh side of the cucumber pieces, then cut the cucumber into 2 cm (¾ inch) triangles and put into a bowl. Dress the cut cucumber with the tiger dressing, chilli oil, chilli oil bits and chopped coriander (cilantro).

To assemble

Slice the eel in half and remove any small bones, then cut into 1 cm (½ inch) slices. Scoop the eel and cucumber pieces into a serving bowl, piling the cucumber high and spooning over the dressing so that it pools around the cucumber.

Serves 2–3

½ cucumber (preferably ridged), halved lengthways and seeded
pinch of salt
pinch of sugar
1 clove garlic, smashed with the edge of a knife
180 ml Tiger Dressing (see page 229)
30 ml Sichuan Chilli Oil (see page 229)
40 g Sichuan Chilli Oil bits
1 tablespoon finely chopped coriander (cilantro) stalks
30 g smoked eel

Note
The chilli oil 'bits' are the blitzed chilli mix that sits at the bottom of the Sichuan oil.

Lu Rou Fan with Egg and Fish Floss Rice

Lu rou fan is a national Taiwanese dish and the ultimate comfort food. Before I ventured into food, I used to judge how good a xiao chi house was by their *lu rou fan* – even if it wasn't their main dish. Ours is inspired by the Tainan version that is sometimes served with a crispy egg and pork floss. Pork floss is a dried meat product seasoned with soy and sugar with a light and fluffy texture. I use it a lot on congee or eat it like a snack. You can't get pork floss here, so we substitute it with fish floss.

The fatty nature of the sauce means it coats the steamed rice perfectly. The key is to not render down the fat of the pork completely. We do this by first poaching the pork belly (side), then cutting it into small cubes and braising it for just the right amount of time. Sometimes it isn't just about how good the braise on the pork is, but the quality of the sauce on the grains of the rice. When Federico, our chef, cooked this dish up as a test, you could see the quality of the sauce by the sheen it took on. We both stood in the kitchen mesmerized by the glistening cubes of pork swimming in the soy braise and paid our respects by eating it.

刈包麵店

Serves 5

For the poached pork:
1 x 250-g pork belly (side)
10 ml Michiu rice wine or cooking sake
2 cm (¾ inch) piece of fresh ginger, crushed
½ clove garlic, crushed

For the braised pork:
¼ tablespoon rapeseed (canola) oil
¼ shallot, diced
1 tablespoon light soy sauce
1 dried red chilli
1 star anise
1½ teaspoons Shaoxing rice wine
¾ teaspoon mirin
1 clove garlic, crushed
¼ red apple, peeled, cored and diced
1 cm (½ inch) piece of fresh ginger, crushed
¼ spring onion (scallion), cut in half
¾ teaspoon rice vinegar
1 small cinnamon stick
¼ teaspoon dark soy sauce

For the rice:
375 g short-grain rice (preferably Chishang rice or Japanese sushi rice)
375 ml filtered water

To serve:
250 ml vegetable oil
5 eggs
5 Pickled Radishes (see page 192)
50 g fish floss (you can find this in Asian supermarkets)

Poached pork

Bring a deep saucepan of cold water and pork belly (side) to the boil. Once boiling, leave in the water for 5 minutes, then remove. Discard the water.

We do a two-stage cooking process for braising the pork. The first stage of gentle poaching makes the pork belly tender and resting it in the liquid lets it rehydrate so the pork belly is really moist. Put the pork belly, skin side down, into a deep saucepan and cover with cold water so that the pork is totally submerged, then add the wine, ginger and garlic. Bring to a boil, then lower the heat to the lowest setting and gently poach for about 20 minutes until the pork is firm and no longer pink and the skin is translucent. Remove the pan from the heat and leave the pork to cool and rest in the poaching liquid until the liquid is cooled or overnight.

When you're ready to braise, lift the cooled pork from the poaching liquid onto a chopping (cutting) board and strain the poaching liquid through a fine-mesh sieve into a measuring jug (large measuring cup). Cut the pork, skin on, into cubes. Keep the poaching liquid as it will be reused for braising.

Braised pork

Heat the oil in a flameproof casserole dish (Dutch oven) or clay pot, add the shallot and pork cubes and gently pan-fry until the shallot is soft and fragrant. Pour in 125 ml of the poaching liquid, then add the remaining ingredients, except for the dark soy sauce, and bring to the boil. Reduce the heat to low and leave to slowly braise, covered, for 2 hours, checking from time to time that the pork remains covered with liquid; if not, add more of the poaching liquid.

Take off the lid and increase the heat to medium, add the dark soy sauce and give it a good stir. Cook for about 20 minutes until the sauce has reduced to a light, sticky consistency. The fat from the belly should melt in the mouth, but the cubes should still maintain their shape; the braising liquid should be drinkable, not overly sticky or salty but glistening with a thin layer of fat on top, and shiny and golden brown in colour. At this stage, you can pick out the spices and discard.

Rice

An hour before serving, wash the rice thoroughly, 3 times, then tip the rice into a bowl, cover with cold water and leave to soak for 30 minutes.

Pour the filtered water into a saucepan and bring to the boil. Drain the soaked rice and add to the boiling water. When the water is boiling again, put a lid on, reduce the heat to low and cook for 18 minutes. Open the lid to check that the rice is cooked and ever-so-slightly glistening but not wet. Put the lid back on, remove from the heat and leave the rice to rest for 10 minutes before serving (this process allows the remaining steam to absorb back into the grains, resulting in fluffy and bouncy rice). At no point remove the lid from the pan.

To assemble

Heat the oil in a small frying pan (skillet) or wok over a high heat. Crack 1 egg into the pan and fry until the edges bubble and crisp up but the yolk is still runny. Remove from the pan and keep warm. Repeat with the remaining eggs, reusing the oil for each egg.

For each serving, wet a rice paddle or spatula with a little water, then gently scoop out a fifth of the rice into a small, shallow bowl. Ladle over 50 g of the braised pork cubes to one side, leaving room for a radish and the fish floss. Drizzle with some of the braising liquid so that the pork is covered and some of the rice is flavoured, but not so much as to make the rice swim in it. Garnish with 1 pickled radish on the inner rim of the bowl and 2 teaspoons of fish floss, then top with a crispy egg.

Crispy Tripe

Tripe is common in Asia, although it is often slow-braised or served cold to give it a bouncy 'QQ' (an Asian term for bouncy-chewy). While I have lots of good memories of tripe, it isn't an easy sell in England, but I love turning offal (variety meats) into something that people find irresistibly moreish once they eat it. The spice mix plays a big role in that – sprinkle it over anything and you'll make it addictive. We have already converted many people, some declaring tripe the best thing they have ever eaten. One person even told us it works as a hangover cure, and another that it was 'like crack'. Enjoy this crispy tripe like you would crisps (chips), washed down with an ice-cold Taiwan Beer.

The tripe needs to be braised at least one day before you want to serve the crispy tripe.

Serves 3

For the braised tripe:
300 g tripe
50 ml rice vinegar
2 teaspoons salt
1 tablespoon vegetable oil
1 star anise
1 cinnamon stick
½ teaspoon red Sichuan peppercorns
5 dried red chillies
50 g fresh ginger, peeled and sliced
3 cloves garlic
25 ml Shaoxing rice wine
125 ml light soy sauce
25 g spring onions (scallions), cut in half
15 g rock sugar

For the spice mix:
2 teaspoons five spice powder
20 g caster (superfine) sugar
2 teaspoons citric acid
20 g onion powder
2 teaspoons smoked paprika
15 g ground white pepper
2 teaspoons ground black pepper
1 teaspoon salt
¾ teaspoon ground star anise

To serve:
vegetable oil, for deep-frying
60 g cornflour (cornstarch)
3 tablespoons Spring Onion Tofu (see page 229)

Braised tripe

First, you need to wash and blanch the tripe to remove some of the strong offal (variety meat) flavour. Put the tripe into a large saucepan, add the vinegar and salt and mix thoroughly with your hands, almost like you are scrubbing the tripe. Cover with water and bring to the boil, then drain.

Preheat the oven to 150°C/300°F/Gas Mark 2. Heat the oil in a flameproof casserole dish (Dutch oven), add the star anise, cinnamon stick, Sichuan peppercorns, dried chillies, ginger and garlic and cook until fragrant. Add the blanched tripe, then pour in the Shaoxing wine and stir to deglaze the pan, scraping up any residue from the bottom. Add the soy sauce, spring onions (scallions), rock sugar and 1 litre water. Put the lid on the dish, transfer to the oven and cook for 2½ hours.

Remove from the oven and leave the tripe to cool in the braising liquid in the refrigerator overnight. Any tripe you don't want to cook the following day can be kept in the braising liquid in the refrigerator for up to 3 days.

Spice Mix

The next day, mix together all the ingredients for the spice mix in a small bowl. You'll only need 6 teaspoons of spice mix for this recipe, the remaining mix can be stored in an airtight container in a cool, dark cupboard for up to 1 month.

To assemble

Heat the oil in a deep, heavy-based saucepan to 180°C/350°F, or until a cube of ginger sizzles and browns in 10 seconds.

Remove the tripe from the braising liquid and smooth it out flat on a chopping (cutting) board. Cut it into thin slices at an angle, then dredge with the cornflour (cornstarch), making sure it is evenly coated. Working in batches, carefully place 1 serving of 100 g tripe into the hot oil and deep-fry for 2–3 minutes until crisp and golden, then remove with a slotted spoon and drain on paper towels. Toss the drained, crispy tripe with 2 teaspoons of the spice mix, making sure the seasoning is evenly distributed. Repeat with the remaining tripe.

Divide the crispy tripe among 3 bowls and serve each with 1 tablespoon of the spring onion tofu on the side.

刈包麵店

Fried Ogleshield Cheese Rolls

We have long been fans of Neal's Yard Dairy, who support and champion the highest-quality cheese across the British Isles. We wanted to use the Ogleshield cheese they sell in a dish, as it has a great melting quality and such a complex flavour. Our Fried Ogleshield Cheese Rolls were born when we opened BAO Noodle Shop. Wrapped in a spring (egg) roll casing and studded with hits of soy-pickled chilli, their appearance seems simple and inexpensive, but the great produce makes this dish.

Serves 5

50 g plain (all-purpose) flour
5 x 21.5 × 21.5 cm (8.5 × 8.5 inch) square spring (egg) roll wrappers
140 g Ogleshield cheese, cut into twenty 9 × 1.5 cm (3½ × ⅝ inch) pieces
30 pieces of Soy-pickled Chillies (see page 231)
vegetable oil, for deep-frying

To serve:
30 g Ogleshield cheese, grated
30 g Pickled Plum Ketchup (see page 231)
30 g Green Sauce (see page 230)

Mix together the flour with 50 ml water in a small bowl – this will be the 'wrapper glue' to seal the rolls.

Cut 1 spring (egg) roll wrapper in half to make 2 triangles. Lay 1 triangle on a board with the long edge nearest you and the point furthest away. Place a piece of cheese at the bottom of the triangle, along the long edge, then top with 3 pieces of soy-pickled chillies and place another piece of cheese on top. Brush the flour and water 'glue' over the edges of the wrapper and fold in the sides so they sit snugly against the cheese. Roll the cheese up and seal the loose tip. Repeat with the second triangle and with the remaining wrappers, cheese and chilli pieces.

Heat the oil in a deep, heavy-based saucepan to 180°C/350°F, or until a cube of ginger sizzles and browns in 10 seconds. Carefully place the cheese rolls, 5 at a time, in the hot oil and deep-fry for 2 minutes, or until crisp and golden. Use a slotted spoon to press the rolls down into the oil so they are submerged while deep-frying, to ensure an even colour. Remove with the slotted spoon and drain on paper towels.

Divide the rolls among 5 plates, sprinkle with the grated cheese and serve with the sauces together on a small plate.

Cull Yaw Dumplings

There is something very comforting about a no-frills boiled dumpling. So plain and simple yet so delicious and heart-warming, especially when steaming hot.

Sourcing a medium-high protein flour from Taiwan (see page 182) was important for this recipe, so that the dumpling skin would have a good bite and the perfect bounce once cooked. Mutton is not a very Taiwanese filling for dumplings, but we knew we wanted to use the minced (ground) cull yaw from Matt Chatfield, the Cornish farmer behind The Cornwall Project (see page 33). It's the quality of the meat that makes a real difference to these dumplings, injecting so much flavour into a single bite.

The *hong you* (red chilli oil) dressing is a classic accompaniment that vendors perfect in their own ways, choosing the balance between spicy, sweet and sour. Ours is spicy and acidic and works well with peppery spring onions (scallions) and diced onion. Make sure you toss the dumplings with the dressing and herbs properly to get the perfect bite with each dumpling.

Any dumplings you don't eat can be frozen and kept for another day (boil them for 6 minutes if cooking from frozen).

刈包麵店

Makes about 25 dumplings

For the dumpling dough:
175 g 12–13% protein noodle or dumpling flour, plus extra
for dusting
pinch of salt
60 ml hot water
50 ml cold filtered water

For the cull yaw filling:
200 g minced (ground) cull yaw (or use lamb)
⅓ teaspoon ground black pepper
⅓ teaspoon ground white pepper
⅓ teaspoon ground cumin
⅔ teaspoon salt
1 tablespoon premium soy sauce
1¼ teaspoons vegetable oil
½ teaspoon sesame oil
65 ml chicken or pork stock (broth)
80 g onion, finely diced

For the dumpling dressing:
70 ml Chinkiang black rice vinegar
45 ml whole bean soy sauce
45 ml mirin

To serve:
3 spring onions (scallions), finely sliced
50 g onion, finely diced
5 teaspoons Sichuan Chilli Oil (see page 229)

Dumpling dough

Combine the flour and salt in a large bowl, then add the hot water, stirring with chopsticks. Add the cold filtered water and stir again until loosely combined, then tip the dough out onto a lightly floured work counter and knead until smooth. The dough will be crumbly at first, but it will become smooth and soft after some persistence–don't be tempted to add any more water. Wrap the dough in cling film (plastic wrap) and leave to rest at room temperature for 2 hours.

Cull yaw filling

Combine all the ingredients except the stock (broth) and onion in a bowl. Using your hand to mix in one direction, gradually add the stock until it is completely absorbed. The meat mixture should be sticky and have resistance. You want to break down the proteins in the meat so that it does not taste mealy and instead has a smooth and bouncy mouthfeel when you eat it. You'll know this has happened when the white streaks of fat in the lamb mince are no longer distinct from the meat itself, so don't be afraid to mix longer than you might normally think to.

Add the diced onion and mix well to ensure it is evenly dispersed through the meat. Try to make the dumplings fresh before using rather than pre-preparing.

Dumpling dressing

Whisk the ingredients together in a small bowl.

To assemble

Unwrap the dough and roll out into a long sausage shape, then divide into 7 g dough balls. Dust a baking sheet, a rolling pin and the work counter generously with flour, then roll out the dough balls into 7 cm (2¾ inch) discs (skins).

Wet a butter knife and scoop out about 12 g of cull yaw filling onto a dumpling skin. Fold the skin in half to cover the filling and press the sides together. You shouldn't need water to close the dumplings as the moisture from the fresh dough will be enough, but if you had stored the discs or used too much dusting flour, then you can use a dab of water. Transfer to the prepared baking sheet and repeat with the remaining skins and filling.

Bring a large saucepan of water to the boil and drop in the dumplings one by one. Make sure you cook the dumplings in small batches so they have room to bounce around happily. Cook for 4 minutes, or until all the dumplings float to the surface of the water. Remove with a slotted spoon and keep warm.

Spoon the dressing and Sichuan chilli oil into the bottom 5 bowls, then place 5 steaming hot dumplings into each bowl, and garnish with the spring onions (scallions) and onion. Serve with the chilli oil.

BAO Drinks

I can't talk about BAO drinks without providing some background on foams – it was the milk foam tea that set us on the pathway to mastering this craft. When Shing and Wai Ting travelled to Taiwan, I had to bring them to Tainan, the food capital in the south of Taiwan, to visit an unassuming foam tea shop on the corner of the main roundabout. The idea of super-smooth sweet foam on top of cold-brewed tea makes so much sense but at the same time it was something completely new and original to them. This was how Dream Drinks (our range of drinks using Asian ingredients and many innovative foams) was born. They are *dreamy* and visually hypnotic, the foam slowly dissolving into the drink or the syrupy gradient swaying like a lava lamp. They are also nostalgic, because the ingredients we use nod to our favourite childhood drinks in Asia – the Yakult in the foam tea or the grape flavour of the grapeade – and are presented in glassware that make you feel like you're a child again.

You will find a variety of foams in the following recipes. For that reason, it is highly recommended to purchase a whipped cream dispenser and chargers to create them. The same effect can't be achieved by whisking or whipping. The resulting foams can be used in desserts or hot drinks.

Foam can be stored in the whipped cream dispenser for a day in the refrigerator. I recommend experimenting with it – try using it for a sweet treat with fresh fruit.

Foam dispensing is something that takes years of practice in order to get the perfect gloss and shine, just soft enough that the foam sinks slowly into the drink. We call anyone who has mastered this while working at BAO a 'Foam Lord'.

Foams

The Yakult Foam

2 bottles of Yakult (130 ml)
50 ml double (heavy) cream
26 ml sugar syrup
3 g egg white

Mix all the ingredients together, pour into a whipped cream dispenser and charge with a CO_2 charger.

The Aloe Foam

150 ml aloe vera juice (such as Aloe King, available from Asian supermarkets)
1 egg white

Mix both the ingredients together, pour into a whipped cream dispenser and charge with a CO_2 charger.

The Milk Foam

133 ml milk
123 ml double (heavy) cream
23 ml sugar syrup
3 ml good quality vanilla extract
1 egg white

Mix all the ingredients together, pour into a whipped cream dispenser and charge with a CO_2 charger.

Tips for achieving the perfect foam:

1. Always do a test squirt into another vessel first.
2. Try to keep your hands as steady as possible.
3. Give the bottle a shake if the foam is too loose.
4. If the texture is still too loose after shaking, you may need to chill it for a little while before using.

For the true Lonely Man – the freezer cocktail:

1. Make or purchase one of our cocktail rescue pouches (see Convni page 233).
2. Store in the freezer.
3. Wait until you feel the need for a cheeky cocktail.
4. Put a glass in the refrigerator or freezer to chill.
5. Pour your patiently waiting frozen cocktail into the glass.

MILK FOAM.

CONDENSED MILK FOAM.

CHING JI FRUITS, TAINAN.

THE BAO HI.

PREPARING THE FROZEN LEMON TOWER.

BAO HI

This drink was inspired by the memory of a Japanese businessman who sat next to us in a yakitori bar in Osaka. He sat down, ordered a draught beer and downed it in one go, then ordered a *chuhai* (a highball drink made with shochu and soda water/club soda), and had a grilled skewer delivered to him straight after. A perfect Lonely Man experience. It was this feeling of finishing work and just being so happy to drink and eat a grilled skewer that we wanted to re-create at BAO Borough, where the menu is inspired by the grill joints from our travels.

There are some crazy fruit bars in Japan, as well as in Taiwan, where the fruit stalls are such a big part of our culture – you can order fruit to be served simply on a plate, ready to eat, or have it blended into a drink. I miss the fruit from Taiwan so much. We created our range of BAO HI drinks with the idea of showcasing British seasonal fruit in a highball format, combining two memories from different places. The BAO HI is our classic drink, with a frozen lemon tower that is so OTT it hits you in the forehead when you take a sip.

This recipe makes more cordial than you need for the BAO HI, but it tastes great with tonic water as a refreshing pick-me-up whenever you need one, and will keep in the refrigerator for up to 1 week or in the freezer for up to 6 months.

You will need to make the lemon towers in advance so that they are completely frozen by the time you make the cocktail. For those feeling lazy you can buy them from our online store.

Serves 4

For the lemon towers:
4 lemons

For the salted citrus cordial:
50 ml lemon juice
50 ml lime juice
100 g caster (superfine) sugar
1 teaspoon citric acid
pinch of salt

For the BAO HI mix:
1 teaspoon peach bitters
125 ml Toki whisky (or other Japanese whisky)
72 ml salted citrus cordial (see above)

To serve:
ice cubes, as needed
400 ml soda water (club soda)

 VE

Tip
If you're not in a rush, before making the cordial you can peel the lemons and limes and mix the peel with the sugar for a while. The longer you leave the sugar and peel together the more citrus flavour will leech into the sugar. When you're ready to make the cordial, just pick the peel out and use the sugar as normal.

Lemon towers

Using a mandoline, slice the lemons thinly into 5 mm (¼ inch) slices.

Lay 4 sheets of cling film (plastic wrap) on the work counter and lay the lemon slices in a vertical line on each one, overlapping one another. Fold the cling film over the lemons so they are fully covered, then freeze flat overnight.

Salted citrus cordial

Combine all the ingredients in a measuring jug (large measuring cup).

BAO HI mix

Combine the peach bitters, whisky and 72 ml of the salted citrus cordial in a jug (pitcher).

To assemble

Fill 4 highball glasses with ice. Combine the BAO Hi mix with the soda water (club soda), then divide among the glasses.

Remove the lemon towers from the freezer and remove the cling film from each one, then place them in the glasses so they stand up out of the drinks.

Peanut Milk

Before going into the recipe, I have to first give a shout out to the peanut-milk man who visits weekly and has a must-order of peanut milk. If it's sold out, he won't come in. He visits BAO Soho to taste the quality of the peanut milk and tells them it's not as good as at Fitz.

This is a much-loved recipe that we have been making almost daily at all the BAO restaurants, right from the beginning. It is not your typical healthy nut milk; in fact, it's the opposite. The milk is infused with sugar, vanilla and roasted peanuts. We have two recipes: the OG version with a milky cream base and the vegan version made with oat milk. Even if you consume dairy, both are delicious. The OG is a bit richer and more indulgent; you savour every sip and it feels like a nourishing shot. The oat-milk version, given below, is silky smooth, but if you want to do dairy, just swap the oat milk and oat cream for cow's milk and double (heavy) cream. If making the dairy version, serve it in small stubby glasses over a cube of ice.

Serves 3

125 g skinned peanuts (groundnuts)
½ vanilla pod (bean), split open and seeds scraped out
270 ml oat milk
25 g light muscovado sugar
100 ml oat cream
ice cubes, to serve

Preheat the oven to 180°C/350°F/Gas Mark 4. Spread out the peanuts (groundnuts) on a baking sheet and toast in the oven for 8–10 minutes until golden brown, being careful they don't burn. Transfer to a food processor and process to a coarse powder (it is best to do this in batches because peanuts have a high fat content and can very easily turn into peanut butter in no time).

Combine the powdered peanuts with 120 ml water in a medium saucepan, then add the remaining ingredients except the ice and cook over a low heat for 45–60 minutes, stirring regularly so the peanuts do not catch on the bottom of the pan and burn, and checking to make sure the mixture doesn't boil over.

Strain the mixture through a fine-mesh sieve or muslin (cheesecloth) into a jug (pitcher), then leave to cool. Chill in the refrigerator until ready to drink – up to 2 days.

To serve, fill 3 tall glasses with ice cubes, then pour over the peanut milk.

QQ HI

This was one of those 'Wow, that is tasty!' moments, which happened the night before we opened BAO Borough. Cameron Flynn, our beverage manager, was playing around with some of the ingredients we had to hand and had the idea of a lager shandy made with grape cordial and topped with aloe vera foam. The hypnotic gradient colours of the grape cordial and the beer topped with the glossy aloe foam made it instantly iconic. When it was presented to me, I took a sip and immediately knew it was going on the menu. Super tasty and fun.

Serves 1

25 ml Grape Cordial (see page 221)
330 ml Taiwan Beer (or light lager)
20 ml Aloe Foam (see page 210)

Place a tall beer mug in the freezer to chill, then remove and pour in the grape cordial. Top up (off) slowly with the beer. Dispense the foam onto the surface of the drink using a circular motion and working from the outer rim of the glass to the middle, ending with a peak.

Melon Floatini

A trip to Osaka really cemented my love of the plastic models of food and drink that are seen on display in café windows in Japan. There was a melon soda ice cream float that would always feature in these window displays, and we took it as inspiration for our own vivid green drink. Instead of topping it with ice cream we paired it with milk foam for a lighter, more drinkable experience. I still remember when we first opened BAO King's Cross and I saw a table of four grown-up men each order this drink; they then sat sipping and indulging in a drink that nods back to childhood. That was a perfect little moment.

Serves 1

25 ml Toki whisky (or other Japanese whisky)
25 ml Midori melon liqueur
50 ml soda water (club soda)
3–4 ice cubes
20 ml Milk Foam (see page 210)
1 glacé (candied) cherry

Pour the whisky and Midori into a hurricane glass, top up (off) with the soda water (club soda) and stir, then add the ice cubes. Dispense the milk foam onto the surface of the drink using a circular motion and working from the outer rim of the glass to the middle, ending with a peak. Garnish with the glacé (candied) cherry for the ultimate retro *kissaten* look.

包飲品

Melon Sour

This is my go-to drink after work at BAO Borough – I always make sure they make it in my special glass with a squiggly glass stem that is kept behind the bar. The drink transports me back to drinking melon soda as a child, but now I need something alcoholic, so the Midori does the job.

Serves 1

For the miso syrup:
10 g white miso
160 g caster (superfine) sugar
85 ml filtered water

Melon sour pre-mix:
10 ml white miso syrup (see above)
10 ml Somerset apple eau de vie
30 ml dry gin
30 ml Midori melon liqueur

To serve:
25 ml lemon juice
25 ml aquafaba (the liquid from canned chickpeas)
ice cubes, as needed
1 maraschino cherry

Put a Martini glass into the freezer to chill.

White miso syrup

Put all the ingredients into a blender and blend at high speed for 20 seconds. There will be more syrup than is needed for this recipe, but it can be stored in a sterilized glass jar (see page 89) in the refrigerator for up to 1 month.

To assemble

Fill a cocktail shaker with all of the melon sour pre-mix ingredients, the lemon juice and aquafaba, then top up (off) with ice cubes. Shake well. Remove the ice by straining the mixture through a cocktail strainer. Return the liquid to the cocktail shaker and dry shake with no ice. Pour through a cocktail strainer into the chilled Martini glass and garnish with the maraschino cherry on the rim of the glass.

Yakult Float

Yakult takes me back to my childhood; I used to freeze it and eat it like a lollipop. Koji-fermented pineapple is classically used in Taiwan with steamed fish. I loved the idea of having a pineapple soda with fermented notes. Instead of fermenting pineapple, we add a touch of vinegar to give a similar effect. The Yakult foam was created through all our experiments with foam making. It adds such a nice acidity and lightness to the drink. It is sweet but savoury with the sea salt and 'fermented' pineapple juice.

Serves 2

For the pineapple syrup:
30 ml pineapple juice
30 g caster (superfine) sugar
½ teaspoon cider vinegar

For the Yakult foam:
2 x 65 ml bottles Yakult
50 ml double (heavy) cream
25 ml sugar syrup
1 egg white

To serve:
4 ice cubes
30 ml lemon juice
160 ml soda water (club soda)
pinch of salt

Pineapple syrup

Combine all the ingredients in a small saucepan and heat gently over a low-medium heat until the sugar has dissolved. Remove from the heat and leave to cool.

Yakult foam

Combine all the ingredients in a jug (pitcher), then pour into a whipped cream dispenser. Charge with a CO_2 charger. The quantity of Yakult foam made is more than required for this recipe, but it will keep for a day in the refrigerator and is great served with macerated strawberries as a dessert.

To assemble

Fill 2 stemmed glasses with the ice. Pour the pineapple syrup into a jug (pitcher), add the lemon juice and soda water (club soda) and mix together, then pour into the glasses. Dispense about 20 ml of the foam onto the surface of each drink using a circular motion and working from the outer rim of the glass to the middle, ending with a peak. Sprinkle the salt on top of the foam from as high as you can to make sure it is evenly dispersed.

Grapeade

My love of Asian grape-flavour Hi-Chew sweets (candy) inspired this drink. The grape cordial combined with the aloe vera juice tastes like chewing bubble gum. Fun and tasty! It takes you straight back to Asia, but at the same time you know you would not be able to get this in Asia, because it is our own special invention!

Serves 2

For the grape cordial:
45 ml grape juice
40 g caster (superfine) sugar
2 g citric acid
2 g tartaric acid

For the aloe foam:
150 ml aloe vera juice (such as Aloe King, available from Asian supermarkets)
1 egg white

To serve:
4 ice cubes
250 ml soda water (club soda)
2 drops vanilla extract

Grape cordial

Combine all the ingredients in a small saucepan and heat gently over a low heat until the sugar has dissolved. Remove from the heat and leave to cool.

Aloe foam

Combine both the ingredients in a jug (pitcher), then pour into a whipped cream dispenser. Charge with a CO_2 charger.

To assemble

Fill 2 tall glasses with the ice. Pour 60 ml of the grape cordial into a jug (pitcher), add the soda water (club soda) and vanilla extract and mix together, then divide between the glasses. Dispense about 20 ml of the foam onto the surface of each drink using a circular motion and working from the outer rims of the glasses to the middle, ending with a peak.

Sweet Potato Sour

This was created with Mr Lyan, Ryan Chetiyawardana, the cocktail bartender and owner of the bars Super Lyan, Lyaness and Seed Library, and it is now a BAO classic. The shape of Taiwan is sometimes likened to the shape of a sweet potato, and that was where the idea came from for this cocktail. The sweet potato gives the cocktail a rich mouthfeel, while the flavour of the sweet potato is quite mild.

We recommend using a Vitamix or Thermomix to make an extra-smooth sweet potato purée.

Serves 2

For the sweet potato purée:
70 g sweet potato, peeled and cut into 2.5 cm
(1 inch) cubes
25 g caster (superfine) sugar

For the sweet potato pre-mix:
75 ml dry gin
15 ml apricot liqueur
15 ml chestnut liqueur

To serve:
30 ml lemon juice
30 ml egg white
ice cubes, as needed
long pepper, grated

Sweet potato purée

Bring a large saucepan of water to the boil, add the sweet potato and cook for about 12 minutes until soft.

Meanwhile, make a sugar syrup. Combine the sugar with 20 ml water in a small saucepan and heat over a low heat until the sugar has dissolved.

Drain the sweet potato, then transfer to a blender, add the sugar syrup and blend until smooth. Transfer to a bowl, then chill the purée in the refrigerator until cool.

Sweet potato pre-mix

Combine all the ingredients in a measuring jug (large measuring cup) and mix well.

To assemble

Put 70 ml of the sweet potato purée, 110 ml of the sweet potato pre-mix, the lemon juice and egg white into a cocktail shaker and shake well to mix. Take off the lid, fill with ice cubes, put the lid back on and shake again.

Fill 2 rocks glasses with ice, then strain the cocktail through a cocktail strainer and a fine-mesh sieve into the glasses. Grate a little long pepper over the top to finish.

Iron Shake

The classic hand-shaken drink from the tea shops in Taiwan, which came before bubble tea, is called *pao mo hong cha*, meaning 'foam tea'. We love that the drink looks like Guinness, which is why it is served in a beer glass. Traditionally it is made with a Taiwanese black tea sweetened with sugar syrup and shaken with ice to create a foamy head. For our version, we decided to combine classic British 'builder's brew' tea, which gives body, with Taiwanese Tie Guan Yin tea leaves, which add complexity and a smoky flavour. A complementary malty flavour comes from a Taiwanese roasted brown sugar called *heitang* – you can find it at Asian supermarkets. This is one of my favourite drinks and it's incredible that it creates foam without any added egg white or aquafaba (canned chickpea/garbanzo bean liquid). You just have to shake REALLY hard!

Serves 2

1 teaspoon Tie Guan Yin tea leaves
3 black tea bags (we use PG Tips)
600 ml filtered water
ice cubes, as needed

For the salted heitang syrup:
65 g heitang sugar (or dark muscovado sugar)
¼ teaspoon salt
30 ml filtered water

Put the tea leaves, tea bags and filtered water into a jug (pitcher) or glass bottle. Cover and leave to steep in the refrigerator for 24 hours.

<u>Salted heitang syrup</u>

Combine all the ingredients in a small saucepan and heat over a low heat until the sugar and salt have dissolved. The mixture should be syrupy. Leave to cool. This makes more syrup than needed for this drink, but it would be great over the Horlicks Ice Cream (see page 73). It will keep in a sealed sterilized jar (see page 89) at room temperature for up to 1 month.

<u>To assemble</u>

The next day, strain the tea into a jug and discard the tea leaves and bags. Add 45 ml of the salted heitang syrup, then pour 620 ml of the tea into a cocktail shaker and fill with ice cubes. Shake vigorously, then strain through a cocktail strainer into 2 beer glasses.

Milk Foam Tea

There is such a rich tradition of tea culture in Taiwan, but recently there has been a lot of innovation in the tea industry, the most famous being bubble tea (made with tapioca pearls). I remember first trying the milk foam tea (a cold-brew tea with a foam on top) from a tea shop in Tainan. The contrast of the clean, beautiful-tasting cold-brew oolong with the creamy foam on top was magical. The texture feels like you are drinking a beer (Japanese beer particularly). The key to this drink is the quality of the tea used. We have a special relationship with a teahouse in Taipei that my late grandfather used to visit every day (see page 107). He would sit there and drink tea while he waited for me to finish school and then come and pick me up. This is where we source all of our tea from. This recipe is trying to re-create that memory of first tasting milk foam tea on a hot sweaty summer's day in Tainan.

Serves 8

For the cold-brew tea:
18 g Baozhong oolong tea leaves
1 litre cold filtered water
50 ml sugar syrup
ice cubes, to serve

For the milk foam:
133 ml milk
123 ml double (heavy) cream
23 ml sugar syrup
½ teaspoon vanilla extract
1 egg white

Cold-brew tea

Combine the tea leaves and filtered water in a jug (pitcher) or glass bottle, stir or shake well and refrigerate for 24 hours.

Strain the tea into a clean jug or glass bottle, discard the tea leaves, then add the sugar syrup. The flavour should be floral and light and not overly sweet, so taste as you add the syrup to make sure it doesn't overpower the subtle flavours of the tea. The tea can be stored in the refrigerator for up to 1 week.

Milk foam

Combine all the ingredients in a measuring jug (large measuring cup), then pour into a whipped cream dispenser. Charge with a CO_2 charger. The foam can be stored in the dispenser for a day in the refrigerator.

To assemble

Fill 8 tall, thin glasses with ice and top up (off) each with 125 ml of the cold-brew tea. Dispense the milk foam onto the surface of the drinks so it sits flush with the top of the glasses. Smooth any excess with a palette knife (frosting spatula), making sure the top and edges of the glasses are clean.

BAO Larder

Fermented Chillies

These chillies take at least 2 weeks to ferment and can be made with either red or green chillies.

Makes 100 g

100 g mild red or green chillies, coarsely chopped
salt, as needed (see method)

Cut the heads off the chillies and chop finely. Weigh the chopped chillies, then transfer to a bowl and mix thoroughly with 2 per cent of their total weight in salt.

Transfer to a sterilized glass jar (see page 89), leaving a 1 cm (½ inch) head space, and seal. Leave to ferment in a cool, dry and dark place for 2 weeks before using. Make sure to 'burp' the jar every night by opening the lid momentarily – this will release the gasses and ensure that the jar doesn't explode!

Once fermented, the chillies can be stored in the refrigerator for up to 3 months

Peanut Powder

This powder is great sprinkled on pork or used as a garnish for the Peanut Ice Cream Roon Bing (see page 125) or Pig's Blood Cake (see page 95).

Makes 200 g

200 g shelled peanuts (groundnuts)
2 tablespoons caster (superfine) sugar

Preheat the oven to 180°C/350°F/Gas Mark 4. Spread out the shelled peanuts (groundnuts) on a baking sheet and roast in the oven for 20–25 minutes, or until golden. Shake the tray or turn the peanuts every 5 minutes to ensure an even colour. Remove from the oven and leave to cool completely.

Transfer the peanuts, in small batches, to a food processor and pulse until you have a coarse powder (it is best to do this in batches because peanuts have a high fat content and can very easily turn into peanut butter in no time).

Tip the peanut powder into a bowl, add the sugar and mix thoroughly until well combined. The peanut powder can be stored in a jar in the refrigerator for up to 1 month.

Soy-cured Egg Yolk

This cured egg yolk started off as a topping for the Pig's Blood Cake (see page 95), but since then it has been a constant across all our menus. At first, when we opened a new restaurant, we tried to avoid using it, but then we thought, 'Screw that!' and made cured egg yolk a mainstay in them all. There will never be a BAO restaurant without cured egg yolks, and therefore there will always be a group of angry chefs who have to painstakingly crack and separate the eggs daily. We have provided the method for making one cured egg yolk, but this can easily be scaled up depending on how many you need to make.

Makes 1 soy-cured egg yolk

50 ml mirin
35 ml light soy sauce
15 ml dark soy sauce
1 egg yolk

Mix together all the liquid ingredients in a small bowl, then carefully lower in the egg yolk and leave to cure for 10 minutes.

Tip

When preparing the egg yolk, make sure to remove all the egg white as well as the cloudy placenta. Hold the yolk gently in your fingers as you separate off the egg white and use the side of the index and middle finger to cut away the small chalaza as you do so.

Salted Duck Eggs

If you want to make your own salted duck eggs, it takes about a month.

Makes 12 salted eggs

12 duck eggs
250 g salt
50 g alcohol above 40% abv, *kao liang* wine or my mother-in-law uses brandy

Clean the duck eggs thoroughly in cold water, checking for any cracks in the shells (it's important that there are no cracks). Dry the eggs properly then place them in a glass jar, or any container.

In a saucepan bring 1 litre of water to the boil, then switch off the heat, add the salt and stir to dissolve. Allow the brine to cool to room temperature. Add the alcohol when the salted water is completely cool.

Pour the cooled brine into the jar and make sure it is sufficient to fully cover the eggs. Half-fill a zip-lock bag with water and place it on top of the eggs to make sure they are totally submerged. Cover the jar with a lid and store at room temperature for a month. From day 25, you can taste-test an egg and decide if you want to keep brining. Once you are happy, take the eggs out of the brine, wash in cold water and keep in an airtight container in the refrigerator for up to 10 days. To keep them for longer, bring your brine to the boil, then cool completely, add fresh alcohol and store the cooked eggs in this liquid in an airtight container. Keep in the fridge for up to 1 month.

Crispy Shallots

At BAO Soho, it's a rite of passage for all the chefs de partie on the BAO section to ruin the shallots. While it may seem like a simple task, it takes a lot of practice. Leave the shallots in the oil a moment too long and they will burn. Pull them too early and they'll be soggy. If the oil isn't hot enough, you'll caramelize the shallots rather than make them crispy. Use too much oil and it might jump out of the pot when it starts bubbling and go all over the walls. Many talented chefs have come through BAO Soho and been momentarily humbled by the shallots. If you want to avoid all that, you can buy crispy shallots from South East Asian supermarkets.

Traditionally Thai shallots are used, but we use banana shallots as we like the longer squiggly shapes that they form. If you can get hold of Thai shallots, by all means use them as they are more fragrant and punchy with flavour. However, they form smaller shapes and won't give you the same volume.

Makes 40 g

1 litre rapeseed (canola) oil
5 banana shallots, very finely sliced

Heat the oil in a deep, heavy-based saucepan to 160°C/325°F, or until a cube of ginger sizzles and browns in 20 seconds, then turn off the heat momentarily and add the sliced shallots using a slotted spoon. As soon as they are in the oil and it is bubbling furiously, turn the heat back on. The shallots are done when they are golden brown, they start to become rigid in the oil and they have floated to the surface (they will continue to cook once you remove them from the oil so don't overcook them). Remove them with the slotted spoon and drain on paper towels, then sprinkle them sparingly with salt to season. The shallots can be stored in an airtight container in a cool, dry place for up to 2 weeks.

包食材櫃

Ginger Spring Onion Oil

Ginger Spring Onion Oil is the holy dip of Asian cooking, and is great with poached chicken, steamed fish or even simply mixed into plain noodles. It is a painstaking task to make huge volumes of it in the restaurants, but the effort is worth it as it lifts everything.

Makes 150 ml

100 ml rapeseed (canola) oil
90 g fresh ginger, finely chopped
40 g spring onions (scallions), white parts only, finely chopped
1 clove garlic, finely chopped
caster (superfine) sugar, to taste
salt

Heat the oil in a frying pan (skillet) over a high heat until hot, then add the ginger, spring onions (scallions) and garlic, and cook for 5–10 seconds. Remove from the heat and season heavily with sugar and salt to taste.

Spring Onion Tofu

A sweet-sour, oniony, creamy dip, we use this as a sauce for pickles to soften their acidity.

Makes 200 ml

90 g silken tofu
½ clove garlic
2 teaspoons rice vinegar
¼ teaspoon salt
pinch of ground white pepper
¼ teaspoon caster (superfine) sugar
90 g spring onions (scallions), coarsely chopped
20 ml rapeseed (canola) oil

Put all the ingredients into a blender and blend at high speed until very smooth and a pleasing bright green colour. The tofu can be stored in an airtight container in the refrigerator for up to 2 days.

Black Garlic Glaze

This might be the most expensive sauce we make as black garlic isn't cheap, but we just love it. It's like a turbocharged soy glaze with sweet and sour notes.

Makes 115 ml

2 tablespoons premium soy sauce
35 ml vegetarian oyster sauce
½ teaspoon smoked paprika
2 cloves garlic, grated
1 tablespoon rice vinegar
1½ teaspoons Taiwanese red rice vinegar
2 tablespoons mirin
15 g Fermented Chillies (see page 228)
25 g black garlic

Put all the ingredients into a blender and blend to a paste. Add a little water to loosen the sauce to a glaze consistency. The glaze can be stored in an airtight container in the refrigerator for up to 1 month.

Rice Dressing

Super simple to prepare, you can make a big batch of this and use it whenever you feel like it.

Makes 140 ml

100 ml rice vinegar
20 g salt
20 g caster (superfine) sugar

In a small non-reactive bowl, whisk together all the ingredients until the salt and sugar have dissolved. Another easy way to do this is to put it into a jar, seal and give it a good shake. The dressing can be stored in an airtight container at room temperature for up to 1 month.

Tiger Dressing

The longer you leave this to infuse, the better. It's great as a salad dressing, on Smacked Cucumbers (see page 197) or over dumplings.

Makes 150 ml

1 jalapeño, halved
1 clove garlic, crushed
80 ml Chinkiang black rice vinegar
2 tablespoons sesame oil
25 g caster (superfine) sugar
2 tablespoons rapeseed (canola) oil
½ teaspoon salt
pinch of ground white pepper

Combine all the ingredients in a small non-reactive bowl and leave to infuse in a cold, dark place, covered, for 1 week.

Pick out the chilli and garlic. Give the dressing a good whisk to emulsify it or pour into a bottle, seal and shake before using. The dressing can be stored in a sterilized bottle (see page 89) in the refrigerator for up to 2 weeks.

Sichuan Chilli Oil

Nothing beats a good chilli oil. This is the version we use at all our sites.

Makes 250 ml

18 g coriander seeds
250 ml rapeseed (canola) oil
4 cloves garlic, lightly crushed
20 g fresh ginger, peeled and sliced and lightly crushed
1 star anise
60 g dried red chillies
15 g Sichuan peppercorns
generous ½ teaspoon salt
1 teaspoon sugar
30 g Korean chilli flakes
25 g whole bean soy sauce
½ teaspoon sesame seeds

In a dry pan, toast the coriander seeds for 3 minutes over low heat, being careful they don't burn. Combine the seeds with the oil, garlic, ginger and star anise in a small saucepan and simmer gently over a low heat for 10–20 minutes to infuse – you want to smell the aroma of the garlic and ginger, but not burn them.

Meanwhile, preheat the oven to 180°C/350°F/Gas Mark 4. Put the dried chillies onto a baking sheet and toast in the oven for 8 minutes, or until reddish brown – they should not blacken. Add the Sichuan peppercorns 3 minutes before the end of the cooking time and toast. Remove from the oven and let cool, then transfer to a spice grinder or pestle and mortar, add the salt, sugar, and Korean chilli flakes and grind to a powder. Tip the spice mixture into a heatproof bowl and place a fine-mesh sieve on top, then place the bowl near to where the saucepan of oil is infusing.

Increase the heat under the infused oil until it becomes very hot (180°C/350°F) and the garlic and ginger start to brown fully. Carefully pour the hot oil into the heatproof bowl through the sieve – the spice powder and oil should bubble vigorously for about 20 seconds. Add the soy sauce and leave the oil to steep, covered, for at least 2 days at room temperature for optimum flavour.

The chilli oil can be stored in a sterilized jar (see page 89) or airtight container in a cool, dark place for up to 1 month.

Homemade Mayonnaise

A homemade mayonnaise makes all the difference.

Makes 240 ml

70 g egg yolks (from about 4 eggs)
2 teaspoons Dijon mustard
pinch of salt
1 teaspoon lemon juice
155 ml vegetable oil

Put all the ingredients except the oil into a food processor or blender and pulse until combined. With the motor running, slowly pour in the oil through the funnel, taking a break every 30 seconds to ensure everything is well combined. When you have about 50 ml of the oil left, you can pour a little faster. When all the oil is incorporated, continue to blend for about 10 seconds to ensure that all the oil has emulsified. The mayonnaise can be stored in a jar or covered bowl in the refrigerator for up to 3 days.

Tip
To make Garlic Mayonnaise grate 10 g or 1 large clove garlic into the homemade mayonnaise and mix well.

Sichuan Mayonnaise

Add a kick to the homemade mayonnaise.

Makes 200 ml

75 ml rapeseed (canola) oil
45 ml Sichuan Chilli Oil (see page 229)
60 g egg yolks (from about 3 eggs)
1½ teaspoons Dijon mustard
¼ teaspoon salt
1 teaspoon lime juice

Whisk together the oils in a jug (pitcher).

Put the remaining ingredients into a food processor or blender and pulse until combined. With the motor running, slowly pour in the oil through the funnel, taking a break every 30 seconds to ensure everything is well combined. When you have about 50 ml of the oil left, you can pour a little faster. When all the oil is incorporated, blend for about 10 seconds to ensure that all the oil has emulsified.

The mayonnaise can be stored in a jar or covered bowl in the refrigerator for up to 3 days.

Spiced Beef Butter

We first encountered this at Lin Dong Fang and it sat tableside for those who wanted to turn their clear broth into a rich spicy broth. It remained with us all these years and we now serve this iteration on our rich beef noodles (see page 184).

Makes 100 g

¼ teaspoon red Sichuan peppercorns
1 dried red chilli
1 star anise
½ cinnamon stick
100 g beef fat
⅛ spring onion (scallion), finely diced
1 clove garlic, finely diced
1 cm (½ inch) piece of fresh ginger, peeled and finely diced
1 teaspoon *doubanjiang* (fermented chilli bean paste)
1½ teaspoons chilli powder
1 teaspoon premium soy sauce

Toast the Sichuan peppercorns, dried chilli, star anise and cinnamon stick in a dry frying pan over a medium heat until fragrant, then remove from the pan and leave to cool. Transfer the spices to a spice grinder or pestle and mortar and grind to a powder.

Melt the beef fat in a separate frying pan over a medium heat, add the spring onion (scallion), garlic and ginger and cook until they turn a light golden brown, then strain through a fine-mesh sieve into a heatproof bowl and discard the spring onion, garlic and ginger.

Return the fat to the pan, then add the ground toasted spices, the *doubanjiang* (fermented chilli bean paste) and chilli powder. Give the mixture a good stir over a medium heat, then remove from the heat and leave to infuse for 2 hours.

Strain the beef fat through a fine-mesh sieve into a bowl to remove any solids (if it has started to set, first melt it gently in the pan over a low heat). Stir in the premium soy sauce and use straight away.

Green Sauce

A vivid green sauce that has an added savouriness from the fish sauce.

Makes 350 ml

240 g coriander (cilantro)
1 clove garlic

dash of rice vinegar
½ tablespoon salt
1½ teaspoons caster (superfine) sugar
squeeze of lemon juice
2 jalapeños, halved, seeded and coarsely chopped
2 teaspoons honey
1 tablespoon fish sauce
100 ml rapeseed (canola) oil

Put half the coriander (cilantro) and all the remaining ingredients except the oil into a food processor or blender and pulse until the leaves have broken down, then add the remaining coriander and blend until smooth (doing this in 2 batches ensures a smooth consistency). With the motor running, slowly pour in the oil through the funnel.

If not using straight away, transfer the sauce to an airtight container. The sauce can be stored in the refrigerator for up to 1 week or in the freezer for up to 3 months.

Tip
Freezing this sauce keeps it bright green. Only defrost the amount of sauce you need, being careful not to expose it to the air too much.

Burnt Chilli Sauce

We burn the chillies and then peel the charred skins off. It's a painstaking process but very much worth it.

Makes 250 ml

60 g green chillies
60 g fresh ginger, sliced
60 g cloves garlic
25 ml lemon juice
1½ teaspoons chopped coriander (cilantro)
1 teaspoon Dijon mustard
55 ml rapeseed (canola) oil
½ teaspoon salt
3 tablespoons light muscovado sugar

Using tongs, carefully hold each chilli over a gas burner (if you have one) or place the chillies on a baking sheet under a preheated grill (broiler) on the hottest setting until blackened all over. When cool enough to handle, peel off the burned skin.

Transfer the chillies to a blender, add the remaining ingredients and blend at high speed to create an emulsion.

The burnt chilli sauce can be stored in a sterilized glass jar (see page 89) or an airtight container in the refrigerator for up to 1 week, or frozen for up to 3 months.

包食材櫃

Hot Sauce

This hot sauce recipe used to be such a closely guarded secret that I would go into the restaurant on Sunday nights, after all the other chefs had left, to finish it. It was only recently that I stopped doing this. Now here we are, offering the recipe up to the world. We've come a long way. You can also buy our hot sauce from our shop (see page 233).

Makes 850 ml

20 g garlic, chopped
165 g fresh ginger, chopped into 1 cm (½ inch) cubes
210 ml rice vinegar
265 ml light soy sauce
30 g chilli powder
20 g hot paprika
185 ml honey
5 teaspoons caster (superfine) sugar

Put the garlic and ginger into a blender, then pour in the vinegar. It should be enough to cover the garlic and ginger; if not, add a little more vinegar. Blend at high speed for at least 3 minutes until completely smooth. Add the remaining ingredients and blend at high speed for 6–8 minutes or until completely smooth.

Pass the sauce through a fine-mesh sieve into a bowl – you want some of the ginger fibres to get through, but to sift out the larger, unpleasant stringy bits (this gives a good consistency to the sauce without having to thicken it with anything else). Squeeze any remaining solids through the sieve into the sauce to ensure you get all the juices and flavours from them.

The sauce can be stored in a sterilized glass jar (see page 89) or an airtight container at room temperature for up to 1 month, or in the refrigerator for up to 3 months.

Pickled Plum Ketchup

I love the colour of this bright pink ketchup. Just like tomato ketchup, use this on everything, and turn dishes pink.

Makes 400 ml

For the pickled plums:
160 ml rice vinegar
40 g caster (superfine) sugar
20 g salt
200 g plums, halved, pitted and thinly sliced

For the pickled plum ketchup:
200 g pickled plums (see above)
65 g caster (superfine) sugar
1 teaspoon salt
2 teaspoons rice vinegar
150 ml rapeseed (canola) oil

Pickled plums:

Combine the vinegar, sugar and salt in a small saucepan and heat gently over a low heat until the sugar and salt have dissolved. Let the mixture cool down before using.

Put the plums into a sterilized glass jar (see page 89), then pour over the cool pickling liquid, leaving a 1 cm (½ inch) head space, then seal. Leave to pickle in a cool, dry and dark place for 2 weeks before using.

Pickled plum ketchup:

Put 200 g of drained pickled plums, the sugar, salt and vinegar into a high-speed blender and blend until completely smooth – the longer the better. We let the blender run for 15 minutes. With the motor running, slowly pour in the oil through the lid to create an emulsion. The plum ketchup can be stored in a sterilized glass jar in the refrigerator for up to 1 month.

Fermented Mustard Greens

There is nothing as joyful as good fermented mustard greens, known as *suan tsai* in Chinese. When we first started BAO, my kitchen was full of fermenting jars, with juices leaking everywhere. The greens should have the perfect amount of acidity and saltiness once fermented, and since they can be used in so many different ways, they are always handy to have in your store cupboard. They're great eaten as they are, as a palate cleanser, or they can also be treated as a seasoning, added to your meat or noodle dishes to provide depth and complexity of flavour. I love using these fermented greens in noodle dishes, and they are a crucial component of the Classic Pork BAO (see page 51). Chinese mustard greens can be bought fresh from specialist or Asian supermarkets. You will need to prepare them at least 2 weeks in advance of using.

Makes 350 g

500 g Chinese mustard greens, washed and chopped into 2.5 cm (1 inch) pieces

2 teaspoons salt (2% of the total weight of the greens)

Put the chopped greens into a bowl and sprinkle over the salt, massaging it into the greens until it is evenly distributed.

Pack the salted mustard greens tightly into a 500 ml sterilized glass jar (see page 89). After about 30 minutes, the salt will draw out the liquid from the mustard greens and this liquid should cover the greens. If it does not, place something heavy on top (like a fermenting weight) to keep the greens submerged in the brine (the greens must be submerged otherwise they will grow mould).

Put the lid on the jar and seal. Leave to ferment at room temperature for at least 14 days, but ideally 1 month. Make sure to 'burp' the jar every night by opening the lid momentarily – this will release the gasses and ensure that the jar doesn't explode!

When the greens have fermented to your liking, either transfer the jar to the refrigerator or eat straight away. The fermented greens can be stored in the refrigerator for up to 3 months.

Soy-Pickled Chillies

Soy sauce adds another dimension to pickles. You can experiment with any vegetables you might have in the refrigerator, but we particularly love these chillies. You will need to prepare them at least 2 days in advance of using.

Makes 1 x 500 ml jar

100 ml rice vinegar
25 g caster (superfine) sugar
20 ml light soy sauce
20 ml dark soy sauce
100 g green snub-nose chillies, very finely sliced

In a small non-reactive bowl, whisk together the vinegar, sugar and light and dark soy sauces until the sugar has dissolved.

Put the chillies into a 500 ml sterilized jar (see page 89), pour over the pickling liquid, leaving a 1 cm (½ inch) head space, and seal. Leave them to pickle at room temperature for 2 days, then transfer to the refrigerator.

The soy-pickled chillies can be stored in the refrigerator for up to 3 months.

Yellow Chilli Marinade

Our yellow chilli marinade is made with mild yellow finger chillies and appears in many different guises throughout our restaurants. In particular, it's amazing as a chicken marinade (see pages 118 and 145).

Makes 220 ml

60 g carrot, coarsely chopped
2 cloves garlic
35 ml lemon juice
½ teaspoon lemon zest
80 ml rapeseed (canola) oil
10 g lemongrass stalks, thinly sliced
30 g tamarind paste
100 g mild yellow chillies, stems removed

Put all the ingredients except the chillies into a food processor and process until smooth. With the motor running, slowly add the chillies through the lid and continue blending until you have a smooth paste.

The marinade can be stored in an airtight container in the refrigerator for up to 3 days or in the freezer for up to 3 months.

Taiwanese Golden Kimchi

This is an incredibly versatile ferment, as it can be served alongside a wide variety of dishes. Having a pot of kimchi in your refrigerator is perfect for when you want an easy accompaniment for any meat dish, or even just to eat with rice.

Makes 4 x 500 ml jars

1.5 kg Chinese (napa) cabbage, chopped
30 g salt
½ teaspoon sesame oil
2 teaspoons rice vinegar
½ clove garlic
100 g white fermented tofu
30 g apple, cored
60 g carrot
1½ teaspoons caster (superfine) sugar
1 teaspoon ground turmeric
2 green snub-nose chillies, halved lengthways

Combine the chopped cabbage with the salt in a colander and leave to drain for 1–2 hours.

Put all the remaining ingredients except the green chillies into a blender, pour in 40 ml cold water and blend at high speed to form a smooth liquid.

Wash the cabbage thoroughly and drain well. Transfer it to a large non-reactive bowl and pour over the liquid. Wearing gloves (so you don't stain your hands yellow), massage the pickling mixture into the cabbage.

Transfer the cabbage mixture to four 500 ml sterilized glass jars (see page 89), then add the chillies, leaving a 1 cm (½ inch) headspace, and seal. Leave the cabbage to ferment at room temperature for 7 days. Make sure to 'burp' the jars every night by opening the lids momentarily – this will release the gasses and ensure that the jars don't explode! After 7 days, transfer them to the refrigerator and leave for another week before using. The kimchi can be stored in the refrigerator for at least 1 month

Master Stock (broth)

The base master stock that we feed into both light and rich broth on pages 184 and 187.

Makes 1 litre

350 g beef shin on the bone
1 kg 40-day aged beef bones
1 whole chicken carcass
1 tablespoon vegetable oil
1½ onions, unpeeled and quartered
15 g fresh ginger, smashed
1 bulb garlic, halved horizontally
1 tomato, halved
pinch of red Sichuan peppercorns
pinch of black peppercorns
1 star anise
1 bay leaf
1 dried red chilli
1 cinnamon stick
1.35 litres filtered water
1 *jujube* (red date)

Put the beef shin, bones and chicken carcass into a large saucepan of water, bring to the boil, and blanch for 5 minutes. Drain, then rinse the bones to remove any residue.

Heat the oil in a large saucepan over a medium heat, add the onion and ginger and cook for 15 minutes until browned, adding the garlic halfway through, then finally add the tomato.

Meanwhile, toast the peppercorns, star anise, bay leaf, chilli and cinnamon stick in a dry, heavy-based frying pan (skillet) over a low heat until fragrant. Leave to cool slightly, then wrap the toasted spices in muslin (cheesecloth) or put them into a spice bag.

Add the meat and bones to the saucepan with the onions, pour in the filtered water and add the spice bag and *jujube* (red date).

Bring to the boil, skimming off any scum from the surface. When boiling, remove the last of the scum, then reduce the heat to very low (the stock should be slowly cooking at about 95°C/203°F). Put the lid on the pan and cook for 8 hours. Strain the stock through a fine-mesh sieve and set aside, discarding the solids.

Convni Store

Our Lonely Man supply company, shipping several products nationwide (UK) that might make your life easier. Scan the QR code at the bottom to view our online shop.

Aged White Soy Sauce

Soy like no other, this is the first pressing of the sauce made from soy beans, aged for 400 days, from Ping Tung, Taiwan. We mainly use it as a dipping soy as it's so good, but it can also be added to sauces to give them that extra depth – I even add them to meat jus to give it that rounded touch without overpowering it.

Gua BAO

If you are short on time and want to focus on making the fillings, we ship our BAO which are made lovingly by our team of bakers.

Plain Noodles

Our Emergency Noodles. I try to always keep a supply of these as you never know when you'll need an emergency meal.

And more…

Glossary

Eggs

Century egg Century egg, also known as 'pidan', is a preserved egg made with quicklime, ash and salt. They have a jelly-like, blackened and semi-transparent white and a creamy dark grey yolk. This description doesn't do it justice as it is truly delicious despite the scary appearance.

Salted duck eggs Make these yourself (see page 228) or purchase them from the Chinese supermarket. Shing and Wai Ting's mother likes to add a salted egg (with the shell on) to the rice cooker to steam when she's cooking rice, and when eating, she picks at it to get a salty hit to accompany the boiled rice. My family loved eating them with plain congee. They are creamy with a slight chalky texture. A lot of Chinese recipes use just the yolk, so you can look out for vacuum-packed salted duck yolks in the freezer area at a Chinese supermarket or find half a dozen salted duck eggs on the shelves.

Rice

Chishang rice A short grain rice from Chishang in Taitung, Taiwan. It is a round and plump prized grain that is available from specialist Chinese supermarkets. It can be substituted with Japanese sushi rice.

Glutinous rice An opaque rice that is sticky when cooked. It is grown in East and Southeast Asia.

Rice wines

Michiu rice wine A clear rice wine made from white rice with around 20% abv, it is commonly used in Taiwanese cooking.

Mirin A rice wine that has a lower alcohol level and a higher sugar content than sake. We use a very low alcohol content mirin that tastes sweet. We use it in an untraditional way to sweeten sauces or dressings.

Shaoxing rice wine A Chinese glutinous rice wine that has a slightly sweet flavour and is an amber colour. Available in Chinese supermarkets and some mainstream supermarkets. It can be substituted with a light-bodied dry sherry, although we never do as it's quite easy to find.

Sauces/Pastes

Doubanjiang (fermented chilli bean paste) A paste made from fermented broad beans, chilli pepper, soy beans, salt and flour. A very savoury paste, classically you can get doubanjiang without chilli, however in our kitchens we use spicy doubanjiang for all our recipes.

Vegetarian oyster sauce A vegetarian substitute for oyster sauce, made with soy beans, sugar and dried shiitake mushrooms, it can also be called mushroom oyster sauce. We use it like we would the classic oyster sauce, to enhance umami and give thickness to sauces and marinades.

Yellow bean paste or crushed yellow bean sauce, is made from crushed soybeans and can be found in most Asian supermarkets.

Soy sauces

Aged white soy sauce We import this rare aged white soy sauce ourselves from Ping Tung, Taiwan. A delicate first pressing of a white soy that is aged for 400 days. The colour is a beautiful rich amber and the taste is light yet deep, sweet and full of umami. It's hard to source in the UK, but you can find it on baolondon.com/shop.

Premium soy sauce A premium light soy. 'Premium' is an indicator that it is the first pressing of the soy. If you can't find 'premium' anywhere, look for the description of the soy to see if it is the first pressing. The consistency of the premium soy sauce is slightly thicker, very dark brown in colour and rounder in taste than the saltier light soy sauce.

Whole bean soy sauce A soy that's fermented with whole soy beans. Most soy sauce is made with crushed beans to speed up the process of fermentation. Soy sauce made with whole soy beans takes longer to ferment, which results in a deep yet mellow flavour that is rounder and softer than usual soy sauces.

Spices

Sichuan peppercorns There are two varieties: red and green. Both have numbing qualities and are used in Sichuan cuisine. They give a tingling sensation on the tongue. We use the red peppercorn more than the green – it has an earthy flavour. Green Sichuan peppercorn has a more numbing sensation and is more floral with citrus notes.

Urfa chilli flakes A Turkish dried chilli that is smoky, sour, slightly raisiny and mild in heat. It is a beautiful dark maroon colour. We learnt of the chilli from our spice supplier, Ren, who gave us a sample. We loved it and have been using it ever since.

Sugar/Flour

Rock sugar A crystalised sugar that has a mild caramel flavour and is less sweet than granulated sugar. It is a pale yellow colour and often comes in big lumps which you need to crush into smaller pieces (best to use a hammer, I used to use a book press! It's the best tool!). Rock sugar is mostly used in braising or pickling.

Tapioca flour (starch) Taiwanese fried chicken uses coarse tapioca starch that gives it a nice bubbly crispy texture when fried. Make sure you find the coarse one as there are many fine tapioca starches available in Asian supermarkets that can either be made into dough, for things like boba, or can be made into a slurry to thicken sauces or omelettes to form a soft QQ texture.

Tofu/Curd

Tofu (firm) Firm tofu is versatile because it can hold its shape well and is easy to handle. It can be pan fried, boiled, deep fried and stir fried. All these methods give a slightly different texture. If you freeze the tofu and thaw it, it creates many holes and will soak up lots of flavour when you cook it.

Tofu (silken) A delicate tofu that is made without curdling, the texture is literally silky smooth. We use it to make sauces. It's a good substitute for egg when making a mayo-like velvety texture. It is also great in a broth or lightly fried.

Fermented bean curd A 'fermented' bean curd is one that has been salted and dried, then soaked in brine. The flavour is determined by the seasoning that the tofu sits in. Red fermented bean curd sits in a red yeast rice and alcohol liquid, hence the red colour. White fermented tofu is the original flavour and uses a salt brine. One of our favourite fermented bean curds sits in *jiuniang* (sweet, fermented rice), resulting in a rounded umami condiment with a savoury sweetness. The texture is similar to a cheese curd.

Vinegars

Chinese red vinegar Also known as *dà hóng zhè cù*, this vinegar is made from fermented red yeast rice, it has a reddish pink tint and tastes tart and sweet.

Chinkiang vinegar A black vinegar made from fermented glutinous rice that is dark brown in colour with a rich, complex and fruity taste. This vinegar originates from the Zhejiang province of China and it is often used for dumpling dipping.

Rice vinegar A clear vinegar made from fermented rice, it tastes mild and is slightly sweet. Not to be confused with rice wine vinegar.

Taiwanese black vinegar A black vinegar with star anise, cumin, onion and celery seeds.

Taiwanese red rice vinegar A spiced red vinegar made from fermented red yeast rice with cinnamon and star anise.

Recipe Notes

Unless specified otherwise, butter is unsalted, eggs are large (US extra large) and organic, milk is full-fat (whole), salt is fine sea salt and all herbs are fresh.

Vegetables and fruits are medium in size and should be peeled and/or washed.

Cooking times given are for guidance only, as individual ovens vary. If using a fan (convection) oven, follow the manufacturer's directions concerning oven temperatures.

To check if cooking oil is hot enough for deep-frying, we recommend using a temperature probe as it is the best way to know that the oil has come to temperature. Alternatively, immerse a cube of ginger into the oil. If it browns in 10 seconds, the temperature of the oil is 180–190°C (350–375°F), which is ideal for most cooking.

Exercise a high level of caution when following recipes involving potentially hazardous steps, such as high temperatures, flames or frying. In particular, when deep-frying, slowly and carefully lower the food into the hot oil to avoid splashes, wear long sleeves to protect your arms and never leave the pan unattended. Steam can be deceptively high, so when lifting the lid off the steamer, ensure your hand is away from the steam.

Some recipes include uncooked, cured or very lightly cooked eggs, meat or fish, or fermented foods. These should be avoided by the elderly, infants, pregnant women, convalescents and anyone with an impaired immune system.

Specialist ingredients can be found online or at specialist supermarkets. Certain ingredients can be found on our online shop: baolondon.com/shop

When no quantity is specified – for oils, salt and herbs, for example – then quantities are discretionary.

The tablespoon and teaspoon measurements given are level. 1 teaspoon = 5 ml / 1 tablespoon = 15 ml.

Index

Note: Page references in *italics* indicate photographs.

To our families who have supported us from day one. To all our team, past and present, who has made BAO what it is today. Without them none of this would have been possible.

The BAO OGs (originals):
With special thanks to Alice Ke-Yin Lin, Andrew Gray, Anais van Manen, Bryan Magsano, Chao Yin Wu, Cameron Malik-Flynn, Carlos Monleon, Hilary Brett, James Fernandez, Keegan Chen, Federico Cassino, Tom Ward, Wei Ti Lai and Zoltan Szekeres

A big thank you to Jyotin, Karam and Sunaina Sethi for giving us the opportunity and Billy Hookway for the support – we miss you!

And a thank you to Kerb, Netil Market and Pacific Social Club for giving us the platform to kick start BAO.

Those who helped contribute to the book:
Authors: Erchen Chang, Shing Tat Chung, Wai Ting Chung
Recipes: Erchen Chang, Anais van Manen, Hsuan Yang
Copy Editors: Lucy Kingett, Leonardo Pereira, Barclay Bram Shoemaker
Art Direction: Darcy Ward, Erchen Chang
Design: MATHs
Photography: Pelle Crépin, Fangyu Cho, Ash James, Pascal Grob, Sirui Ma, Roberto Pansolli
Artwork: Erchen Chang, Marcelo Colmenero, Doug John Miller

Phaidon Press Limited
2 Cooperage Yard
London
E15 2QR

Phaidon Press Inc.
65 Bleecker Street
New York, NY 10012

phaidon.com

First published 2023
© 2023 Phaidon Press Limited

ISBN 978 1 83866 620 0

A CIP catalogue record for this book is available from the British Library and the Library of Congress.

All rights reserved. No part of this publication may be reproduced, stored in a retrieval system or transmitted, in any form or by any means, electronic, mechanical, photocopying, recording or otherwise, without the written permission of Phaidon Press Limited.

Commissioning Editor: Sophie Hodgkin
Production Controller: Lily Rodgers
Typesetting: Cantina

The Publisher would like to thank Anne Heining, Lucy Kingett, Joanne Murray, Laura Nicholl, Elizabeth Parson and Caroline Stearns for their contributions to the book.

Printed in Italy